America Revisited

Books by Eugene J. McCarthy

AMERICA REVISITED:
150 YEARS AFTER TOCQUEVILLE

MR. RACCOON AND HIS FRIENDS

THE HARD YEARS: A LOOK AT
CONTEMPORARY AMERICA AND
AMERICAN INSTITUTIONS

OTHER THINGS AND THE AARDVARK

THE YEAR OF THE PEOPLE

THE LIMITS OF POWER:
AMERICA'S ROLE IN THE WORLD

A LIBERAL ANSWER TO THE
CONSERVATIVE CHALLENGE

THE CRESCENT DICTIONARY OF AMERICAN POLITICS

FRONTIERS IN AMERICAN DEMOCRACY

America Revisited

150 YEARS AFTER TOCQUEVILLE

By Eugene J. McCarthy

DOUBLEDAY & COMPANY, INC.
GARDEN CITY, NEW YORK
1978

ISBN: 0-385-03106-8
Library of Congress Catalog Card Number 77-92222
Copyright © 1978 by Eugene J. McCarthy
All Rights Reserved
Printed in the United States of America

Library of Congress Cataloging in Publication Data

McCarthy, Eugene J., 1916–
America revisited.

Bibliography.
Includes index.
1. United States—Civilization—1970–
2. United States—Civilization—19th century.
3. Tocqueville, Alexis Charles Henri Maurice Clérel de,
1805–1859. 4. Beaumont de La Bonniniere, Gustave
Auguste de, 1802–1866. I. Title.
E169.12.M255   973.926

Grateful acknowledgment is made to the following sources for permission to
reprint their copyrighted material:
Brandt & Brandt, two lines of poetry by Stephen Vincent Benét.
City Lights, "American Buttons," translated by Ferlighetti from *Dogalypse:
San Francisco Poetry Reading* by Andrei Voznesensky. Copyright © 1972
by City Light Books.
E. P. Dutton & Co. and J. M. Dent & Sons Ltd., excerpts from *The Social
Contract & Discourses* by Jean-Jacques Rousseau, translated by G. D. H.
Cole. An Everyman's Edition.
Sir Cedering Fox, Goran-Printz-Pahlson, "When Beaumont and Tocqueville
Visited Sing-Sing," translated by Sir Cedering Fox in *First Issue*. Copy-
right © 1972 by Sir Cedering Fox.
Harper & Row, Publishers, Inc., excerpt from *The Lively Experiment* by
Sidney E. Mead. Copyright © 1963 by Sidney E. Mead; excerpts from
Democracy in America by Alexis de Tocqueville, edited by J. P. Mayer
and Max Lerner, translated by George Laurence. English translation copy-
right © 1966 by Harper & Row, Publishers, Inc. Reprinted in England
by permission of Fontana Paperbacks.
New York *Times*, excerpt from January 19, 1953, article. Copyright © 1953
by The New York Times Company.
George Wilson Pierson, excerpt from *Tocqueville & Beaumont in America*
by George Wilson Pierson. Copyright 1938 by George Wilson Pierson.
Simon & Schuster, passage from *Religions of America: Ferment & Faith in
an Age of Crisis, A New Guide and Almanac* by Leo Rosten. Copyright ©
1975 by Cowles Communications, Inc.

Contents

Introduction
Meditating Great Projects

On *May 9, 1831,* two Frenchmen, Alexis de Tocqueville, age twenty-five, and Gustave de Beaumont, age twenty-nine, after nearly forty days at sea, landed at Newport, Rhode Island, being unable that day because of adverse winds to reach New York Harbor.

Tocqueville and Beaumont, French aristocrats, were both magistrates of the courts of France. Together they conceived the idea of a trip to the United States, officially to study American prison reforms. As with many political junkets, the formal and official purpose was secondary to another. Their larger purpose was to study democracy in action, to examine the emerging institutions of the United States.

The young magistrates had some difficulty in getting permission to be absent from their duties for the eighteen months of their projected travels. The court calendar then, as always seems to be the case, was reportedly crowded. Moreover, they had to be cleared by two of the ministries of the French Government—the Ministry of the Interior and the Ministry of Justice. Although they obtained leave for their trip to America, they failed in a secondary effort to have one or the other of the ministries pay their travel expenses. As is commonly noted in press releases or newsletters of our members of Congress today, the two Frenchmen traveled at "their own expense." In this case, it was at the expense of their families.

The scope of their mission was noted by Beaumont in a letter to his father:

We are meditating great projects. First of all we will accomplish to the best of our ability the mission given us; it is a rigorous duty which we ought to perform conscientiously. But while working on the penitentiary system we shall see America; in visiting its prisons we shall be visiting its inhabitants, its cities, its institutions, its customs; we shall come to know the mechanism of its republican government. . . . This government is not understood in Europe. People speak of it endlessly, for the sake of making false comparisons between it and countries which do not in any way resemble it. Would not that be a fine book which would give an exact conception of the American people, would paint its character in bold strokes, would analyze its social conditions and would rectify so many opinions which are erroneous on this point?

So they came, and so the book *Democracy in America* was written by Tocqueville nearly one hundred and fifty years ago. It still provides the best frame of reference, both descriptive and analytical, for the examination of American democracy and social institutions.

The country to which Tocqueville came included all of the lands east of the Mississippi and those lands to the west that were part of the Louisiana Purchase. Texas had not yet joined the Union. The annexation of California and other Mexican territories had not been made; nor had the Oregon country been added to the nation. Nor, of course, were Alaska or the island additions a part of the United States in 1831.

The American population for the most part was Anglo-Saxon and Protestant. It was estimated at about thirteen million persons, most of them along the eastern coast. Significant movement beyond the eastern mountains was just beginning. Massachusetts, according to Tocqueville the most densely populated state in the Union, had 76 inhabitants to the square mile; Connecticut had 62. The population of New York City was about 200,000; the population of Boston was about 60,000. Baltimore had 80,000. New Orleans and its suburbs had 50,000; Nashville, some 5,000; Louisville, 10,000.

Great spaces of the West remained unsettled. The Indians, under pressure of a growing white population, aided by military action, were being pushed farther westward, or into less fertile and less productive areas of the eastern states.

Tocqueville did not see all of America or foresee all that was to come. Not all of his judgments about the character and trends of American democracy have stood the test of time. He did not foresee the great waves of immigration of the late-nineteenth and early-twentieth centuries, which significantly changed the ethnic and cultural composition of the United States. He did not foresee the later changes in transportation and communication, the growth of great cities, or the corporate control of industry and of finance. But he came with a clear eye to examine and note the beginning of a democratic society in its purest historical test, untrammeled by monarchic or despotic traditions, or by tribal controls and restraints, having what appeared to be unlimited resources in land, and having only one great undemocratic burden, that of slavery.

Newport, Rhode Island, was Tocqueville's and Beaumont's first experience of America. This is Tocqueville's description of the town:

It's a collection of small houses, the size of chicken coops, but distinguished by a cleanness that is a pleasure to see and that we have no conception of in France. Beyond that, the inhabitants differ but little superficially from the French. They wear the same clothes, and their physiognomies are so varied that it would be hard to say from what races they have derived their features. I think it must be thus in all the United States.

Beaumont, the novelist and limited artist, was detailed and perceptive in his report:

. . . we wandered about the town. It has 16,000 inhabitants, a magnificent harbor, newly fortified, tiny houses modeled one would say on the kitchen of Beaumont-la-Chartre, but so clean they resemble opera scenery. They are all painted. There is also a church whose bell tower is in a rather remarkable architectural style. I sketched it on Jules' album. We had been told that the women of Newport were noteworthy for their beauty; we found them extraordinarily ugly. This new race of people we saw bears no clear mark of its origin; it's neither English, nor French, nor German; it's a mixture of all the nations. This race is entirely commercial. In the small city of Newport there are 4 or 5 banks; the same is true in all the cities in the Union. . . .

The ship on which Tocqueville and Beaumont had sailed to America, and on which they also returned to France, the *Havre*, was American-built and American-owned. She belonged to the First Havre Line or Havre Old Line, which had been started by Francis Depau in 1822. In addition to the *Havre*, the Old Line had ships with names like *Henri IV, Sully, François I, De Rham,* and *Charlemagne;* they sailed on a regular schedule between France and America.

The *Havre* carried French wines and other luxuries to America, and it also transported French and Swiss emigrants who wished to settle in the United States. On the return trips it carried various American products.

The *Havre* was built in 1828–29 by Smith and Dimon of New York City. She had two decks, a square stern and three masts. She probably had square rigging. She was 126 feet in length, 29 feet in breadth, and her depth of hold was 14 feet 6 inches. She measured 480 tons. This was quite a respectable size for ships of the period, though the *Havre* was not among the very largest.

The *Havre* was a good ship. She was copper-sheathed—that is, had copper plating on her hull below the waterline. The copper protected the wooden hull from barnacles and such. The *Havre* was listed in the 1832 *Lloyd's Register of Shipping* as a first-class or A-1 ship.

The Tocqueville-Beaumont trip to America of 37 days was a little faster than the *Havre*'s average sailing time to America. The ship was captained by Elisha Keen, described by Tocqueville as "an excellent man and a good sailor" but one who mismanaged the provisioning of food.

The *Havre* carried 180–90 people (including its 18 sailors), a cow, a donkey, sheep, ducks, chickens, and turkeys. The cow apparently provided milk for the cabin passengers; the other livestock, except for the donkey, were on board to provide fresh meat for them. The animals gradually disappeared from the little ship's farm and appeared in different form on the dinner table of the cabin passengers. Beaumont found that the ship served excellent wine and had fresh bread every day. He added, "Our food would also be good if we had a good cook, but he is so bad he spoils everything he touches." Because of poor management, the *Havre* was running short of food and was even rationing sugar before she reached land.

Tocqueville reported that 30 of the passengers were accommodated in cabins, 13 between decks, and 120 in the bow. This seems close to the passenger notice about the *Havre* printed in the New York *Daily Advertiser* of May 12, 1831, which said there were 156 in the steerage.

On February 20, 1832—nearly a year after their arrival in America—Tocqueville and Beaumont boarded the *Havre* in New York for the trip back to France. This time they were in the hands of Captain Frederick Augustus De Peyster, a New Yorker of Dutch descent and a veteran of the War of 1812 and the China trade. The journey home was a good one; there was no poor management reported under Captain De Peyster.

The Newport landing was not by design. It was more by necessity and by demand of the passengers, who were weary of the trip and who faced adverse winds and the shortages of food and water. The reports of the Newport stop indicate that some of the passengers stayed on board and that some who made the first landing at Newport returned to the ship to sail to New York. Not so Tocqueville and Beaumont. After staying on the *Havre* for the night, they returned to the town in the morning, and then had their first experience with an American steamboat.

It was an experience which was to mark the rest of their travels in America. Tocqueville seemed unable to resist boarding American lake and river boats. His journals are a litany of their names and of praise for them. He described the steamer out of Newport as

> a tremendous steamship which, coming down from Providence, was making for New York. It is impossible to picture to oneself the interior of this immense machine. Let it suffice you to know that it contains three great saloons, two for men, one for women, where four, five, and often eight hundred people eat and sleep comfortably. You can judge of its speed, since in spite of a contrary sea and wind we covered in 18 hours the 60 leagues which separated us from New York.

On May 11, 1831, Tocqueville arrived in New York City and began his serious observation of American life and institutions.

The following is the itinerary of the young Frenchmen. The dates are approximate; the mode of travel is sometimes a matter of speculation. Without interviews or observations, the travels alone are most impressive—a marvel of endurance and persistence.

April 2–3, 1831	lv. Le Havre on the *Havre*
May 9	arr. Newport after 37 days at sea; spend another night on board
May 10	lv. Newport on a steamer
May 11	arr. N.Y.C. after 18-hour voyage
May 29	up the Hudson River to Sing Sing (Mt. Pleasant)
June 7	return to N.Y.C. by steamboat
June 30	lv. N.Y.C. by sloop; reach Yonkers in 2 or 3 hours
July 1	steamboat to Calwell steamboat *North America* to Albany
July 2	arr. Albany
July 3	excursion to Shaker meeting at Niskayuna (now Watervliet)
July 4–5	lv. Albany by stage during the night
July 5	arr. Utica
July 7	stage to Syracuse horseback to Lake Oneida to Auburn to Canandaigua
July 18	lv. Canandaigua by steamboat, then stagecoach; arr. Buffalo
July 19	lv. Buffalo by steamboat *Ohio* for Detroit (via Erie, Salem, Ashtabula, Grand River, Cleveland, and Sandusky) for 2 days and a night, 300 miles
July 21	arr. Detroit
July 23	by horseback to Pontiac
July 24	by horseback from Pontiac to Flint River, arr. at night
July 25	by horseback from Flint to Saginaw, arr. at night

July 28	lv. Saginaw on horseback
	arr. Flint
July 31	arr. Detroit by horseback
Aug. 1	lv. Detroit on steamboat *Superior* (for Sault Ste. Marie, Mackinac, Green Bay and return to Detroit)
Aug. 2	arr. at Fort Gratiot on Lake Huron
Aug. 4	lv. Fort Gratiot
Aug. 6	arr. Sault Ste. Marie
	excursion by canoe to Lake Superior at Pointe-aux-Pins
Aug. 7	arr. Mackinac
	lv. Mackinac during night of Aug. 7–8
Aug. 9	arr. Green Bay
Aug. 10	lv. Green Bay
	arr. Mackinac
Aug. 12	lv. Mackinac
Aug. 14	arr. Detriot on steamboat *Superior*
Aug. 17	arr. Buffalo by steamboat
Aug. 18–19	Niagara Falls
Aug. 20	Lake Ontario, on steamboat *Great Britain*
Aug. 24	lv. Montreal on steamboat *John Molson;* 24 hours to Quebec
Aug. 31	lv. Quebec on steamboat *Richelieu*
Sept. 2	arr. Montreal
	lv. Montreal on steamboat *Voyageur* to St. Jean
	lv. St. Jean on steamboat *Phoenix* on Lake Champlain
Sept. 2–4	arr. Whitehall
Sept. 4–5	stage to Albany
	arr. Albany
Sept. 7	lv. Albany
	arr. Stockbridge, Mass.
Sept. 9	arr. Boston
Oct. 3	lv. Boston for Hartford
Oct. 8	lv. Hartford by steamboat for N.Y.C.
Oct. 9	arr. N.Y.C.
Oct. 11	by steamboat and stage to Philadelphia
Oct. 12	arr. Philadelphia

Oct. 28	lv. Philadelphia
	arr. Baltimore
	stay 2 weeks, then return to Philadelphia
Nov. 22	Philadelphia to Pittsburgh—72 hours by stage
	lv. Pittsburgh on steamboat *Fourth of July;* accident and rescue by another steamboat, near Wheeling, VA (now WV)
Dec. 1	arr. Cincinnati
Dec. 4	lv. Cincinnati for New Orleans by steamboat
Dec. 5	halted by ice in river
Dec. 6	disembark at Westport, KY; walk 25 miles to Louisville
	by stage—2 days and 2 nights to Nashville
Dec. 11	lv. Nashville by stage
Dec. 12	Sandy Bridge Inn in Tennessee, stranded by carriage breakdown and Tocqueville's illness
Dec. 16	by stage to Memphis
Dec. 17	arr. Memphis
Dec. 25	down the Mississippi on steamboat *Louisville*
Dec. 26–27	stranded on sandbar
Jan. 1, 1832	arr. New Orleans for 3-day stay
Jan. 3–4	lv. New Orleans by steamboat
	arr. Mobile
	lv. Mobile by stage
Jan. 15	arr. Norfolk
Jan. 16	steamboat on Chesapeake Bay to Washington, DC
Jan. 17	arr. Washington, DC
Feb. 3	stage to Philadelphia
Feb. 4	to N.Y.C.
Feb. 20	lv. N.Y.C. on ship *Havre* for France

During the nine months of their American travels, Tocqueville and Beaumont used all major means of transportation, with the probable exception of canal boats. They used steamboats, sailing boats, stagecoaches, and canoes. They went on foot and on horseback.

Despite the competition from steamboats, sailing ships were still widely used along the East Coast and on its largest bays and rivers. (The two Frenchmen traveled on a sloop from Manhattan to Yonkers and found it a very pleasant sail.) Sailing vessels were still vital to the coastal trade in the East.

The young Frenchmen used canoes at least twice in the West. They crossed the river to reach Saginaw, Michigan, in an Indian canoe, which Tocqueville described as about ten feet long and made from a tree. He wrote: "One saw no oars, heard no noise of paddles. It glided swiftly and without effort, long, narrow and black, like a Mississippi alligator making toward the bank to seize its prey."

At Sault Sainte Marie, they went on an excursion up to Lake Superior and back in a canoe paddled by French Canadians. On the way back they shot the rapids on St. Mary's River.

Steamboats were widely used in America of the 1830s—on the eastern rivers, the Great Lakes, and the Mississippi system. In the East and on the Great Lakes, they were used chiefly to carry passengers, but on the Mississippi and other western rivers they were used a great deal for both cargo and passengers. Some of the steamboats were fairly large; most in the West measured at least between 100 and 200 tons. (In steamboat-tonnage measurement, a ton usually equaled 100 cubic feet.) Some, especially the ones used exclusively for passengers, were grandly decorated.

A steamboat in the East might last for ten to twenty years or more, but rarely as long as a good sailing vessel. The life span of western steamboats was very short—only four to five years. The ones in the West were built of less durable wood and often were handled more roughly and carelessly. And navigation conditions in the West were far more treacherous. Submerged tree stumps and trunks ("snags") ruined many steamboats; fires and boiler explosions destroyed others.

Steamboat racing, both formal and informal, was widely practiced in America. It was done partly for sport and partly for business competition. Winning races and setting new speed records helped a line's reputation, and sometimes the first boat to reach a landing would get all the passengers waiting there. But racing sometimes led to serious accidents; more than once a captain built up steam to such a point that the boilers exploded.

Though Tocqueville did not experience a boiler explosion, he certainly had heard about the problem. In his notes he compared

the Sing Sing system of prison discipline to American steamboats: "Nothing is more comfortable, quick and, in a word, perfect in the ordinary run of things. But if some bit of the appara-
tus gets out of order, the boat, the passengers and the cargo fly
into the air."

At the time of Tocqueville's visit, most American steamboats
accommodated their higher-paying passengers in dormitory-like
rooms called saloons or cabins. There would be one large room
for the women and another for the men. Each room had a row of
berths on one side, often separated by curtains from the lounge
area. The men's cabin generally was used for meals for both
sexes. Some boats had staterooms for the use of individuals or
families.

The "deck passengers" traveled on the main deck or lower
deck. Their fares were much lower—between 25 per cent and 50
per cent of the cabin fares. But their accommodations were
much rougher; most of them had no beds, and the passengers
had to provide their own food and cook it on a stove shared by
all the deckers. Their area often was unsanitary—and usually
more dangerous than the upper decks because it was closer to the
boilers. Wood was used as fuel for the steamboats, and the common practice of storing it near the boilers increased the danger.

There was real price competition in steamboating, as in other
forms of transportation, at the time of Tocqueville's visit. This
competition, added to the technological improvements which
increased steamboat speeds, meant that the cabin fare for the
New Orleans–Louisville journey dropped from a range between
$100 and $125 around 1818 to a range between $25 and $30 in
the 1830s.

The New York *Daily Advertiser* of May 10, 1831—the day after
Tocqueville landed in America—listed some eastern steamboat
fares in its advertisements. An ad for a steamboat on the New
York–Providence run told readers that the fare had been "reduced to four dollars," not including meals. Another steamboat
line said its price for the same run was "reduced to $6, including
meals." The North River Steam-Boat Line charged $2 for the
New York–Albany trip. One line charged $3 for the New York–
Hartford run, while another charged only $2.50.

Tocqueville's first encounter with an American steamboat was on the trip from Newport to New York City. He and Beaumont also used steamboats for most of the trip up the Hudson River to Albany. They traveled by steamer again from Buffalo to Detroit. Their boat, the *Ohio*, ran into much rain and took three days to reach Detroit. After their horseback trip in the Michigan wilderness, they took the steamboat *Superior* from Detroit to Green Bay and back. The journey to Green Bay was essentially a sightseeing trip, pleasant and uneventful. There was dancing on deck, and the little orchestra even played the "Marseillaise" for the French passengers. After the excursion, Beaumont and Tocqueville returned to Buffalo by steamboat, visited Niagara Falls, and went by steamboat to Montreal and Quebec and then down to Whitehall, New York. One of the boats they used in Canada was a new one called the *Great Britain*. On Lake Champlain they traveled on the *Phoenix*.

Beaumont and Tocqueville also went by steamer on their trip from Hartford to New York and for part of the trip from New York to Philadelphia. But their most eventful trip started in November at Pittsburgh, on a steamer named the *Fourth of July*. There was snow on the banks of the Ohio River, and much ice in the river itself. While traveling at night near Wheeling, the boat struck a reef and started to go under. The 200 or so passengers thought they were doomed. Many years later, Beaumont described it this way: "Tocqueville and I throw a glance at the Ohio, which at this place is more than a mile wide and whose current is drawing down enormous cakes of ice; we grasp each other's hand in farewell. . . ." But the reef itself kept the boat from going under, and the passengers were rescued by another steamboat and set ashore. The *Fourth of July*, however, was lost. The passengers continued down the river on a third steamboat the following day. After various interruptions and the use of other means of travel, Tocqueville and Beaumont finally reached New Orleans. On their return, they apparently took a steamer from New Orleans to Mobile and one from Norfolk to Washington.

Tocqueville and Beaumont rode horseback on several occasions. The Frenchmen were bothered by the sun at the beginning of their horseback journey to Lake Oneida, and they were tormented by mosquitoes in the Michigan forests. Apart from these few complaints about this mode of travel, they found it tolerable.

The Erie Canal had been completed in 1825 by the state of New York. Though not the first canal in the United States, it was the longest and the best publicized. Its great success had encouraged a boom in canal-building elsewhere in New York and also in other states. By the time of Tocqueville's visit, the following were among the canals already built: Blackstone, Chesapeake and Delaware, Cumberland and Oxford, Delaware and Hudson, Dismal Swamp, Erie, Lehigh, Louisville and Portland, Middlesex, Santee and Copper, and Union.

The Main Line Canal was still under construction; when completed, it would extend from a point near Philadelphia to Pittsburgh. The optimistically named Chesapeake and Ohio Canal was under construction in Maryland. But it was not to be open all the way to Cumberland until 1850, and it was never to reach the Ohio River. The state of Ohio had joined the canal boom; it was building the Ohio and Erie and also the Miami and Erie.

Though originally built to haul cargo, the canals also proved attractive to travelers; and special boats were built for passengers. These often left much to be desired in the way of meals and sleeping accommodations. Boats on the Erie Canal, for example, had cushioned benches that folded out into beds; but above them more beds were suspended by cord or chain from the ceiling—an arrangement somewhat risky for both those on top and those below. During the day, passengers on the roof or upper deck sometimes had to duck or even lie on the deck to avoid low bridges. (As a canal boat approached a very low bridge, some passengers enjoyed calling out, "All Jackson men bow down!") But the canal boats were convenient and reasonably cheap. They were safer and quieter than steamboats. And they were more comfortable than stagecoaches, although slower.

Tocqueville and Beaumont could have gone from Albany to Buffalo on the Erie Canal, instead of going by stage. But they apparently did not use canals for any of their journey through America, though Tocqueville several times noted the importance of canals in his travel diaries.

American railroads were still in their infancy. Only about 100 miles of railroad were in operation by the end of 1831; this compared with well over 1,000 miles of canals. Part of the Baltimore and Ohio Railroad was open, however, and the B & O reached Frederick, Maryland, by early 1832. There was passenger service on part of the B & O and on a few other short railroads. Some of the railway cars were horse-drawn. The early railway cars looked like stagecoaches, though new designs would be developed later.

A hint of the future was given during Tocqueville's visit when, in June of 1831, the steam locomotive *York* was tested for the B & O. This engine took the sharpest turns at fifteen miles an hour and reached the amazing speed of thirty miles an hour when running on a straight line.

The roads in America were generally poor, as the two Frenchmen often noted in their travels. Roads were bumpy in dry weather and muddy after rains. Tree stumps often were left in roads, and it was considered an achievement to have the stumps cut low enough so that axles would not strike them. An exception to the general rule was the National Road, or Cumberland Road, which was built by the federal government and built very well. Neighborhoods or local governments tried to keep other public roads in minimal repair.

There were also privately owned turnpikes, built in the hope of making profits from tolls. Most turnpike companies proved to be financially unsuccessful. Even though their roads were usually much better than public roads, they were not nearly as helpful in moving freight as in carrying passengers. They were also expensive and difficult to maintain. And some people built "shunpikes," which were detours around tollgates. Where there were no shunpikes, drivers could wait until sunset, when toll collectors went off duty, and then drive through the tollgates free.

A stagecoach of this period usually could seat at least nine passengers on the three seats inside. (A tenth passenger could ride outside on the seat beside the driver.) Inside passengers in the front rode with their backs to the driver; those in the middle and back rode facing forward. The middle had no back for bracing; it was especially uncomfortable on rough roads. Small pieces of luggage were carried under the seats; larger pieces were placed in a compartment called the "boot" which was attached to the back of the coach on the outside. The roof might be slightly rounded, without a rack, and thus useless for luggage. By the mid-1830s, the coach evolved further to a style generally called the Concord Coach (after Concord, New Hampshire, where the best coaches of that style were built). The Concord Coach was flat-topped, with a rack on top for luggage. It was to be widely used all over the country, and especially in the Far West.

Tocqueville noted that American carriages were suspended on leather alone. The "thorough braces" were wide straps of leather that were riveted or laced together to great thickness and strength, then passed under the carriage itself and attached to the rest of the structure. Despite the Frenchmen's complaints about bumpy rides, the thorough braces were considered by Americans to provide a smoother ride than could be had in earlier carriages. Americans of that era were grateful for small favors.

Coaches which made regular runs on the turnpikes often were named for a famous person or a state, city or foreign country. At one point, there was even a coach called *Erin Go Bragh*. When a President traveled over the National Road, a new coach, or one especially redone for his convenience, would be provided by the company he patronized. It would be named after him or his office—for example, the *General Jackson* or the *President*.

There was genuine price competition between coach lines, and coach fares had dropped significantly after 1800. The 1832 fare between Boston and New York was about eleven dollars. Stage companies made extra money by carrying mail for the government. The mail coaches, which also carried passengers, were usually much faster than the regular ones.

Tocqueville and Beaumont used stages a great deal and often complained of bad roads and bumpy rides. Their first long stage trip was the one from Albany to Buffalo. Then, after a period of traveling chiefly by steamboat, they probably used stages in New England and on their trip from Philadelphia to Baltimore and back. They went by stage from Philadelphia to Pittsburgh, traveling night and day for about seventy-two hours. It was a November trip, and a most uncomfortable one.

Their next encounter with a stage came when they found the Ohio River frozen below Louisville and decided to go overland to Memphis in order to find a steamboat there. The roads were bumpy and the weather was very cold. After Nashville, the carriage broke down, and they had to walk at one point. But they finally reached Memphis by stage. On their return from New Orleans, they went by steamer to Mobile, then took stages again on their way back to New York. Apparently those rides were uneventful.

If Tocqueville and Beaumont were to come to America in this year, they would probably fly. It would take seven hours to fly from Paris, instead of the thirty-five days it took them to sail from Le Havre in 1831. They might even take a flight on the Concorde and arrive in three and one-half hours.

Their first view of New York would be from the air as their plane circled for landing, with the pilot's calling attention to Ellis Island and the Statue of Liberty, the Battery, the Staten Island Ferry, the Hudson River piers, the World Trade towers, the Empire State Building, Central Park, the United Nations buildings, and so forth. And then on to the landing, followed by the taxi trip through the midtown tunnel or over one of the bridges to Manhattan Island.

If they came by boat, they would pass the Statue of Liberty at the entrance to the Hudson River. They would see the Battery, quite different from what it was when Beaumont recorded it in one of his sketches in 1831. They would come to a city not of 200,000 persons, but to a city of 8 million. A city close to the continent, yet still an island city, stopping just short of being America. Holding the visitor uncertain, although already cast toward the new and strange land. Its taxicabs driven by persons in transition, immigrants or the sons and daughters of immigrants. Jews, Greeks, Lebanese, Armenians, Puerto Ricans, Jamaicans, and others—some having entered the United States legally, others illegally. The new and the not-so-new of the city. Showing their national origins, their religion, and their politics on the dashboard. Some ready to talk, some silent.

Tocqueville and Beaumont might arrange a boat trip up the Hudson to Albany, but it is much more likely that they would go by automobile to Sing Sing and then to Albany. They undoubtedly would go by car the 200 miles from Albany to Buffalo, viewing the cities of Utica, Schenectady, Syracuse, and Oneida along the highway.

Always the same pattern of approach to each city—beyond the suburbs a scattering of trailer homes and then motor courts in line (Haven's Rest, Trailside), the roadside stores, furniture (always furniture), restaurants of no distinction (Sarah and John, Flo and Pete). An occasional glimpse of well-ordered, well-cared-for suburbs saved from the moving stream of the highway by miles of anchor fence and a moat of grass. Exits promising food, gas and lodging, and in the distance the reaching signs of the gasoline stations—Gulf, Exxon, Texaco, Shell, and the lesser names like Super. Then the city proper with McDonald's, Gino's, Hot Shoppes and Howard Johnson's, and the more mysterious Colonel Sanders and Pizza Palace. Supper clubs with shingled mansard roofs promising cocktails and an occasional topless lunch and dinner, if you can stand it. And now, passing over the heart of the city, leaping over roads, streets, rivers, railroad yards, even houses in the westward rush, the smoke of factories in the distance or below. And then the diminuendo, the same fading from city, to service, to suburbs, to survival, a distance of farms and then a repeat—trailer homes, once again the same names, the same signs, the same architecture, the same road, flowing under the cars, the landscape, the cities. Sometimes the factory smoke changes—gray, to orange, to white.

English and Greek names indiscriminately mixed with the Indian names. Oneida, Rochester, Syracuse, Utica, Schenectady, Erie, Buffalo, Albany. Upper New York—it cannot sustain the great city of the sea, of the islands. It tips west to the Great Lakes, its rivers run there. It tips north, its rivers run north now to the St. Lawrence, away from the city. All but the Hudson, moving inexorably against the trend, having carried Henry Hudson, Washington Irving, and now carrying Pete Seeger, who would save it from its rising to its standing against the Atlantic tide.

The passage from Buffalo to Detroit would not be by steamboat, but certainly by airplane, flying over Erie, Salem, Ashtabula, Grand River, Cleveland, and Sandusky. It would take not two days and a night, as it did in 1831, but one hour. All passenger travel is now gone from the Great Lakes, except for incidental passage which can be booked on ore boats or an occasional freighter.

In most of these travels, up the Hudson to Albany, across the state of New York and over Lake Erie and its shores, some traces of the earlier condition of the country might be observed. But on the trip from Detroit to Pontiac, and from there to Flint and on to Saginaw, scarcely a trace of the world of 1831 would be found. The wilderness of the horseback trip described by Tocqueville is wholly gone. The dark and shadowed trail over which Tocqueville and Beaumont were led by Indian guides is now the supertrail of the automobile, the new symbol of American strength, power, prosperity, and mobility.

Detroit was a town of two or three thousand souls in 1831. Today it is a city (with suburbs) of two or three million persons. The road from Detroit to Pontiac, which Tocqueville and Beaumont traveled on horseback, passed through a thinly settled area in which log huts were the standard dwelling. Pontiac was a community of "twenty very neat and pretty houses, forming so many well-furnished shops, a transparent stream, a clearing a quarter of a league square . . ."

The road from Detroit to Pontiac is now a six-lane highway, lined by one-story buildings of assorted size but of generally common purpose—to serve the automobile and those who drive or ride in it. At nearly every intersection there are four filling stations, each offering a different gasoline. There are new-car-sales buildings and lots, used-car lots, car washes, an automobile factory, car and truck and trailer sales and leasing centers, specialty service shops for mufflers, distributors, tires, brakes, auto glass, shock absorbers, seat covers, transmission service, radiator service. There are repair shops, even one called the Cadillac Collision Clinic, paint shops, drive-in food services, and roadside restaurants, motels, drive-in banks, drive-in theaters, parking spaces. Only an occasional church, cemetery, or golf course breaks the line of service to the automobile culture.

And beyond Pontiac on the way to Flint, which Tocqueville described as "these flowered wildernesses" in which he experienced "tranquil admiration, a vague distaste for civilized life, a sweet and melancholy emotion, a sort of wild instinct which

makes one reflect with sadness that soon this delightful solitude
will be completely altered."

Route 10: not all unpleasant, one-story suburban offices set in
open space, with new plantings of grass and trees, and then islands of automobile service facilities, again filling stations, car
washes, tire sales, car sales, car rentals, drive-in restaurants,
banks, liquor stores, carpet and furniture stores, Kinney Shoes,
and all the better-known food service chains, from McDonald's
to Gino's, to Colonel Sanders.

And in between a waste of scrub oak and box elder, waiting
for the real estate developer, looking as though it had but partially recovered from what Tocqueville described as he neared
Flint: a land "cut by hills and valleys. Several of these hills were
most savage in appearance." Flint River in 1831 was marked by a
few cabins. Today it is marked as the home of the Buick motor-
car and the Chevrolet truck.

Beyond Flint, on the way to Saginaw, the real wilderness
began for Tocqueville and Beaumont. It was for this stretch that
they used Indian guides. Here, wrote Tocqueville, all traces of
man disappeared. "A majestic order reigns above your head.
Near the earth, on the contrary, everything offers the image of
confusion and chaos. Trunks incapable of longer supporting their
branches have broken at half their height and present to the eye
only a torn and pointed top. Others, long shaken by the wind,
have been precipitated to earth in one piece. Torn from the soil,
their roots form so many natural ramparts behind which hun-
dreds of men could easily find cover. Immense trees, retained by
the surrounding branches, hang suspended in the air, and fall
into dust without touching the earth."

The trail from Flint to Saginaw is now a six-lane highway.
There is little of natural grandeur along the route. No great
pines or oaks, but rather second- and third-growth scrub oak and
poplar and willows and dead trees in swamps, denied natural
drainage by the straight-line highway. Only indications of a wilderness that once was, a billboard calling on cougar hunters who
might need the services of a gunsmith or outfitters. And in the
stretch of road, two raccoons, killed by passing automobiles.

There is no trace, easily observed, of Tocqueville in Saginaw,
or of the Indians and wild ducks that he found there. One street

bears the Indian name Tuscola, and there is a small community near Saginaw called Indian Village. Saginaw is one of the principal centers for the production of steering equipment for General Motors cars. The city today fulfills the prophecy of Tocqueville that "In a few years these impenetrable forests will have fallen, the noise of civilization and of industry will break the silence of the Saginaw."

The Canadian trip would be made principally by airplane, with possible automobile side trips to points of historic interest. Instead of outposts and trading posts, the visitors would see the cities of Montreal and Quebec, both changed from 1831. Considering their endurance and their enthusiasm for America, they might return from Canada by car along the same route they followed by boat and stage—to Albany, to Stockbridge and Boston, to Hartford and on to New York City—a not unpleasant trip. Two days later they might go by car from New York to Philadelphia and on to Baltimore; after two weeks, back to Philadelphia by the Turnpike or Route 1—a dangerous and unpleasant trip. More likely than not they would fly from Philadelphia to Pittsburgh rather than risk the Pennsylvania Turnpike; and then, unless they were curious enough to take one of the few remaining boats in service in the United States (on the Ohio or on the Mississippi), they would probably fly from Pittsburgh to New Orleans. They would see, but only from the air, cities like Cincinnati, Nashville, and Memphis. They might well miss Mobile altogether, and bypass Baltimore while heading for New York and their return to France.

Or they might fly to Los Angeles and San Francisco, stopping to see Chicago on the way back. On the western flights they would take in the land in great gulps or leaps, almost too much to swallow and certainly to digest. They would see the scars of strip mining in Illinois and in Kentucky, in Ohio and West Virginia. Reservoirs and waterways, the artificial lakes of the TVA, the slow-flowing Mississippi and the gray Missouri, the dry riverbeds of the West, and the scar of the Colorado.

Great reaches of fields cut in straight lines all the way across Colorado to the very base of the Rocky Mountains, and beyond, naked as uncovered breasts or old bones. The mountains, great thrusts of rocks, some snow-capped like Rainier, Mount Hood,

and St. Helena. And in a dry season whole ranges rise brown
and green and finally barren gray. And they would see the des-
erts of the Southwest.

At night, the clustered lights of the small towns, and single
lights of farmyards scattered across the plains. And then the
great valleys of light approaching Los Angeles, and hills of light
in San Francisco, that startled city hung on the edge of the
continent. An uncertain city, a stranger of a city, there at the end
of our land, with the highest suicide rate of any city in America.

Tocqueville and Beaumont would probably talk to essentially
the same kind of person they met on their earlier trip. Their letters of recommendation (more likely transatlantic telephone
calls) would be to the talking and writing professionals—
newspapermen, politicians, columnists, and commentators. Instead of a sketch pad, Beaumont would undoubtedly have a
camera, if not a cameraman, and the tape recorder might well
supplement Tocqueville's journal. The America they would see,
and the institutions they would observe and study, would be
startlingly different in some respects, and scarcely changed in
others.

The chapters which follow this introduction are an effort to
compare and contrast the America of 1978 with that which
existed and which was observed and commented on by the
French visitors of 1831.

1

Indians: To Be Free

Whereas prison study was the official and formal reason given by Tocqueville for his trip to America, many lines in his journals suggest that his greatest personal interest was in the Indians of America.

With great expectations he anticipated seeing his first Indians. He had read the books of Chateaubriand and of James Fenimore Cooper, and undoubtedly carried in his mind an image of "the noble savage" when he wrote in his journal: "I was expecting to find the natives of America savages, but savages on whose face nature had stamped the marks of some of the proud virtues which liberty brings forth. I expected to find a race of men little different from Europeans, whose bodies had been developed by the strenuous exercise of hunting and of war, and who would lose nothing by being seen naked."

His first sight of Indians was at Oneida Castle, a village about 180 miles from New York. The Indians ran after Tocqueville's carriage, asking for alms. His view of these Indians was slight and passing. It was at Buffalo, some time later, that his romantic anticipation was shocked by reality. The Indians whom he saw there were "small in stature, their limbs, as far as one could tell under their clothes, were thin and not wiry, their skin, instead of being red as is generally thought, was dark bronze. . . . Their physiognomy told of that profound degradation which only long abuse of the benefits of civilization can give, but yet they were still savages. Mixed with the vices which they got from us was something barbarous and uncivilized which made them a hundred times more repulsive still. . . .

"Having wandered to some distance from the town, we ran into a crowd of Indians who were returning to their village. Most of them were more or less drunk. An Indian woman was rolling in the dust of the road, uttering savage cries. Close to the last houses we saw an Indian lying at the edge of the road. It was a young man. He was motionless and, we thought, dead. Some stifled groans that painfully broke from his breast showed that he was still alive and struggling against one of those dangerous fits of drunkenness brought on by brandy. The sun had already sunk, and the ground was damp. Everything indicated that the wretched man would breathe his last sigh there, if he was not helped. . . .

"When we got back to the town," Tocqueville continued his narrative, "we told several people about the young Indian whose body was stretched on the road. We spoke of the imminent danger to which he was exposed; we even offered to pay the expense of an inn. All that was useless; we could not persuade anyone to budge. Some said to us: 'Those men are used to drink to excess and sleep on the ground; they never die from accidents like that.' Others recognized that the Indian would probably die, but one could read on their lips this half-expressed thought: 'What is the life of an Indian?' The fact is that that was the basis of the general feeling. In the midst of this American society, so well policed, so sententious, so charitable, a cold selfishness and complete insensibility prevails when it is a question of the natives of the country. . . . This world here belongs to us, they tell themselves every day; the Indian race is destined for final destruction which one cannot prevent and which it is not desirable to delay. Heaven has not made them to become civilized; it is necessary that they die. Besides, I do not at all want to get mixed up in it. . . ."

He was in the territory in which Chief Red Jacket of the Senecas had managed to hold his people together on their reservation until his death, after which the Ogden Land Company, a New York group of land speculators, began to move to take over the reservation. Through the established methods of bribery and deception, they succeeded in getting most of the tribal land. During the administration of Martin Van Buren, the Senate approved a confirming treaty, denounced by the President but passed by the controlling vote of Vice-President Richard M. Johnson, who was reputed to have killed Tecumseh.

Approximately a hundred years later, in 1960, the Tuscarora tribe lost a case to the Niagara Power Project in the name of progress and under the threat of the bulldozer. In a dissenting opinion to the Supreme Court decision which rejected the Indian case, Justice Hugo L. Black, joined by Chief Justice Earl Warren and Justice William O. Douglas, wrote: "The record does not leave the impression that the lands of their reservation are the most fertile, the landscape the most beautiful or their homes the most splendid specimens of architecture. But this is their home—their ancestral home. There they, their children and their forebears were born. They, too, have their memories and their loves. Some things are worth more than money and the costs of a new enterprise. . . . I regret that this Court is to be the governmental agency that breaks faith with this dependent people. Great nations, like great men, should keep their word."

Later in his travels, Tocqueville was to see Indians whose character was closer to his ideal of the Indian, and Americans who were more understanding and more concerned about the fate of the native Americans. His first experience was the worst. It was because he was seeing the Indians in the border zone, where their abuse and corruption by the whites was evident in its grossest form.

These were Indians whose ancestors had been displaced and then displaced again and again by the relentless pressure of white settlers beginning nearly three hundred years earlier when, in 1625, colonists in Massachusetts asked Samoset, a Pemaquid chief, to give them twelve thousand additional acres of land. He put his mark on a paper, thus executing the first deed of Indian land to the English colonists. Later immigrants did not bother to go through legal formalities. By the time Massasoit, chief of the Wampanoags, died in 1661, his people were being pushed back into the wilderness. His son Metacom, called King Philip by the colonists, organized a confederacy to save the tribal lands.

The Indians had success in their initial attacks on settlements, but after months of fighting, the Wampanoags and the Narragansetts were virtually exterminated. King Philip was killed and his head exhibited at Plymouth for twenty years. The good men of Plymouth sold captured Indian women, including Philip's wife and son, into slavery in the West Indies.

The pattern in New York was much the same: beginning in 1641 when Willem Kieft ordered the massacre of the Raritans, and during the following centuries when the Six Nations of the Iroquois were defeated and driven westward.

Farther south, too, the Indians were driven inward, away from the coastal cities and the lands east of the Alleghenies and the Appalachians, and then even farther to the west as settlers began to pour over and around the mountains into the fertile plains of the Midwest. In Ohio, the Miamis were forced to give up most of their territory. Many members of the Sauk and Fox tribes, driven by the settlers who came into Illinois territory after the War of 1812, fled across the Mississippi into what was to become the state of Wisconsin. They left their names on a river in Wisconsin, the Fox, and on the Sauk River in Minnesota. Black Hawk, leading an alliance of Sauk and Fox in a last stand in Illinois, lost his war and was taken captive soon after Tocqueville returned to France.

Most of the Ojibways, descendants or relatives of those Tocqueville saw in Buffalo, moved west to Michigan and north to Canada along with the Ottawas. The Menominees and Winnebagos, who now have one of the more popular camper trailers named after them, and the Potawatomi, who supported Black Hawk, were all moved or moving west to areas later to become states like Indiana, Illinois, Wisconsin, Iowa, and Minnesota.

Tocqueville's most satisfying experience was with the Indians of the Great Lakes region. Settlements in that area were thin, and the Indians relatively free to lead their natural lives. There the Indians trusted the white men, and the white men trusted the Indians. In Pontiac, Tocqueville was assured by a Mr. Williams that the Indians, mainly Chippewas in that area, were persons of intelligence and integrity, in no way like the Indians that Tocqueville had seen in Buffalo, as Williams was in no way like the whites of Buffalo in his attitude toward the Indians. When

asked whether there was danger in traveling through the territory of the Indian tribes, Williams replied with indignation:
"No, no; you can proceed without fear. For my part, I should
sleep more calmly among the Indians than among the whites."
And later on the same journey, they were assured by a white
woodsman, whom they met on the trail, that rather than being
afraid of the Indians, he "would rather live in their midst than
among the whites. No, no," he said, "I am not afraid of the Indians; they are worth more than we, if we have not brutalized
them by our liquors, poor creatures!"

Tocqueville was to make few additional observations on Indians until later in his visit to America. On his way to New
Orleans he came to know what was happening to the Indians of
the Southeast. By this time, the Indians of the Northeast had all
but been destroyed. The Wampanoags of Massasoit and of King
Philip were gone, as were the Chesapeakes, the Chickahominys,
and the Potomacs of the Powhatan confederacy. The Montauks,
Nanticokes, Catawbas, Miamis, Hurons, Eries, Mohawks, Senecas, and Mohegans had been scattered if not obliterated.

Andrew Jackson, known to the Indians as Sharp Knife, took
office as President of the United States in 1829. Jackson had
made a reputation as an Indian fighter. He was also a slave
owner. For other reasons, he is still honored at annual Democratic party fund-raising dinners.

Jackson's early Indian fighting was excused as a part of international conflict and rivalry with the Spanish in Florida. But
after the Florida treaty of 1821, foreign involvement could no
longer be used as justification for Indian fighting in that land
area. Nonetheless it continued: the Cherokees, Chickasaws,
Choctaws, Creeks, and Seminoles—still numerous—held on to
their tribal lands and refused to be driven off.

In Jackson's first message to Congress, he recommended that
these Indians be removed to the west beyond the Mississippi,
where he recommended "the propriety of setting apart an
ample district west of the Mississippi . . . to be guaranteed to
the Indian tribes as long as they shall occupy it." In 1830, the Indian Removal Act became law.

Jackson, it is reported, believed that Indians and whites could not live together in peace, that his plan would take care of this conflict, and that there would be no more broken promises.

Jackson was not alone in this view. Efforts to maintain Indian reservations within the eastern states, not just in Jackson's territory but farther north, had not been very successful. Well ahead of Jackson's administration, President Monroe had accepted the need for a removal program, and plans for removal began to take shape. Most plans called for assent by the Indians and for compensation. The record shows that the assent was often very superficial, the compensation less than adequate, and that bribery and liquor were important forces in getting agreement from the Indians. John Quincy Adams slowed the programs; but his slowing down of progress, as it was believed to be, built up pressure for acceleration under Jackson.

Liquidation of Indian reservations in the old Northwest was pressed hard and with success between 1829 and 1843. With friendly support from the White House, the Shawnees, the Delawares, and the Wyandots, among others, moved west of the Missouri. It was in 1832 that Black Hawk, recrossing the Mississippi to find vacant prairie in which to plant a corn crop, was set upon by the militia of Illinois, which pursued the starving Indians back into Wisconsin, killing women and children along the way. An officer commanding one company of the expedition was Abraham Lincoln. It was during Lincoln's administration some thirty years later that the long walk of the Navajos began.

Jackson's immediate challenge was from the four great Indian nations of the Southwest: the Chickasaw, the Creek, the Choctaw, and the Cherokee. White land occupancy was restricted in the East because of Indian rights and tenure in northeastern Georgia, in areas of western North Carolina and southern Tennessee, in eastern Alabama, and in the northern two thirds of Mississippi. In these twenty-five million acres lived nearly sixty thousand members of the four tribes.

The Jackson administration was wholly co-operative, adding philosophical as well as legal and military support to removal. Thomas Benton, senator from Missouri, spoke of a national imperative (an early form of Manifest Destiny) for the removal of the Indians, an action which, he said, was according to God's will. Jackson himself described the progress of America as demonstrated by a land "studded with cities, towns, and prosperous farms, embellished with all the improvements which art can devise or industry execute, occupied by more than 12,000,000 happy people, and filled with all the blessings of liberty, civilization and religion," in contrast with what had been forests "ranged by a few thousand savages."

In 1832 Jackson appointed a Commissioner of Indian Affairs as part of the War Department to see that laws affecting Indians were carried out.

In 1834 Congress passed an act to regulate trade and intercourse with the Indian tribes and to preserve peace on the frontiers. According to the act, all of the United States west of the Mississippi, except for the states of Missouri and Louisiana and the Territory of Arkansas, would henceforth be Indian country. No white person was to trade in the Indian country without a license. No white persons were to be permitted to settle in Indian country, and the military forces of the United States were charged with responsibility for enforcing the laws.

Even before the laws could be put into effect, a new wave of white settlers rushed west to form the territories of Wisconsin and Iowa. The government shifted the "permanent" Indian frontier from the Mississippi River to the ninety-fifth meridian: a line which ran from Lake of the Woods, now a part of the border between Minnesota and Canada, southward through what later became the states of Minnesota and Iowa, and then along the western borders of Missouri, Arkansas, and Louisiana, ending at Galveston Bay, Texas. To keep the Indians west of the ninety-fifth meridian and also, in principle at least, to keep the settlers east of that line, a series of military posts were built, running from Fort Snelling on the Mississippi in Minnesota, to forts Atkinson and Leavenworth on the Missouri, forts Gibson and Smith on the Arkansas, Fort Towson on the Red, and Fort Jesup in Louisiana.

In the Southeast the government began making treaties with the Indian tribes: with the Choctaws of Mississippi, providing for their removal within three years; with the Creek nation in 1832, providing for the liquidation of their reservation in Alabama.

In 1833 the first public auctions of Choctaw lands occurred.

According to Edwin Miles, the people of Mississippi were so grateful to Jackson for making those lands available that "they were inclined to disregard differences of opinion that he might entertain on issues of less importance."

The Jackson administration, reflecting the President's disposition, helped the southern states separate the tribes from their lands. Jackson appointed John Berrien as Attorney General rather than the preferred candidate, William Wirt, because he mistrusted the latter's stand on Indian removal. When Wirt later became lawyer for the Cherokees, Jackson denounced him as a wicked man. Jackson removed a head of the Indian Affairs office because the man was believed to be sympathetic to the Indians, and replaced him with a more reliable person. When the Supreme Court ruled in *Worcester* v. *Georgia* that Georgia had no right to extend its laws over the Cherokee nation, the President refused to enforce the decision. His refusal was immediately interpreted by whites as a license to intrude on Indian lands and as an encouragement to states' rights in dealing with Indians.

The removal procedures were varied: direct and indirect, legal and illegal, violent and nonviolent. As a rule, force was avoided and the removal accomplished within reasonable limits of legality. Federal law for the most part recognized tribal and treaty rights. State laws did not, but rather treated the Indians as individuals under state law. Federal law offered allotments or reservations to Indians who cultivated their lands and wished to become citizens, while encouraging trans-Mississippi movements. Money was appropriated, and the President was authorized to negotiate removal treaties with the eastern tribes.

Fraud, bribery, and alcohol played their part. When these methods failed, or where special circumstances arose, force and cruel methods were used. The war that drove the Seminoles out of Florida followed broken American promises. So, too, the Creek uprising and oppression followed frustration and fraud. Action against the Cherokees, the Choctaws, and the Chickasaws was particularly indefensible since, even by European standards, they were civilized. They lived in fixed communities and practiced an advanced agriculture; some even held black slaves. The Cherokees had a written language, printed the Bible and other books in their own language, and published a weekly newspaper, *The Cherokee Phoenix.*

Tocqueville, making his way to New Orleans in 1831, witnessed a part of this Indian history at Memphis. A riverboat captain was persuaded to risk the ice-clogged river because of additional fares to be paid by the government to transport Choctaws on their way west. There appeared, he wrote, "a large troupe of Indians, old men, women, children, belongings, all led by a European and steering toward the capital of our triangle. These Indians were Chactas (or Tchactaws), following the Indian pronunciation . . .

"The Chactas," he continued, "were a powerful nation living on the frontiers of the States of Alabama and Georgia. After long negotiations they finally, this year, succeeded in persuading them to leave their country and emigrate to the right bank of the Mississippi. Six to seven thousand Indians have already crossed the great river; those arriving in Memphis came there with the object of following their compatriots. The agent of the American Government, who was accompanying them and was responsible for paying their passage, when he learned that a steamboat had just arrived, ran to the bank . . ." Tocqueville continued: "But we had not left yet; it was a question of embarking our exiled tribe, its horses and its dogs. Here began a scene which, in truth, had something lamentable about it. The Indians advanced mournfully toward the bank. . . . In the whole scene there was an air of ruin and destruction, something which betrayed a final and irrevocable adieu; one couldn't watch without feeling one's heart wrung. The Indians were tranquil, but somber and taciturn. There was one who could speak English and of whom I asked why the Chactas were leaving their country. 'To be free,' he answered. I could never get any other reason out of him. We will set them down tomorrow in the solitudes of Arkansas. One must confess that it is a singular fate that brought us to Memphis to watch the expulsion, one can say the dissolution, of one of the most celebrated and ancient American peoples. . . ."

This commentary was supported by Tocqueville's interview with Sam Houston of Tennessee and later of Texas fame. Tocqueville met Houston, according to his journal, on December 27, 1831, at the mouth of the White River, where the boat had stopped to let the Choctaws get off. Houston boarded the boat for the remaining trip to New Orleans.

Houston spoke of the history of the Indians, of the civilization of the Cherokees especially, and then rated in order after them the Creeks, the Chickasaws, and the Choctaws. Houston was hopeful that the granting of lands to the Indians would provide a refuge and that, if the government took the trouble to encourage them, the Indians there would civilize themselves.

There were two things from which Houston thought the Indians should be protected: one was strong drink, for, he said, "Brandy is the main cause of the destruction of the natives of America"; the other, Christianity. "My view," said Houston, "is that it is a very bad plan for civilizing the Indians to send missionaries among them. Christianity is the religion of an enlightened and intellectual people; it is above the intellectual level of a people as little advanced in civilization, and so much the slaves of mere material instincts as the Indians. In my view, one should first try to win the Indians away from their wandering life, and persuade them to cultivate the soil. The introduction of the Christian religion would follow naturally on the change that had taken place in their social condition. I have noticed that only Catholicism has been able to succeed in making a durable impression on the Indians. It strikes their senses and speaks to their imagination."

Tocqueville was less optimistic than Houston. Leaving out the issue of brandy and of Christianity, he wrote in *Democracy in America:* "From whatever angle one regards the destinies of the North American natives, one sees nothing but irremediable ills: if they remain savages, they are driven along before the march of progress; if they try to become civilized, contact with more-civilized people delivers them over to oppression and misery. If they go on wandering in the wilderness, they perish; if they attempt to settle, they perish just the same."

It is the pessimistic view of Tocqueville, the Frenchman, rather than the optimism of the American frontiersman Sam Houston that has prevailed. Within a quarter of a century after the establishment of the ninety-fifth meridian line as the permanent Indian frontier, the line had been bent or broken in both the

northern and southern ends, and miners and traders had moved
through the middle section of the line.

The final move against the remaining Indians began after
1860. Following the outbreak of the Sioux in Minnesota and their
suppression, war between Indians and whites in the western
reaches of the United States was almost continuous. Some two
hundred pitched battles between soldiers and Indians took place
in the years 1869 to 1876. In Colorado large holdings of the Utes
were taken over by the government and opened to settlers and
miners; later the Utes were forced to a reservation in Utah. The
discovery of gold in Idaho spelled the end of the peaceful lives
of the Nez Percés. After a series of battles with soldiers who
heavily outnumbered his warriors, Chief Joseph of the Nez
Percés surrendered: ". . . Hear me, my chiefs! I am tired; my
heart is sick and sad. From where the sun now stands I will fight
no more forever." And so it went until the symbolic ending of Indian freedom in the Ghost Dance and massacre at Wounded
Knee. By 1890 the Indian had lost his physical freedom but lived
on in a cultural wilderness.

Now, nearly 150 years after Tocqueville's visit, it is estimated
that there are over 1,000,000 Indians in the United States. About
650,000 live on or near reservations. The states with the largest
Indian populations, according to the 1970 census, are Oklahoma,
Arizona, California, and New Mexico. There are also significant
numbers of Indians in some midwestern, eastern, and southern
states: North Dakota, South Dakota, Wisconsin, and Minnesota,
for example, in the Midwest; North Carolina in the Southeast;
and New York in the Northeast.

By every generally accepted measure of cultural and economic
well-being, the Indians of the United States fall far below average standards. Poverty and unemployment mark the reservations. In 1977, of Indians living on reservations and able to
work, about 40 per cent were unemployed. Many of them were
not even seeking jobs because they knew that none were available. The high school dropout rate of Indians is estimated at
roughly 35 per cent. While the Indian birth rate is twice as high
as the national average, the Indian suicide rate is also twice as
high. The incidence of tuberculosis and several other diseases is

much greater among Indians than among the general population.

In contrast with their earlier status, Indians are now citizens of the United States and of the individual states in which they reside. They vote and pay taxes. Indian men were subject to military conscription when it was in effect. Most Indian children now attend regular public schools instead of federal schools (or Indian schools, as they have been called).

Reservation lands are still held in trust by the United States, and the Bureau of Indian Affairs still has extensive power over the lives of Indians. In contrast with earlier times when Indian tribes were treated (at least on paper) as quasi-sovereign nations, their tribal governments are now, by virtue of laws and court decisions, more like subordinate versions of state governments, or like county governments with somewhat enlarged sovereignty and responsibility.

Indians own about 2.2 per cent of U.S. land. This statistical figure is quite meaningless, since the land which they own is, for the most part, the poorest and least productive in the nation. The Indians were driven from the best lands of the country to lands that are isolated, unsuited to farming, and lacking in mineral wealth. Most reservations needed subsidies from the time they were first established. In the nineteenth century, reservation Indians received "rations"; now they receive "surplus commodities."

Many hoped that Indians would become self-sufficient economically, especially through farming. (White farmers without subsidies are scarcely self-sufficient, even on good land.) But most reservation lands are far from the rich agricultural areas of the country. Even where Indian land is suitable for farming, as it is in parts of the West, Indian water rights have often been lost. Reservation lands in many areas of the West are suitable only for cattle or sheep ranching. Unfortunately, however, ranching requires few workers per acre—hence the high unemployment rates of so many reservations. There is a parallel between the Indian removal history of the United States and the enclosure movement of medieval England, which displaced the serfs and turned the lands over to sheep raising and the woolen trade.

Although a few tribes have found mineral wealth on their lands—and at a time when it could not be taken from them —their situation is hardly typical. "While tales of tribal Indians inundated with great wealth have been colorful, more significant in the long run have been the cases of more modest assets—such as those of the Navajo—which have provided the economic basis for a variety of tribal developmental programs and afforded some stability and power to tribal governance."

In 1971 Congress passed the Alaska Native Claims Settlement Act, which ended aboriginal title to half a million square miles of land and established a complex system of compensation for oil produced on the land, including the right of native corporations to regain some of the land.

Indian rights and Indian claims have received widespread and serious attention in recent years. In some cases redress of grievances and restoration of rights have been pursued through regular legal channels; in other cases, by militant acts such as seizure of property and violation of laws. The results achieved have been mixed, but for the most part they have been, compared to past history, affirmative and supportive of Indian claims.

In 1970 Congress by law restored 48,000 acres of land to the Taos Pueblo Indians of New Mexico. This was land that the government had taken for national forest purposes in 1906 without compensating the Indians. In 1972 by President Nixon's executive order, 21,000 acres of land were restored to the Yakima tribe in Washington State. This was land apparently taken from the Indians by the federal government by mistake in 1908.

In 1954 the Menominees of Wisconsin became the first tribe to be liberated under the terms and purposes of a congressional resolution passed in 1953. The resolution read in part:

> It is the policy of Congress, as rapidly as possible, to make the Indians within the territorial limits of the United States subject to the same laws and entitled to the same privileges and responsibilities as are applicable to other citizens of the United States, and to end their status as wards of the United States, and to grant them all the rights and prerogatives pertaining to American citizenship. . . .

Final termination of the Menominees was delayed until April 1961. Then, according to the provisions of the termination bill, the Indians on the Menominee Reservation were to be removed fully from federal trust status and be free to manage their own affairs, including valuable forest lands and a tribal sawmill. A dozen other tribes, most of them in the west, were "terminated" in this period.

Termination, as a policy, was seriously questioned when it was adopted. Twenty years after the termination of the Menominees, their tribal rights were restored in what President Nixon described as "an important turning point" in Indian history.

An earlier Nixon statement, of July 8, 1970, had announced a new policy, reversing that of the Eisenhower administration. Mr. Nixon declared:

> Because termination is morally and legally unacceptable, because it produces bad practical results, and because the mere threat of termination tends to discourage greater self-sufficiency among Indian groups, I am asking the Congress to pass a new concurrent resolution which would expressly renounce, repudiate and repeal the termination policy as expressed in House Concurrent Resolution 108 of the 83d Congress [passed in 1953]. This resolution would explicitly affirm the integrity and right to continued existence of all Indian Tribes and Alaska native governments, recognizing that cultural pluralism is a source of national strength. It would assure these groups that the United States Government would continue to carry out its treaty and trusteeship obligations to them as long as the groups themselves believed that such a policy was necessary or desirable. . . . In short, such a resolution would reaffirm . . . that the historic relationship between the Federal Government and the Indian communities cannot be abridged without the consent of the Indians.

On December 22, 1973, President Nixon signed into law an act restoring the Menominee Indians of Wisconsin to federal services. Under the provisions of the act, the emancipation of 1961 was reversed, putting the Menominee land into trust and generally restoring the tribal relationships of earlier times.

The fishing rights of some Indian tribes have been clarified.

Financial settlements have been made in response to court action in a number of cases. Land restorations and grants continue to be made on a limited scale—one of the most recent being the enlargement of the Havasupai Indian Reservation in the Grand Canyon. The Havasupai tribe were removed or driven from the lands on the canyon rim almost a century ago; since then they have lived on two small areas of land at the bottom of the canyon.

More radical actions have been less successful, insofar as success can be measured directly, although they have served to attract attention to and win sympathy for the Indians.

One of the occupations receiving most attention was that of Alcatraz in San Francisco Bay in 1969. Nineteen months later the United States Government removed fifteen Indians from the island.

From June 14 to July 1, 1971, Indians occupied a Nike missile site in Chicago in protest over lack of suitable housing.

On June 6, 1971, about forty Indians camped on Mount Rushmore in South Dakota. They demanded that the federal government honor an 1868 treaty which, the Indians said, gave them the right to all land in South Dakota west of the Missouri River. Their demands were not honored.

The most disturbing Indian protest was the ten-week siege of the town of Wounded Knee on the Oglala Sioux reservation near Pine Ridge, South Dakota. The siege began on February 27, 1973, when nearly 200 members and supporters of the American Indian Movement took over the town. The protesting Indians charged that the administration of the reservation was corrupt and called for the repeal of the Indian Reorganization Act of 1934. The dispute was temporarily settled to no one's satisfaction with the rejection of the leaders of the siege in a tribal election in February 1974.

The most successful Indian takeover was that of the Bureau of Indian Affairs building in Washington, DC, which was occupied by Indians from November 2 to November 8, 1972. The Indians represented a group called the Trail of Broken Treaties Caravan. In response to their demands, one official in the Bureau of Indian Affairs resigned, an Indian was appointed to a new position created in the Interior Department, and procedural changes were initiated, giving Indians hope for more attentive response to their problems.

On New Year's Eve, 1974, a band of forty Menominees seized land and buildings near their reservation in Wisconsin. The property belonged to the Alexian Brothers, a Roman Catholic religious order dedicated to medical care. The Brothers subsequently agreed to turn over the buildings, which had not been used since 1969. But in the summer of 1975, the Brothers announced that they were canceling the agreement; they said that tribal leaders had decided they did not want the property.

The largest Indian claim to receive judicial attention is that of the 3,000 Passamaquoddy and Penobscot Indians in the state of Maine, who are asking that their title to over one half of the state (12.5 million acres) be restored and that they be paid 25 billion dollars in back rents and damages. The technical legal basis for the assertion of the claim is that a 1794 treaty between the Indian tribes and the state of Massachusetts (from which Maine later separated) is not binding because that treaty was never ratified by Congress as required by the Indian Non-Intercourse Act of 1790. In January of 1975, a federal judge ruled that that act did apply to the Passamaquoddy Indian tribe and that the act established a trust relationship which had not been respected in the 1794 treaty. The lower court decision was upheld in the United States Court of Appeals in Boston and was not appealed to the Supreme Court within the time allowed for appeal. Further legal action is anticipated; and it is expected that a compromise will be worked out, including financial settlements with the tribes and possibly the return or transfer of some portion of the state's 750,000 acres of public lands to the Indians. Some private titles also are in jeopardy, and exchange or transfer of private holdings may also be a part of the settlement.

Claims similar to those of the Maine Indians are being made in other states, including Massachusetts, where the Wampanoag tribe on Cape Cod is claiming the town of Mashpee, along with 17,000 acres of land. The same tribe is also claiming about 5,000 acres on the island of Martha's Vineyard. In Rhode Island the Narragansett tribe is claiming 3,200 acres in the town of Charlestown. In Connecticut, the Schaghticoke tribe is claiming 1,300 acres; and the Western Pequot tribe, 1,000 acres. In New

York, the Oneida tribe is asserting a claim to 300,000 acres in the area between Syracuse and Utica. And in South Carolina, the Catawbas are claiming 144,000 acres, including the city of Rock Hill.

Some of these legal difficulties might have been avoided if state government officials had read Tocqueville, for there is a note written in the margin of his journal to this point: "There is a law forbidding a white to buy an Indian's land. The United States does not recognize the Indians' right to alienate their land except in their capacity as a people, and when the purchaser is the United States itself."

Despite successful claims by some of the tribes against the government, despite procedural changes in dealing with Indian problems, and despite widespread sympathy for the Indians, the fact remains that little overall progress has been made toward solving what is called the "Indian Problem."

Almost every decade in the last thirty years has been marked by a new approach to the problem. In the fifties, there was pressure to terminate federal trusteeship responsibilities and to give the Indians full citizenship. Under this policy, significant land transfers occurred, and in some states Indians were brought under state civil and criminal jurisdiction. The prohibition against the sale of alcoholic beverages to Indians outside Indian jurisdictions was repealed, and a local-option system was established within the reservations. The Division of Indian Health was transferred in 1955 from the Bureau of Indian Affairs to the U. S. Public Health Service.

Indian defenders and supporters were encouraged. Oliver La-Farge, for example, was moved to write in the late fifties:

The progress has been great, and it has been spotty. You cannot make over a race in 25 years, despite what the allotment theorists believed. It takes more than one generation to make the jump from a home in which no English is spoken, where the very sight of a white man is a rarity, where the thinking is the same as it was 300 years ago, to full competence in our alien and complex way of life. If, while the Indians are struggling desperately to make the great adjustment, the last remnants of their land base are lost to them; if, as they fear, the Indian Reorganization

Act will be junked some day, their struggle will be hopeless. It is the Government's responsibility to enable [Indians] to keep and use what they already have, to allow them an ordinary choice, and not the flat alternatives of migrate or starve.

The Bureau of Indian Affairs characterized the decade of the sixties as one of "New Direction," marked by a "New Trail" toward "equal citizenship rights and benefits, maximum self-sufficiency, and full participation in American life." There was to be a shift away from termination of federal trust relationships and a replacement of the caretaking role, supposedly rejected in the fifties, with new forms and concepts of assistance to the Indians. This was to take the form of assistance in improving Indian housing, education, medical care, in alleviating unemployment and poverty. A resolution passed by Congress in 1967–68 enunciated a new policy and purpose toward the Indians and the Alaskan Natives, declaredly reversing the policies which followed from the congressional resolution of 1953.

Nonetheless, in the seventies Indian discontent continues and concern for their plight, despite limited and spotty improvements, continues. The situation proves in part what Henry Knox, first administrator of federal Indian policies in George Washington's administration, said—namely, "that the civilization of the Indians would be an operation of complicated difficulty; that it would require the highest knowledge of the human character and a steady perseverance in a wise system for a series of years cannot be doubted." The experience of nearly 200 years does not sustain the optimism of the rest of his remarks: "But to deny that, under a course of favorable circumstances, it could be accomplished, is to suppose the human character under the influence of such stubborn habits as to be incapable of melioration or change."

The historical excuse for mismanagement and abuse of the Indians in the nineteenth century was that there was not time enough; America was growing and expanding so quickly that no one paused long enough to deal rationally and fairly with the Indians. According to this interpretation, when there was space enough, the Indians lost to time. Sydney Mead, in his book *The Lively Experiment,* describes the predicament, if it was that.

The Pilgrims during that first terrible winter soon discovered
what later generations of Americans came to know almost in-
stinctively, that

> "There is no time to grieve now, there is
>   no time.
> There is only time for the labor in the cold."
>   [Stephen Vincent Benét]

Francis Parkman, the cultivated New Englander, lured on to
suffer the primitive vicissitudes of the Oregon Trail by his consuming passion to study the Indians in their native habitat, recorded in epigrammatic lines one great truth about his fellow
Americans. Hunting for food one day, he shot an antelope:
"When I stood by his side, the antelope turned his expiring
eye upward. It was like a beautiful woman's, dark and bright.
'Fortunate that I am in a hurry,' thought I; 'I might be troubled
with remorse, if I had time for it.'"

Mead continues: "In all the dark pages of American history,
none is darker than that on which is written the story of the Indians. And that page, too, if not made bright, is at least grasped
with tragic understanding when read in the context of time. Bernard De Voto, whose historical writings were all informed by
poetical insight, writing of the Indians in their last great preserve in the vast land 'across the wide Missouri,' stresses this
point.

Perhaps the Indians might have been adapted to the nineteenth-
century order and might have saved enough roots from their own
order to grow in dignity and health in a changed world—if there
had been time."

The problem today is not one of time. It is in part one of
space, but basically one of misunderstanding and uncertainty on
the part of both Indians and those who speak for American civilization. There is growing knowledge of Indian culture and history, and realization that this culture is quite different from that
commonly accepted as the American ideal or standard. The Indian heritage generally stresses extended families, tribal solidarity, community ownership, decisions by consensus, respect for
the elders of the tribe. The emphasis in the broader and charac-
teristic American culture, on the other hand, is on the nuclear,

isolated family, on individual effort and ownership, on fierce competition at the individual level, on decisions by majority votes.

It is now recognized that there are, and have always been, great cultural differences among the various Indian tribes. At the time of the first contact between Europeans and the American Indians, there were, according to one study, more cultural and linguistic differences among the Indians than there were among Europeans. The same study observes that as late as 1960, there remained some fifty different Indian languages still in use in America. Many Indians think of themselves as, for example, Sioux or Cherokee first and as Indians only in a broad racial or cultural category.

Christian religious sects are re-examining their missionary role relative to Indians. Typical of this re-examination, or of the conclusions from such re-examination, is a 1975 report of the Minnesota Catholic Conference: "New beginnings demand that we take an honest look at the past. We realize and acknowledge that our deeds, although done in good faith, were sometimes, in fact, a disservice to Indian people." The report asserted that Indian religion "demands appreciation," supported diverse "cultural communities," and said that, above all, "Indians have the right to be Indians."

Solution, or even partial solution, is not easy. Indians themselves are uncertain, as well they might be, as to what should be done. Older Indians on the reservations often favor the status quo, not only because they are used to it but also because they have seen past changes and reforms fail. Some Indians favor industrial development on reservations; some oppose such development, especially if it is not subject to Indian control. Some stress retention or revival of traditions in language, songs, religion. Others are content with a compromise, retaining basically Indian ways of doing things by community, consensus, and kinship, at the same time that they enjoy some of the benefits of American technology and civilization.

There is time, and there is more space available to Indians than we have come to believe. There is, if accepted, a place in America for cultural differences, certainly to the limited extent that they are being sought by the Indian peoples of America.

We must not expect the return of the "noble savage," but the establishment of conditions which allow and encourage Indians to live with dignity—conditions of reasonable economic and cultural security.

2

Black Americans: Great Misfortunes

Tocqueville's interest in America was one of interpretation rather than of observation. He was, therefore, little interested in the institution and practices of slavery. But having acknowledged its existence, he proceeded to make judgments about its effects on democracy and especially to predict the difficulties of the future. Even these comments and projections were almost incidental, since he saw slavery as an intrusion into democratic society, a contradiction which would have no place in the European or French democracy which he anticipated.

Tocqueville's own observations about slavery, as reported in his notebooks, are relatively restrained. Most of the entries are quotations from white Americans of the middle and upper classes. There are indications, however, of Tocqueville's own attitudes toward slavery. He expressed sympathy for the slaves, but seemed content to simply observe them at work and to discuss slavery with the slave masters and other white men who were willing to comment. There is no record of his actually having talked to slaves. He seemed to have a detached interest, principally in the effects of slavery on the white people and on the political future of the country.

The notebooks contain interesting quotations on the economics of slavery. Some Americans thought slave labor to be generally more expensive than free labor. Some made distinctions, holding that wheat was better cultivated by free labor, but that tobacco growers could make economical use of slave labor, since slave women and children could be used in tobacco cultivation.

The notebooks also contain reports of legal and *de facto* discrimination practiced against "free" black people in the North. Blacks in Philadelphia, he was told, had the legal right to vote, but they were afraid to exercise that right because they might be badly treated if they tried. One Philadelphian explained: "The law with us is nothing when it is not supported by public opinion." Tocqueville noted that both jails and cemeteries in Philadelphia were segregated.

In Ohio and Maryland Tocqueville was told that discrimination against free blacks was quite deliberate. Thus he quoted a young lawyer in Ohio as saying: "We try to discourage them [black people] in every possible way. Not only have we made laws allowing them to be expelled at will, but we hamper them in a thousand ways. A Negro has no political rights; he cannot be a juror; he cannot give evidence against a white. . . ." And a lawyer in Maryland, where free blacks already faced significant discrimination, said: "I am very much afraid that the incoming Legislature may pass unjust and oppressive laws against the blacks. People want to make it intolerable for them to remain in Maryland. One must not hide it from oneself; the white population and the black population are in a state of war. They will never mix. One of the two must give way to the other."

Although the Nat Turner slave rebellion had occurred shortly before his visit, Tocqueville made no mention of it in his notebooks. It may well have been on the minds of some of the people in Kentucky and Maryland whom he interviewed. A man in Kentucky told Tocqueville that in recent years the people of that state had undergone a mental revolution in their attitude toward slavery. Many Americans interviewed by Tocqueville seemed to think that the problem could not be settled rationally, that white and black could not live together, that one or the other would prevail. The Kentuckian was quoted as saying: "We do not know what to do with the slaves. Our fathers did us terrible harm by introducing them among us."

On the basis of his own limited observations and the comments of those with whom he discussed slavery, Tocqueville, in his book *Democracy in America,* made extensive and, in some cases, incisive and prophetic comments on slavery in America. At one point in the book Tocqueville said that "the Negro hardly notices his ill fortune." But in other places he wrote of the degradation and rootlessness of the slaves, their awareness of their plight, and the despair, if not self-hatred and resentment, among them. "From birth," he wrote, "he [the slave] has been told that his race is naturally inferior to the white man and almost believing that, he holds himself in contempt. He sees a trace of slavery in his every feature, and if he could he would gladly repudiate himself entirely."

Tocqueville observed that, whereas the physical conditions under which the slaves lived had been improved, the Southerners "have, if I may put it in this way, spiritualized despotism and violence. In antiquity men sought to prevent the slave from breaking his bonds; nowadays the attempt is made to stop him wishing to do so." This may well be an overrefined observation as to what the slave owners had in mind. Certainly, a partial result of the Christianization of slaves was, whether intentional or not, to make them more obedient and willing to accept their lot.

On the issue of discrimination, Tocqueville wrote that, whereas the legal distinctions between white and black were decreasing in some parts of the United States, prejudice seemed unshakable. He attributed this to the fact that, as distinguished from ancient slavery, in which the slave was usually of the same race as his master, in America the slave was of a different race and "hardly recognized as sharing the common features of humanity." In the South, he observed, legislation was harsher against the blacks, "but customs are more tolerant and gentle." There was, he noted, less obsession with segregation, and there was miscegenation. "In the South," he wrote, "the master has no fear of lifting the slave up to his level, for he knows that when he wants to he can always throw him down into the dust."

In the free states he found racial prejudice to be even stronger. There the blacks were subject to legal and *de facto* discrimination. They had no land. They had the poorest and meanest jobs. If they had legal and civil rights, they were afraid to exercise them, and segregation extended even to the cemetery. He predicted that the white population in the free states would continue to grow and that the blacks "will be no more than unlucky remnants, a poor little wandering tribe lost amid the huge nation that is master of the land; nothing but the injustices and hardships to which they are subjected will call attention to their presence."

Tocqueville saw slaveholding in retreat in the northern states, pointing out that in Maryland it was on the verge of being abolished, and noting that even in Virginia the problem of slavery was under discussion. But he expressed the belief that the abolition of slavery in the North encouraged northern slave owners to send their slaves to the South. As a consequence, northern slaves were not free; they simply became southern slaves.

Taken altogether, he saw no way out of the slavery problem. Even if the South were to abolish slavery, he judged it would have trouble handling the great number of free black people. (There were 1,980,384 slaves in the South in 1830.) Also, basing his judgment on his observations of race relations in the North, he said that abolition would increase the southern whites' aversion to the black people.

In the event of emancipation, which he seemed to think inevitable, he saw only two possibilities: "the Negroes and the whites must either mingle completely or they must part." He saw war as a likely possibility and speculated that, if the Union endured, the blacks would lose because of the overwhelming strength of the whites. But if the war should occur after dissolution of the Union, then the whites might be driven out of the South, "leaving the Negroes in possession of a country which Providence seems to have destined for them, since they have no trouble in living there and can work the ground more easily than the whites can." Whereas Tocqueville did not accept the argument that whites were unable to work in the Deep South, he conceded that work would be harder for whites there than in New England, and that both crops and climate in the South argued for the use of slave labor.

He reflected on the possible success of a movement, then being talked about, to transport American black people to Liberia and saw it as an impractical way to try to solve the problem. He thought that transport could not be organized on a scale large enough to overcome the natural increase of the black population in the United States. And he predicted that "the Negro race will never again leave the American continent, to which the passions and vices of Europe brought it; it will not disappear from the New World except by ceasing to exist."

He foresaw the end of slavery. "Either the slave or the master will put an end to it. In either case, great misfortunes are to be anticipated."

Tocqueville was very close to the truth in most of his comments on slavery. He accepted what seemed to be the common judgment of those whom he interviewed, that slavery was not economically sound; and he observed that those parts of the country with few slaves prospered more quickly than those with many slaves. This pattern he said, continued to hold as settlers moved west and was finally demonstrated by comparison of Ohio and Kentucky, separated only by the Ohio River. Ohio, he said, was populated by people who were industrious and prosperous, while the inhabitants of Kentucky were lazy and less prosperous. This condition resulted, he concluded, from the fact that labor was honorable in Ohio but considered degrading in Kentucky, and that free men worked more quickly than did slaves.

The issue of the profitability of slavery in the 1830s and later has caused much debate among economic historians. Some of the disagreements are over facts such as the actual costs of keeping slaves. Many slaveholders kept inadequate records, if they kept them at all. Other records have been lost.

Kenneth Stampp's book *The Peculiar Institution* (1956) is something of a revisionist book. Many, if not most, earlier historians had accepted the view that slavery was not profitable. Stampp sought to prove that it was. He and other historians argue and seek to prove that slave labor was as productive and as profitable to use as free labor.

Tocqueville, or those who advised him, apparently overstated the slowness of slave labor, overestimated the costs of providing for young and old slaves, did not take into account the fact that old slaves often did work, and did not realize that plantation life provided more than enough work for field hands year round. There was also money to be made from selling the natural increase of the slave population, from renting slaves, and from being middlemen in the internal slave trade.

Tocqueville seems to have exaggerated the proportion of white slaveholders to white non-slaveholders. In his notebooks he wrote that in his travels in Kentucky and Tennessee "Almost all the farmers we saw, even the poorest, had some slaves." And in *Democracy in America*, when he compared Ohio and Kentucky, he said that "on the left bank [Kentucky] no white laborers are to be found, for they would be afraid of being like the slaves; for work people must rely on the Negroes . . ." And again he wrote: "No family in the South is so poor that it does not have some slaves." This mistaken report may be due to his route of travel through the South, since apparently it did not take him into those areas where there were white farmers and craftsmen who had no slaves.

Statistics are scarce for the years around 1830, but by 1860, as Kenneth Stampp reports, there were only 385,000 slave owners in the South out of 1,516,000 free families. He notes that the proportion varied greatly in different parts of the South: for example, one third of the families in Louisiana owned slaves, while in Kentucky and Tennessee only one fourth of the families owned slaves.

In 1830 there were approximately 2.3 million black people in the United States, about 18 per cent of the population. Of these, according to *Historical Statistics of the United States*, there were 181,501 free blacks in the southern states—a greater number than the total number of blacks in the North (166,757). Sociologist E. Franklin Frazier concluded from his studies that the free blacks of the South were economically better off than the free blacks in the North who had to compete with the European immigrants. The differences were apparently slight. Whereas some free blacks in the South became wealthy, Frazier said that most of them lived close to the subsistence level. Some blacks in the North did accumulate property. John Hope Franklin says that in 1800, free blacks in Philadelphia owned almost 100 houses and lots, and in 1837 blacks in New York City owned $1,400,000 worth of taxable real estate.

Tocqueville apparently missed the beginnings of the abolitionist movement, which were evident at the time of his visit. In 1829 a free black named David Walker had published a militant pamphlet against slavery. There were many black antislavery groups in the North by 1830, and in that year a black convention was held in Philadelphia with delegates from five states. Several abolitionist papers were being published at the time of his visit, including at least two in the South and William Lloyd Garrison's *The Liberator.*

This was the general situation in which Tocqueville made observations which, over one hundred years later, still described with startling accuracy race relations in both the North and the South. For he wrote: "In almost all the states where slavery has been abolished, the Negroes have been given electoral rights, but they would come forward to vote at the risk of their lives. When oppressed, they can bring an action at law, but they will find only white men among their judges. It is true that the laws make them eligible as jurors, but prejudice wards them off. The Negro's son is excluded from the school to which the European's child goes. In the theaters he cannot for good money buy the right to sit by his former master's side; in the hospitals he lies apart. He is allowed to worship the same God as the white man but must not pray at the same altars. He has his own clergy and churches. The gates of heaven are not closed against him, but his inequality stops only just short of the boundaries of the other world. When the Negro is no more, his bones are cast aside, and some difference in condition is found even in the equality of death." This quite accurately describes the treatment of people of the black race in the South, and to a large degree in the North, at the beginning of the drive for racial equality in the 1940s.

Today? the black population, which in 1830 was 2.3 million persons—about 18 per cent of the total U.S. population—had increased in absolute numbers to 25 million by 1978. But the black percentage of the total population had declined to 12 per cent. Whereas nearly all of the black population in 1831 was in the southern states, today it is about equally divided between North and South.

Tocqueville could not have foreseen the great migration of black people from South to North which occurred in the twentieth century, most of it within the years since 1940. In that year, 77 per cent of American black people lived in the South. But by 1975, only 52 per cent of American blacks lived in the South, while 39 per cent were in northern states, and 9 per cent lived in the West. He, perhaps, could not have anticipated anything like the civil rights movement of the last three decades. Had he considered it, however, I believe he would have thought its success essential to what he considered the most difficult problem facing the America which he saw—namely, that of slavery and racial differences.

The place of the black in American society has improved significantly in recent years. The grossest and most humiliating manifestations of discrimination have all but disappeared. Discrimination in public places has been outlawed. School segregation has been declared illegal, although the process of eliminating that discrimination in fact remains unfinished. Equal protection under the law is for blacks, as for the poor generally, a goal rather than a reality; although here again, at least in isolated and well-publicized cases, there has been progress.

The most widely noted increase in black participation in American life has been the growth of black political power. Black candidates have been elected (and, in several cases, re-elected) as mayors of major cities: Cleveland, Ohio; Gary, Indiana; Newark, New Jersey; Los Angeles, California; Atlanta, Georgia; and New Orleans, Louisiana.

More black people have been elected to the Congress of the United States, representing both northern and southern constituencies. And especially in the South, following the phenomenal increase in black voter registration in recent years, black persons have been elected to local offices. In 1960, before passage of the Voting Rights Act, 29 per cent of southern blacks of voting age were registered. In 1976, 63 per cent were registered.

In addition to the Ambassador to the United Nations, one United States senator, seventeen members of the House of Representatives, and mayors of major cities, it is estimated that there are over 4,000 black city council members, aldermen, state legislators, and other elected officials in the country. This is less than 1 per cent of the nation's elective offices, but a significant change compared to what black citizens held ten or twenty years ago.

Some progress has been made toward reducing employment discrimination and toward improving job opportunities for blacks. Black workers in significant numbers are being admitted to the hard-to-crack building-trades unions. Government and industry have expanded employment opportunities for blacks.

Yet in America black people remain poor in disproportionate numbers.

In 1976 the median family income for whites in America was $15,537; the median family income for blacks was $9,242—some $6,000 per year less. In 1976 about 25 million Americans were classified as living below the minimum income level; 8 million of them were non-white. The percentage of whites under the low-income mark was about 9 per cent, down from 18 per cent in 1959, while the percentage of non-whites under the mark was about 29 per cent, down from 56 per cent in 1959.

Unemployment, a serious problem for many Americans since the end of World War II, is more serious for blacks than it is for whites. While the overall unemployment rate in October 1977 was 7 per cent, the rate for blacks was almost double that; and the rate among young black workers was 37.9 per cent, compared with 14.8 per cent for young white workers. Young blacks remain the victims of the last-hired, first-fired principle of American employment practices.

Many of the problems and difficulties of the black population in America are shared by poor whites and by the poor of other races. But the black problems, because of the numbers involved and because of historical factors, appear to be the most difficult of solution. Racism continues to be the most serious and difficult cultural challenge to America, as Tocqueville judged it would be.

Most of the improvements in the lot of racial minorities have been effected by positive action—that is, action determined and formalized, sometimes by legislative requirement, sometimes by court orders, sometimes by unusual personal or group efforts—rather than by the normal operation of culture or of social institutions. Usually the action involves a limited number of persons from the minority group who are selected, and then educated or trained if necessary, or directly employed. In some cases they are included as a result of quota requirements imposed on government contractors or used in direct government employment at federal, state, and local levels.

The general evidence is that normal social selection, without reference to race, is not yet working. Whereas public housing, for example, generally includes more than the percentage of minority members in the general community, middle-income and suburban housing communities do not contain a representative percentage of minorities. The reason is in part economic and in part cultural. Segregated housing and segregated communities, despite open-housing laws, will undoubtedly continue to be the mark of American cities until there is economic integration, and a consequent reduction in the income differentials that now distinguish the races of America.

In addition to open-housing, job quotas, and other programs, there is busing of school children in order to achieve racially balanced schools, as well as to improve the standard of education for minority students. There is no clear demonstration yet as to the efficacy of busing as a means of achieving a better integrated society. The public schools were meant to be instruments for the elimination of undemocratic differences in American society, such as religious prejudices and discrimination based on differences in income. Racial integration of the schools is a third test. Any easy or immediate success should not be expected. For the most part, the bused and integrated children return to segregated neighborhoods after the school sessions. Until changes are brought about in the American economic system, the minorities will carry a continuing burden of poverty, of unemployment, and of what, by virtue of economic forces, amounts to segregated low-paid employment, well beyond the end of their educational experience.

There is an additional problem, that of "reverse discrimination," an issue which is encountered with increasing frequency and which is being given court recognition. Certainly the use of racial quotas in determining employment, or in admitting persons to schools, runs counter to the American concept of equal competitive opportunity for all. The use of quotas is a challenge, if not a contradiction, of that principle. Much as quotas may be defended by considerations of the general good, and the evidence of generalized discrimination against minority races, they reverse the concept of individual rights.

As principles based on physiological characteristics are more generally applied, it is possible that the additional standard of age may be applied in a challenge to the rule of seniority. There have been court decisions ordering the rehiring of persons who were dismissed in reductions in force, when it has been demonstrated that, had it not been for discrimination based on race or sex, the person dismissed would have had more seniority than those who were retained.

Organized labor is conscious of this threat to seniority, one of the worker rights most strongly supported by unions. Labor publications carry warnings of threats to seniority, which is described as the most precious asset of a union member next to his/her union card.

Seniority rights are in one of the areas where legislators fear to tread. The burden of decision, as was the case with discriminatory voting laws and the busing of school children, is left to the courts. This further supports Tocqueville's observation that everything in the United States is justiciable.

3

Prisoners: Nobody Thinks
of Rendering Them Better

Tocqueville and Beaumont, in keeping with the official justification for their relief from court duties in France, did not wait long after their arrival in America before starting an investigation of American prisons. On May 29, 1831, about two weeks after reaching New York, they arrived at Mount Pleasant to visit Sing Sing Prison.

At the time of the Tocqueville-Beaumont visit, prison reform was not wholly new. There had been efforts in the colonial period, especially on the part of the Quakers. But in the postrevolutionary years, reform achieved new impetus and aroused interest in European countries.

In the colonial period, for the most part, prison terms were not used as punishment for crime. Those accused of breaking the law were held in jails, which were not built very differently from homes. They were not high-security buildings; they were used primarily for holding people before trial, or between trial and sentencing, or as places of limited punishment for debtors.

Punishments, when ordered, were generally physical and quite severe. The stocks, the pillory, whipping, in some cases branding and other mutilations, were used to punish offenders. The death penalty was in common use for serious crimes, and even for lesser ones if repeated by the same person. Whereas the punishments were harsh, they were usually administered quickly and not accompanied by any long period of imprisonment. Many colonial towns banished nonresident offenders after their physical punishment.

The Quakers, who out of religious belief had long opposed the harsh punishments derived from English practice in the colonial period, were among the first to initiate prison reform after Independence. In 1790 they built the first "penitentiary" (the word itself was an innovation) as part of the old Walnut Street Prison in Philadelphia. The purpose of the new section was to reform prisoners, accepted as a Christian duty, rather than to punish or kill them. The principle was isolation, on the theory that in solitary the offender would rethink his life, repent, and be reformed. It was also believed that while in the process of his own meditative reform, the criminal would not be exposed to the evil influence of other prisoners who had not progressed in penitence and purification.

The Walnut Street Prison was less than a success. The reform of character that had been anticipated did not generally follow.

Ideas about prison reform and prison discipline had moved beyond those of the Walnut Street Prison experiment by the time of Tocqueville's visit.

There are three books which report his comments and observations: *Democracy in America; Journey to America* (his notebooks); and the special report which he and Beaumont prepared, *On the Penitentiary System in the United States and Its Application to France.*

Tocqueville made little mention of prisons in his major and best-known work, *Democracy in America,* quite possibly because the subject was covered at length in the separate report on prisons. But he did make a few observations in *Democracy* that were a little more free than those in the prison report, and worthy of special note.

"I doubt," he wrote, "whether in any other country crime so seldom escapes punishment." He attributed this to public interest in finding and arresting anyone guilty of crime. (We still have the custom of citizens' arrest, though it involves considerable risk and is not often practiced.) "In Europe," he wrote, "the criminal is a luckless man fighting to save his head from the authorities; in a sense the population are mere spectators of the struggle. In America he is an enemy of the human race and every human being is against him."

Taking the law into one's own hands has a long tradition in

the United States. Tocqueville noted the practice of vigilantes and the use of duels for personal settlement of disputes, especially in the new states of the Southwest, which in his time meant Tennessee, Alabama, Mississippi, and Louisiana. The posse and the Ku Klux Klan were later manifestations of the same disposition.

He noted the American disposition to maintain limited and short-term interest, to accept that one success is total success or that there is no need to prove anything beyond that success. One swallow may make a spring. He reported that prison-reform efforts had become popular and had resulted in the building of new prisons and the beginning of attempts to change instead of simply to punish prisoners. But the reforms could not be accomplished immediately, and he noted that the public tended to lose interest in the old prisons, which "seemed to become more unhealthy and more corrupting at the same rate as the new ones became healthy and devoted to reform. . . . And beside some prison that stood as a durable monument to the gentleness and enlightenment of our age, there was a dungeon recalling the barbarities of the Middle Ages."

The book *On the Penitentiary System in the United States and Its Application to France* was a report based on thorough study of Sing Sing, Auburn, Cherry Hill, and Wethersfield prisons, interviews with wardens, supervisors, prisoners, and others, and observations of some of the older prisons in America. Although Beaumont apparently wrote the main text of this long report, Tocqueville provided footnotes and comments, and the report was published under the names of both men.

The two young Frenchmen could not be described as bleeding hearts or as men who were soft on criminals. They did not look on criminals as victims of society or as simply unfortunate or unlucky people. Nor did they accept simple explanations, if we are to judge from Tocqueville's comments when he was told in Philadelphia "that almost all crimes in America are due to the abuse of strong drink, which, being sold cheaply, the lowest classes could consume at will. 'How comes it,' Tocqueville asked, 'that you do not put a duty on brandy?' The response: 'Our legislators have often thought about it,' but that is a difficult undertaking. There is fear of a revolt, and those who voted for such a law could be certain not to be re-elected.' 'So,' Tocqueville replied, 'with you, drunkards are in a majority and temperance is unpopular.'" And so it remained until Prohibition.

Tocqueville and Beaumont believed that criminals deserve punishment, even severe punishment. With this in mind, they reported on American prisons and practices of punishment, and on popular attitudes toward both. They had come to America to observe the new penitentiary system. Most of their report, therefore, was devoted to this system rather than to the older prisons which existed in most American states. It is important to note, however, that they did make a few comments on the older prisons. They reported that nine states had adopted new systems, most of them following the example of the Auburn system, but that the other fifteen states were still using the old systems. In those states the prisons were overcrowded and unhealthy. Prisoners who had committed crimes of varying gravity, prisoners of different ages and sometimes of opposite sex, were mixed. The indicted and the convicted, witnesses and accused, criminals and debtors, were mixed. The old prisons, they reported, were lacking in discipline; silence was not enforced nor labor required. There were many escapes and many deaths.

Ohio, they reported, had a good penal code but barbarous prisons. In Cincinnati they found that half of the prisoners were in irons. And in New Orleans prisoners were mixed with hogs. "In locking up the criminals, nobody thinks of rendering them better, but only of taming their malice; they are put in chains like ferocious beasts; and instead of being corrected, they are rendered brutal."

They also reported on the makeup of the prison population. The combined prison population of Connecticut, Massachusetts, New York, Pennsylvania, and Maryland, according to their information, was about 24 per cent black. The percentage of blacks increased as one went further south, reaching over 50 per cent in Maryland. Women made up only about 9 per cent of the combined prison population of Connecticut, New York, Pennsylvania, and Maryland. With the exception of the Wethersfield Prison in Connecticut, the new penitentiary system had not been applied to women; but corporal punishment of women generally was not allowed.

The two prisons studied most carefully by Beaumont and Tocqueville were the Cherry Hill Prison in Philadelphia and the Auburn Prison in New York. They said that both of those prisons were distinguished from older American prisons and from European prisons in three ways. First, they tried to prevent prisoners from corrupting each other. In the Cherry Hill system this was done by keeping prisoners physically separated from one another. In the Auburn system it was done by forbidding them to speak to each other during the day when they were together, and by locking them in separate cells at night. Second, they provided work for the prisoners. This would, it was believed, give prisoners good work habits and in some cases teach them new skills. There was the additional consideration of possible profit to the states from the sale of prison-made products. Third, they attempted moral and spiritual reformation of prisoners. Tocqueville and Beaumont observed that, although this did not seem very successful, they nonetheless believed that it helped bring about a civil reformation so that prisoners might return to society and become useful citizens. They observed also that the new penitentiaries were far better than the old and that the two penitentiaries that had existed long enough to provide evidence (Auburn and Wethersfield) had a lower rate of recidivism than did the older prisons.

Philadelphia's Cherry Hill Prison, officially known as the Eastern State Penitentiary, reflected the Quaker tradition. Beaumont and Tocqueville spent much time studying this prison and interviewing its prisoners. Confinement at Cherry Hill meant that a prisoner had absolutely no contact with other prisoners; he did not even see them except by chance. Each prisoner was kept in a cell with a small exercise yard attached to it. Work such as shoemaking or weaving was brought to the prisoner in his cell in a kind of putting-out system of manufacture. According to the report, the prison superintendent visited each prisoner at least once a day and the prison inspectors at least twice a week. The prisoners might also see the prison chaplain if they wished to do so. Their reading material was restricted to the Bible and occasional "tracts containing edifying anecdotes." There was no school at Cherry Hill, but the superintendent and inspectors gave reading lessons to prisoners of good disposition. Some inmates reportedly learned to read by themselves.

Tocqueville, having obtained a dispensation from the normal policy whereby visitors could not speak with prisoners, was allowed to speak to them alone. He reported that the health of most was good, very good, or excellent. He expressed the opinion that the special experience of Cherry Hill made a deep impression on the prisoners, but was careful to hedge his observation by adding that "experience alone can show whether the impression is durable."

The theory of the confinement was that the prisoners would have time to think about their crimes and to repent. Some did become quite religious, Tocqueville reported, perhaps because the Bible and the chaplain were among their few distractions from punishment. He reported also that the men found work a great consolation from solitude, that the prisoners were generally subdued and very unhappy, that they missed their families, and that after speaking with strangers for a while most of them became agitated and began to cry.

Some of the prisoners told their interviewer that although the discipline at Cherry Hill was severe, they preferred it and Cherry Hill to the old Walnut Street Prison, which they described as a school of vice and crime. Some of the inmates saw complete isolation from other prisoners as protection from post-release blackmail or temptation back into a life of crime.

The Auburn system was different. At Auburn solitary confinement had been rejected after an 1821 experiment in which eighty selected convicts were isolated. The results were bad. Within three years the test convicts had either died or become insane or declined in health to the point where the governor pardoned the survivors. Auburn then settled into its own system, which became much more popular than that of Cherry Hill and set the pattern for the development of the penitentiary system in other states. At Auburn prisoners were kept in individual cells at night but worked in a common workshop during the day. They were not allowed to speak to each other at any time. Absolute silence was strictly enforced.

Even at the time of the Tocqueville-Beaumont visit, the Auburn Prison system was accepted as successful. It had been es-

tablished at Sing Sing Prison and copied in six or seven states
outside of New York. The young French observers seemed to
think that the Auburn system was superior to Cherry Hill in
developing true habits of obedience. Prisoners under the Auburn
system retained some freedom to disobey, although they were
punished if they did, while prisoners at Cherry Hill were physically unable to disobey in most instances simply because of the
isolation. There was, therefore, in the Auburn system opportunity for more self-discipline.

Auburn included chaplain services and Sunday worship. The
chaplain thought that the religious influence was helpful, although the French interviewers speculated that there may have
been an element of delusion about the degree of successful reformation.

At Auburn prisoners carried out work that was the subject of
contracts between the prison authorities, or the state, and outside business. Like most American prisoners, they received no
pay—a fact which Beaumont and Tocqueville thought somewhat
unfair. They suggested that the system used in the Baltimore
Prison was much fairer. The Baltimore practice was to allow a
prisoner to do additional work, for which he would be paid, after
he had finished his assigned task for the day. His earnings were
accumulated and paid to him when he finished his term and left
the prison.

The types of punishment for offenses against prison discipline
varied among the different penitentiaries. Cherry Hill generally
followed a more passive or denying approach. Offenders were
commonly placed in a dark cell and had their rations reduced.
This punishment usually brought the prisoner to heel within two
days. There was another punishment, hinted at but not explained
or pursued, of taking away the prisoner's tools so that he could
not work. The whip was used at other prisons: often at Sing
Sing, less often at Boston and Baltimore, still less at Auburn, and
with "extreme mildness" at Wethersfield. Beaumont and Tocqueville indicated that their studies and inquiries showed that whipping was less harmful to prisoners than was solitary confinement.
"At Auburn the prisoners are treated much more severely," they
wrote. "In Philadelphia they are much more unhappy. In Auburn, where they are whipped, they die less frequently than in

Philadelphia, where, for humanity's sake, they are put in a solitary and somber cell."

There was no mention of recreation. The prisoner worked all day and rested all night. "And before his sleep as after it, he has time to think of his solitude, his crime and his misery."

The Frenchmen reported that there was even more equality in prisons than in American society as a whole. There were no special cells for special prisoners, no maximum security and minimum security distinctions. All prisoners wore the same clothes and ate the same food. There was no reward for good behavior or for hard work. This met with the approval of Beaumont and Tocqueville, for, in their opinion, the worst criminals would benefit by a reward system while others, who might deserve lighter treatment, would not get it.

One of the encouraging aspects of the American system was that ex-convicts could easily find jobs—a condition that the Frenchmen believed discouraged a return to crime. They also noted that there was no central information bureau on ex-prisoners and their whereabouts. Persons released from prison in America, they were told, usually left the state, changed their names and started a new life elsewhere.

Tocqueville and Beaumont found that "Houses of Refuge" were established in a few cities for the care and training of young offenders, including neglected children who had become vagrants. These houses were run along the general lines of strict vocational training schools, with reform-school discipline. The child was sent to a house of refuge by a magistrate without specification of how long he was to remain. The house remained the child's guardian until he reached the age of twenty, unless the directors of the house freed the child before that age. They might also bind him out as an apprentice after he had spent some time in the house. Beaumont and Tocqueville thought the houses of refuge a good idea and believed that they saved children from lives of crime.

Finally, they made some observations about the cost of American prisons and about their size in relation to their effectiveness. They concluded that small prisons were best for discipline and also for reformation. Sing Sing's chief defect, they said, was that it had too many prisoners (1,000). They wrote that Wethersfield (in Connecticut), "the smallest penitentiary in America, is also the best."

Among the more interesting interviews recorded in Tocqueville's notes on his journey to America were two on prisons and criminals.

One was a conversation with Hugh Maxwell of New York on June 27, 1831. Maxwell, a district attorney, was one of the founders of a house of correction for young offenders. Of the penitentiaries, he said that whereas he thought the discipline excellent for keeping order and getting useful work out of prisoners, he did not think it had "effective influence on their dispositions or behavior." Maxwell expressed the view that the adult criminal could not be reformed however one treated him; in fact, the American penitentiary "hardened" him.

Another interview was with Elam Lynds at Syracuse on July 7, 1831. Lynds had been warden of Auburn Prison and in the face of much opposition had introduced the Auburn system. Later he had taken with him one hundred convicts from Auburn and had built the first cell block at Sing Sing. The facts that the prisoners worked without manacles or other restraints, that they had few guards, that they slept in tents yet none tried to escape, were looked upon as tributes to the strength of Lynds and his system.

Lynds was without doubt a hard and opinionated man. He told the Frenchmen that when he undertook his reforms at Auburn he was strongly opposed. "There were outcries against tyranny," he said. "However I had my way in the end. When there was the question of building Sing Sing and I offered to undertake it with prisoners working in the open fields, people would not believe that it was a practical possibility. Now that I have brought it off, many people are still ill-disposed or jealous towards me."

He said that he thought his system would work anywhere, but better in France than in the United States because "French prisons are under the immediate control of the government which can give solid and consistent support to its officers. Here [in the U.S.] we are the slaves of a perpetually changing public opinion."

Lynds said that in his experience among the prisoners at Sing

Sing, one fourth of whom were foreigners, the Spanish from South America were the worst, the French the best. He favored whipping as the most effective and humane punishment, and believed solitary confinement to be "often ineffective and almost always dangerous." He believed that little reform was accomplished in prison beyond the teaching of trades; that the chaplain's exhortations and the prisoners' own reflections did not make good Christians; and that good behavior in prison was usually the mark of the worst criminals, who, because they were more adroit and clever than the others, saw the advantages of being model prisoners. Lynds opposed giving prisoners remission because of good conduct in prison. He had little time for the theorists who had learned about human nature in books and not in life. The key to successful prison management, according to Lynds, was to break the spirit of the prisoner and reduce him to a state of passive obedience. If this were accomplished, he believed that the manner in which the prison was constructed and the nature of work for the prisoners became secondary considerations.

A Swedish poet, Göran Printz-Påhlson, has tried to catch the spirit of Lynds's prison in this poem.

When Beaumont and Tocqueville Visited Sing Sing

When Beaumont and Tocqueville visited Sing Sing
in order to collect material for a thesis on prison care
in America,
they saw a vision of the future.

Joined in wordless hatred, unchained prisoners
worked side by side in a dull silence.
The guards, as if on the edge of a volcano,
controlled their panic, a listless force.
Dark houses, half finished cell blocks.

Thus, through decades, the dream of America
was destroyed in front of their eyes:
hot dog stands grew like footprints on muddy roads,
billboards crowded close to the best views,
a smiling Indian sold souvenirs from Woolworth's,

and Natty Bumppo comes home from the office
annoyed that there are no spaces left to conquer,
checks that no one has entered illegally, to steal,
looks in the closet for Russians and Jews, turns on the T.V.
and sits down to write a hate letter to the Reader's Column.

Silent, unchained prisoners—a dream
that will torment Europe through innumerable nights,
worse than the fear of chaos
and more realistic.

Tocqueville and Beaumont were generally accurate in their report on U.S. prisons and were sustained by observers of the same time and by historians of later days. But record-keeping was much less thorough in their day and the worship of statistics had not yet begun. David Rothman, who wrote *The Discovery of the Asylum*, is of the opinion that statistics on physical and mental health under the competing systems of Auburn and Cherry Hill cannot be relied on, since "partisans did little more than set down subjective judgments in the guise of absolute numbers." This happens today, one might add. Rothman also challenges the claims about profitability of prisons in the early nineteenth century. He suspects that there was juggling of figures in order to show profits and concludes that "prison labor never brought great returns and in many instances was unable to meet the daily expenses of operation, let alone cover the costs of construction."

There were a few things which Beaumont and Tocqueville either failed to observe or thought unimportant. Prison uniforms had been introduced in the 1790s and were used at the time of their visit. It was also common practice to cut prisoners' hair short (in a time when men wore their hair long). The principal reason for both uniforms and cropped hair, apparently, was to provide identification and thus to discourage escape and make apprehension easier. There is a possibility that the second practice may have been designed also for humiliation or a weakening of the spirit, with a history going back at least to Samson, continued in the Marine Corps, and exercised by some judges as punishment for juvenile offenders today.

Tocqueville and Beaumont erred in degree in their report on Cherry Hill. Whereas communication between prisoners there was very limited, it did occur despite precautions taken by prison authorities. Although the prison had been built carefully on the principle of absolute separation of prisoners, some talking was possible through pipes and also between upper and lower floors in the few cell blocks that were two stories high, when those on the lower floor were in their exercise yards. (Air vents and ventilator shafts are still a problem for prison authorities.) Cherry Hill records often mentioned attempts to communicate as the reason for punishing prisoners. The drive to communicate is a deep one. To talk with contemporaries or to leave a mark, as in the caves of Auvergne, for someone not there or not yet born is a strong urge. It is manifest in a pure way in prison.

Beaumont and Tocqueville were mistaken in believing that the only punishment used at Cherry Hill was that of putting prisoners in a dark cell and reducing their food rations. The records show that this punishment was used more than any other, but there were variations on it. For example, the cell might be unheated. One sixteen-year-old boy was kept in a dark cell for forty-two days and fed so little that he was found to be starving when finally examined by the prison doctor.

Cherry Hill used an American version of the Chinese water torture. This was a special type of shower; water was poured on the prisoner from a point high above him. The measure of suffering varied with the temperature of the water and the volume. A report following an investigation of Cherry Hill in 1834 noted that one nineteen-year-old prisoner was given the treatment outside in weather so cold that the water froze upon him.

The straitjacket was sometimes used on unruly prisoners. A particularly cruel punishment, the iron gag, was also used at Cherry Hill.

Today, almost 150 years after the Tocqueville visit, few of the problems observed by Tocqueville and others in his day seem to have been solved. The Auburn system, rather than that of Cherry Hill, has become the general model for both construction and administration. Separate prisons for women and reformatories for younger offenders have been added to the institutions for handling prisoners in the United States.

At the end of 1975 there were 242,750 inmates in federal and state prisons. A small part of that total—about 24,000—were in federal prisons; the rest were in prisons maintained by the states. California and Pennsylvania together had as many inmates as there were in all federal prisons. Only about 4 per cent of the state and federal prisoners were women.

The breakdown of population in county and city jails is similar. In 1972, there were about 141,600 prisoners in the jails. About 38 per cent of them were awaiting trial. Ninety-four per cent of the jail inmates were males; 41 per cent were black; less than 4 per cent were under eighteen years of age.

It is estimated that, of all persons in state prisons and related institutions in 1974, 47 per cent were black, whereas black persons constituted only 11 per cent of the general population.

Prison reform is as much a concern to Americans today, perhaps even more so, than it was in 1831. Despite experience, new social disciplines, medical advances, and psychoanalysis, progress has been less than noteworthy. It makes little sense to say, "The prisons aren't working," unless one specifies which of a number of goals or purposes are not being achieved.

One purpose of prisons, the oldest of all, is to punish criminals. Most observers agree that our prisons do punish. They punish criminals first of all by denying them freedom. They are denied spatial freedom and left with little more than time. Serving time in a limited space, and with limited opportunities to work or live with other persons, was the basic principle of the old Cherry Hill Prison, though it was believed that these restrictions would not punish as much as they would reform.

There are other forms of punishment in our prisons beyond the limitation of freedom. Some of these punishments clearly achieve the level of "cruel and unusual punishments" forbidden by the Eighth Amendment to the Constitution.

At Arkansas' Tucker Prison Farm, prisoners until the late 1960s were flogged and tortured with electric shocks. California's Vacaville Center has used a more sophisticated technique—namely, intense pain as an "aversion therapy." The pain has been administered not as punishment but for "rehabilitation."

Severe beatings by guards still do occur. There are reports of the excessive use of solitary confinement in many prisons. One of the worst abuses is the placing of young or weak male prisoners in situations where they are almost certain to be the victims of homosexual rape by other prisoners.

The use of drugs, especially of new drugs, is the latest form of punishment, although administered in the name of rehabilitation. California used a drug called Anectine on about thirty prisoners late in the 1960s. The drug paralyzes the voluntary muscles for one to two minutes. Bernard Weiner, in "The Clockwork Cure," reported that the person who receives Anectine "is overwhelmed by a feeling of suffocation, of drowning, of sinking into death. While in this fearful state, the inmate is told that when next he has an impulse to smash or attack, he will stop and think and remember the sensation he is experiencing under Anectine."

Weiner also reported that Prolixin, a drug that causes strong nausea, was used over a thousand times in the California system in 1970 and that electroshock therapy was used at the Vacaville Center almost five hundred times in 1971. He wrote that "reports out of the California State Hospital for the Criminally Insane at Atascadero repeatedly mention that genital electroshock was used on sexual offenders as aversion therapy." There were indications that in 1971 California prison administrators were considering the use of brain cauterization for some violence-prone inmates.

Punishment in some cases goes beyond the prison term. There are federal laws and many state laws that deny civil rights to ex-convicts. These restrictions are not always limited to felons; some are applied to persons convicted of lesser offenses. Many are not limited in time, as a prison sentence might be, but remain in effect throughout the life of the former convict. The penalties range from denial of the right to vote and to hold public office to the denial of opportunity for public employment or employment in occupations licensed by the state. As late as 1971 thirteen states still imposed on prisoners who had been given life sentences the additional penalty of "civil death," under which the person's marriage can be ended legally, his or her children made subject to adoption, and his or her property subject to redistribution—all of this despite the fact that most life sentences end in parole.

There is no question but that imprisonment in the United States is punishment; that our prisons do punish those who are committed. There are, of course, other goals and purposes of imprisonment. One is to separate the prisoner from society so that he cannot victimize people. In the physical sense our prison system does accomplish this purpose. Not many prisoners escape.

Most prisoners are released sooner or later, either because their sentences are for limited periods or because they are able to obtain parole. Many resume criminal activities after release. Because of recidivism, some advocate that criminals should receive long but indefinite sentences and be released only when judged "safe" for society. This theory was tested in Maryland under a special law for "defective delinquents." So great was the protest against indeterminate sentences that they were eliminated in 1977. This method makes equal punishment for crime impossible and rests on the questionable thesis that society has a right to punish or incarcerate persons for estimated probability of recidivism—a thesis comparable to that used to move Americans of Japanese descent into concentration camps during World War II on the grounds that they might prove disloyal.

We know little about the effect of imprisonment as a deterrent. Certainly the experience of imprisonment, or the anticipation of it, must deter some people from crime. We do not know how many it does deter, what kind of people may be deterred or from what kinds of crimes. Nor is there very clear evidence that imprisonment reforms prison inmates. Prisons in fact may be corrupting and even schools for crime.

Homosexual rape, although not reported in every prison, is a common and serious problem. The same is true of stabbings and physical attacks by one prisoner on another or by one gang of prisoners on another. San Quentin Prison experienced a veritable reign of terror in 1972. It was attributed to black-white hostility which resulted in frequent stabbings and reached a point at which white guards were siding with white convicts and black guards with black convicts.

The availability and use of drugs in prisons is another corrupting reality.

As in 1831, failure and inadequacy of prisons and prison methods have stirred the concern of many people. There is no lack of proposals for reform.

Those proposals that relate to the management of the prisons themselves are easiest to evaluate. The larger questions of reforms related to deterrence, rehabilitation, and the like are much more speculative.

Overcrowding, for example, is a definable and manageable problem if society is willing to meet the costs. Providing dormitories for prisoners is regarded as a reform by some, but others see it as a form of overcrowding which increases the danger to inmates from other inmates. A Quaker study, called *Struggle for Justice*, contends that "dormitory housing, an ill-conceived reform, which is a horror to inmates, has been widely adopted because it is cheaper to build and operate."

Overcrowding seems to intensify almost every other problem within the prison or jail: mixing of the nonconvicted and the young with older, more experienced criminals; racial hostility; homosexual rapes; drug traffic; noise; general invasion of privacy; inadequacy of education, library facilities, work programs, and vocational training. More, larger, and better facilities, or fewer prisoners, or shorter sentences are obvious answers.

Racism in prisons is a new problem, or at least newly recognized. Institutional discrimination against black prisoners still exists in some prisons, especially in southern states. Even in northern states it is said to exist on an informal basis. A common complaint is that there are too few black prison administrators and guards in prisons with large numbers of black inmates. Where segregation is not imposed, self-imposed segregation in dining halls, in exercise yards, and in other areas of prison life may develop or be organized. One should not expect better social relations within the prisons than exist on the outside. Limited possibilities of reform to avoid racial tension within prisons is possible, but satisfactory improvement is not likely to come until relations outside the prison are improved.

In the same way, one must question whether the drug problem inside prisons can be solved if the same problem cannot be solved on the outside.

If prisons do little or no good, except to keep criminals under restraint (especially those who might commit additional crimes if at large), and to satisfy society's disposition to punish wrongdoers (whether that disposition arises from culture or from human nature), and if there are going to be limits on either purpose, the hard questions must be asked:

One: Who should be sent to prison?
Two: How long should they be kept there?
Three: Under what conditions should they live in prison?
Four: Under what terms should they be released?
Five: What of capital punishment?

There is general agreement that those guilty of crimes of violence should be imprisoned, for punishment if for no other reason, and to remove them at least temporarily as threats to public safety. There are mixed views on how people guilty of nonviolent crimes should be treated. California recently has placed great stress on probation as an alternative to imprisonment for nonviolent offenders. In 1960 about one third of California's prisoners had been convicted of robbery, murder, assault, and rape. But in 1976 about half of the state's prisoners had been convicted of such crimes.

The elimination of drug abuse, drunkenness, and homosexual and other sexual acts, especially among or between consenting adults, from the criminal code altogether—or the use of punishments other than imprisonment—would greatly reduce the prison population and the burden on the courts. It is argued that easing the punishment for these acts would encourage them. However, there is no evidence that imprisonment is an effective deterrent. It may be an excuse for not dealing with the social or psychological problems which may be responsible for the original criminal acts.

Another proposed alternative to prolonged prison terms is the requirement of restitution in cases of theft, forgery, and embezzlement. Restitution is sometimes required now under the law, but apparently more often by insurance companies than by the state. In the case of automobile theft, perhaps a penalty plus the Hertz mileage rate would satisfy the demands of society.

The use of probation without a prison sentence, or following a short but definite one, is reported to be particularly effective with first offenders. California has stressed probation in recent years, and the state government has found probation cheaper than imprisonment. It may be no more effective than long imprisonment with repeating criminals. If so, cost may be the determining consideration.

Another reform often suggested is that the length of prison terms be reduced. Proponents of this change say that long terms are self-defeating. They contend that juries are more reluctant to convict, even when the evidence for conviction is strong, if the sentence seems too severe. They assert also that longer sentences work against rehabilitation; that the longer a person is in jail, the more likely he is to come back. John Irwin, in a study called *The Felon*, describes the habit of "jailing," through which a person long accustomed to prison adjusts to it so completely that he finds it difficult to live on the outside. Other observers say that the rate of recidivism is unrelated to the length of prison terms. Whatever the case may be, it is a fact that the United States generally imposes much longer sentences than do other Western nations, and our crime rate does not prove the effectiveness of longer sentences.

James Hoffa, in testimony before a Senate subcommittee on prisons a few years ago, expressed his opinion that a prison term of more than two years for nonviolent crime does not serve any rehabilitative purpose. Testifying before the same subcommittee, attorney F. Lee Bailey supported the Hoffa position: "I have studied to some extent, both directly and in consultations with other experts, the European system, which works far better than ours and which is known to be far different. Their prison terms are consistently very low, and I agree wholeheartedly with Mr. Hoffa's statement that anything in excess of two years is probably wasted . . ." Possibly anything in excess of a year is wasted, or anything beyond the incarceration which places the mark of criminal service on the person.

If we assume, as we must, that persons will continue to be sent to prison in this country for reasonably long periods of time, the question of how they should be treated while under sentence will continue to challenge us. Some proposals for the care and treatment of prisoners today are very close to those which were made and accepted in 1831. In fact, some critics of today's prison system suggest that major difficulties today arise from changes made years ago in the spirit of humanitarian and liberal reform. One such reform which they say causes trouble is that of attempting to make the punishment fit the criminal. This reform was supposed to allow judges and parole boards to consider such factors as the offender's motives, background, chances of reformation, and so forth. Critics charge that the consequence has been great inequality in prison terms, to the point where the inequities themselves constitute a miscarriage of justice. Another result has been to encourage—almost to force—prisoners to play the dishonest game described by Elam Lynds in 1831 in order to affect judges and parole boards.

The indefinite sentence, too, has come under critical fire. California used to have indefinite sentences, such as one-to-five years, or five-to-twenty, or ten-to-life. Good behavior in prison was the condition for early release. At least two major difficulties resulted from this practice. One was that prisoners found it a special torment not to know when they would be released. With a fixed term of five years, a prisoner knows that he may get out earlier through parole, but that in any case he will not serve more than five years. Under the California system, until the parole board fixed his sentence he did not know whether he should anticipate parole after one year, five years, or an indefinite time. He thus lived from one parole-board hearing to the next, hoping at least that the board would set a definite term. Often it did not. The second problem is that giving so much power to a parole board resulted in much "programing" by inmates. "Programing" occurs when a prisoner enrolls in some prison program (such as counseling or vocational training), not because he believes such a program will help him, but simply to make a good impression on the parole board. California now has definite sentences for most crimes.

Somewhat related to the indefinite sentence is the practice of plea-bargaining, although this is more a matter of judicial process than of prison policy. Plea-bargaining often results in variable sentences for the same crime.

There is the continuing question of capital punishment, with support of capital punishment usually rising during periods of high crime rates, especially crimes of violence, and declining when the execution is personalized. This issue remains more psychological and political than scientific or rational. Currently the swing in the United States is to the restoration and extension of

capital punishment and to the refinement of the procedures leading up to execution. Many states are rewriting their laws to meet
objections raised by the Supreme Court in reviews of previous
state laws.

The recent case of Gary Gilmore, the Utah prisoner who asked
that he be executed, confused the opponents of capital punishment. On the defensive, opponents of capital punishment are
usually reduced to advocating more humane (if one can use
that word) methods of execution. Part of the shock of the Gilmore case was his demand that he be killed by a firing squad.
Even though the practice of having one unloaded shell in the
gun of one member of the firing squad was followed, the line of
responsibility between society and the death of the prisoner
remained quite direct. The Gilmore case ran contrary to the general disposition to try to blur that line through the use of more
advanced methods of execution. The guillotine, for example, was
considered more advanced and more humane than crude be-
heading with an axe. It was more accurate, more impersonal,
using gravity rather than human strength as the source of its immediate force. The electric chair and the gas chamber are currently favored over the firing squad.

Separate from this irresolvable question is the debatable and
challenging one of prison reform. The Federal Bureau of Prisons,
concerned about charges that prisons are too dehumanizing and
unnatural, has tried to make federal prisons more like the outside
world. Civil rights are to be denied, but not all human rights.
Books in Lewisburg's prison library and in its commissary, for
example, are not censored. Movies are selected by the prisoners
without official censorship. James Hoffa, who spent several years
in Lewisburg, complained in his appearance before a Senate
subcommittee that most of the books in the prison library were
about crime and sex—as, he said, were the prison movies.

Conjugal visiting within prisons, or weekend furloughs that
allow prisoners to be with their wives, have been proposed and
tested in a limited way, as have prisons with both male and fe-
male inmates. The results, insofar as they can be judged, have
been good. Some states report a reduction of homosexuality and
a general improvement of prison climate. But the serious problem of homosexual rape—which, the experts say, is often more a

manifestation of racial antagonism than of sexual deprivation—has been little affected.

In the past ten to twenty years, there has been increasing stress on psychiatric aid to prisoners, on group therapy, and on other forms of psychological treatment. The results, like those of the chaplains in Tocqueville's time, remain inconclusive.

The best rule seems to be to keep people out of prison if possible, except for the most dangerous and hardened criminals. Among proposed alternatives to prison is the requirement of restitution, mentioned previously. Probation before imprisonment, under close supervision and with assistance in employment and other problems, is viewed by some experts as less expensive and more effective than present practices.

Certainly the prisoner should be followed and helped after release. Most civil penalties should be canceled upon release or within a reasonable time thereafter. And obviously the conditions that lead to crime, or that require heroic virtue if crime is to be avoided by those subjected to them, must be changed.

Which leaves us with Thomas More's judgment that "it is not possible for all things to be well, unless all men are good—which I think will not be this good many years."

4

Religion: The Nation with the Soul
of a Church

Alexis de Tocqueville, in his visit to America, was especially interested in the role of religion in the new democratic society. In the course of his travels, he spoke to many persons about the influence of religion on American life: to ministers, to priests, and to laymen (both politicians and nonpoliticians). He attended Roman Catholic Mass and also a Shaker service.

Most of those to whom he spoke shared his view that religion was necessary to a republic; that the restraint provided by the acceptance of religious authority resulted in respect for law; and that religion exerted a great and good influence on American society. John Quincy Adams said that he considered religion one of the chief guarantees of American society. Joel Poinsett, who had been U.S. Ambassador to Mexico, stated that religion "is one of the things that most powerfully helps us to maintain our republican institutions" and that the religious spirit "exercises a direct power over political passions, and also an indirect power by sustaining morals." Poinsett stated further that many educated Americans believed this to be the case and that consequently they did not "show the doubts they may have about the reality of Christianity, but even hesitate to join new sects such as the Unitarians. They are afraid that they may lead indirectly to the destruction of the Christian religion, which would be an irreparable ill for humanity."

The head of the Presbyterian seminary in Auburn, New York, also stressed the need for religion in America. "I do not believe," he said, "that a republic can exist without morals, and I do not

believe that a people can have morals when it has no religion. I
judge then that the maintenance of the religious spirit is one of
our greatest political interests." A planter from Georgia stated
the same case with slight variation, saying that Protestantism "is
indispensable for a republican people. With us religion is the
surest guarantee of freedom. Religion progresses hand in hand
with freedom, and pours its blessings on its principles. If ever we
cease to be religious, I shall feel that our condition is very dangerous."

Tocqueville was impressed by the way in which religion and
politics seemed to complement each other in America. He remarked: "Religion regards civil liberty as a noble exercise of
men's faculties, the world of politics being a sphere intended by
the Creator for the free play of intelligence. Religion, being free
and powerful within its own sphere and content with the position reserved for it, realizes that its sway is all the better established because it relies only on its own powers and rules
men's hearts without external support." He added: "Freedom
sees religion as the companion of its struggles and triumphs, the
cradle of its infancy, and the divine source of its rights. Religion
is considered as the guardian of mores, and mores are regarded
as the guarantee of the laws and pledge for the maintenance of
freedom itself."

The American colonial tradition was for the most part one of
religious establishment and of conformity within the respective
colonies. Those who did not wish to conform were invited to
move on or, in some cases, were driven out. Thus, Roger Williams moved to Rhode Island. Others moved to the West, in
keeping with the concept of religious freedom proclaimed for
the Massachusetts Bay Colony by Nathaniel Ward, namely that
"all Familists, Antinomians, Anabaptists, and other Enthusiasts,
shall have free liberty to keep away from us, and such as will
come to be gone as fast as they can, the sooner the better." In
somewhat the same vein, John Cotton, surprised by the disturbance resulting from the banishing of Roger Williams, said: "The
Jurisdiction (whence a man is banished) is but small, and the
Countrey round about it, large and fruitful: where a man may
make his choice of variety of more pleasant, and profitable seats,
then he leaveth behinde him. In which respect, Banishment in

this countrey, is not counted so much a confinement, as an enlargement."

What was the state of religion and of the churches in America in 1831, forty years after the Bill of Rights had guaranteed religious freedom and had forbidden support of an established religion? The general attitude was one of toleration.

The divisiveness to follow with the growth of the Catholic population, and with the rise of special sects like the Mormons, had not yet become evident. Abolitionism with religious identification was just beginning. Temperance societies were in their infancy. Religion had not yet been politicized.

By 1831 the Methodists and Baptists were on the way to becoming the majority religions in America. Certainly they had more churches, if not more people, than the other religions. The Jacksonian faith in democracy and in majority determination carried over into religion, and societies of the like-minded were formed.

The circuit rider carried the message before the churches were built. His message, the Methodist message, was also that of the camp meeting, which by 1830 had become almost a Methodist monopoly. Held irregularly, the camp meeting was intense and personal, leading men to be saved by the grace of God. The typical camp meeting, of the kind Tocqueville heard about in the West and the South, is described by Cushing Strout as follows:

> In the camp meeting frontier religion found its characteristic expression. Gathered in homemade tents for several days, thousands of families would eat, drink, sing, shout, pray, and cry together. Seated on rude benches in front of the platform built for a battery of preachers, the frontiersmen were convicted of their sins; warned to flee from the wrath to come; and exhorted to pray for the anxious souls who sat on the mourners benches, awaiting their second birth in the crisis of conversion. Hucksters pitched their wares at the sidelines, whiskey poured from the smuggled-in kegs, while the toughs who had come to jeer guzzled freely, fought, or found a woman. Respectable girls and their swains courted as they could; sometimes sexual and religious anxiety nourished each other. . . .

Two main forces gave form to religion as it bore on politics in the 1830s. One was rationalism, the theme that had marked the

Constitutional Convention, with spokesmen such as James Madison and Benjamin Franklin. The other was a continuation of the pietism of the eighteenth century; it was marked by individualistic religion, emphasizing personal religious experience as more important than formal creeds and rituals.

At the time that the Constitution was adopted, fortunately, no one church predominated in the colonies. Congregationalists prevailed generally in New England, Anglicans in the South and in part of New York. Anglicans in New England and Presbyterians in the South were in the category of dissenters. Any desire or plan for uniformity of religion in the new nation was thus precluded by circumstances. Since uniformity was impracticable, the men who wrote the Bill of Rights faced this choice: either general toleration and no established church or establishment with acceptance of dissenting sects (the pattern in England today). They decided to write the no-establishment clause and to guarantee freedom of worship.

The realities were such as to reduce differences that might have been expected to arise between rationalists and pietists. Accommodation was made easier because the rationalist Deists were not aggressively anti-church. They pragmatically accepted most, if not all, of the identified religions of the day. Rationalists were intellectually committed to toleration, to voluntarism, and to self-government. This made it easier for them to accept a kind of democratic religion when it appeared in the pietist and revivalist forms. Because they accepted that religion was useful to society and possibly to believers, and because they were under no pressure to conform, the rationalists found in their inquiries and reflections no firm bases for rejecting religious doctrine.

Religious toleration of the early nineteenth century was not wholly the result of openness of mind or of ideological commitment. The toleration that marked religious relations among the various sects apparently was as much pragmatic as it was a matter of conviction or principle. Tocqueville quoted Joel Poinsett to the effect that religious toleration in America was not an absolute by any means: "'I am convinced,' Mr. Poinsett said to me today (16th January 1832), 'that even nowadays in America the Lutherans would burn the Calvinists, the latter the Unitarians, and the Catholics all the others, if the civil power was given to any of those persuasions. There is always deep hatred between them.'" Tocqueville also quoted a priest as replying, when asked which sects in America were most hostile to Catholicism: "All sects are united in their hatred of Catholicism; but only the Presbyterians are violent. It is they too who are the most zealous."

Space and time conceptions also influenced American religion. Space in the 1830s was in great supply—not only for westward movement of settlers, but also for religious liberty and for missionary activities. Time was in short supply, or so it seemed. While the frontier was open and moving, religion had to be quick; blessings had to be ready, immediate. For baptism, marriages, and burials, almost any minister would do. The loneliness and isolation of the frontier encouraged the circuit-riding preacher, the revival meeting, and the democratization of religion.

The churches in those years did not try to impose their moral standards on society through political action. Gambling, drinking, card-playing, and other forms of sport and indulgence were opposed within the range of religious persuasion and power. As late as 1839, the *Western Christian Advocate* (a Methodist paper) advised against political discussion at church meetings. The function of the church, it said, is not to reform politics but to save souls.

Generally, at least in principle, the elimination of religious controversy and disagreement seems to have been accepted as good. Tocqueville wrote: "All the clergy of America are aware of the intellectual domination of the majority, and they treat it with respect. They never struggle against it unless the struggle is necessary. They keep aloof from party squabbles, but they freely adopt the general views of their time and country and let themselves go unresistingly with the tide of feeling and opinion which carries everything around them along with it." He added: "They try to improve their contemporaries but do not quit fellowship with them. Public opinion is therefore never hostile to them but rather supports and protects them. Faith thus derives its authority partly from its inherent strength and partly from the borrowed support of public opinion."

Yet Tocqueville, hedging a little on his optimistic view of religious harmony in America, agreed with those Americans who held that Christian sects were basically hostile to each other and that they regularly condemned each other to eternal fire. He added this comment: "The Indian, more tolerant in his rude faith, does not go beyond exiling his European brother from the happy hunting grounds he reserves for himself . . . he dies peacefully, dreaming of the evergreen forests which the pioneer's axe will never bring down, where deer and beaver will come to be shot through the numberless days of eternity."

By 1830, signs of religious disagreement affecting politics were beginning to show. The new religions, or their followers, were beginning to identify with the new politics, the popular politics of Andrew Jackson. And there was evidence that the tranquil rule of the majority anticipated by Tocqueville might not be fully realized. By 1834, the Catholics were singled out for special attention when a mob stirred up by Lyman Beecher burned the Ursuline convent in Charlestown, Massachusetts. Ten years later, two Catholic churches were burned during a riot in Philadelphia. *The Book of Mormon* was published in 1830; soon after, pressure on the Mormons forced them to go West in a series of moves: to Missouri, then to Illinois, finally to Utah.

Meanwhile there was another religious reality in America, one which was quite detached from sectarian division and theological dispute. It has been described by religious historians as the "American civil religion." It has remained largely unchanged in its basic tenets and commitments since colonial times. For community or civil purposes, it overrides sectarian objections and distinctions.

Tocqueville sensed the existence of this civil religion, noting that, "The religious atmosphere of the country was the first thing that struck me on arrival in the United States. The longer I stayed in the country, the more conscious I became of the important political consequences resulting from this novel situation."

The relationship he perceived was quite definable, a rather clear realization of Rousseau's ideal of civil religion as stated in *The Social Contract:*

> Now, it matters very much to the community that each citizen should have a religion. That will make him love his duty; but the dogmas of that religion concern the State and its members only

so far as they have reference to morality and to the duties which he who professes them is bound to do to others. Each man may have, over and above, what opinions he pleases, without it being the Sovereign's business to take cognizance of them; for, as the Sovereign has no authority in the other world, whatever the lot of its subjects may be in the life to come, that is not its business, provided they are good citizens in this life.

There is therefore a purely civil profession of faith of which the Sovereign should fix the articles, not exactly as religious dogmas, but as social sentiments without which a man cannot be a good citizen or a faithful subject. While it can compel no one to believe them, it can banish from the State whoever does not believe them—it can banish him, not for impiety, but as an antisocial being, incapable of truly loving the laws and justice, and of sacrificing, at need, his life to his duty. . . .

The dogmas of civil religion ought to be few, simple, and exactly worded, without explanation or commentary. The existence of a mighty, intelligent, and beneficent Divinity, possessed of foresight and providence, the life to come, the happiness of the just, the punishment of the wicked, the sanctity of the social contract and the laws: these are its positive dogmas. Its negative dogmas I confine to one, intolerance, which is a part of the cults we have rejected.

One might conclude from some of the writings of Jefferson, Franklin, and others that the civil religion of the new republic conformed to Rousseau's description. But the real religion—civil, if we wish to call it that—was much less rationalistic and much more a product of tradition and of fundamentalist, biblical origins. It was not the clear, integrated body of beliefs and values described by Will Herberg, when he said that civil religion is essentially "the American Way of Life":

It is an organic structure of ideas, values, and beliefs that constitutes a faith common to Americans as Americans, and is genuinely operative in their lives . . . Sociologically, anthropologically, it is *the* American religion, undergirding American national life and overarching American society . . . And it is a civil religion in the strictest sense of the term, for, in it, national life is apotheosized, national values are religionized, national heroes are divinized, national history is experienced as a *Heilsgeschichte*, as a redemptive history.

The American civil religion is distinguished by these marks:

1) Acceptance of divine providence as having a special concern for America.

2) Acceptance of a special mission to the world and of a covenant.

3) Acceptance of the idea that religious belief serves the state well; that men are better citizens, better soldiers, better politicians if they are religious in the common conception of religion.

Belief in the special mission of Americans and of America was expressed early in colonial times, when it was common for religious and civil leaders to speak as did William Stoughton of Massachusetts, who asserted that "God sifted a whole nation that he might send choice grain over into the wilderness." In the same spirit and in the same century, Edward Johnson, a colonial historian, said to his fellow settlers in Massachusetts: "Know this is the place where the Lord will create a new Heaven and a new Earth in new Churches and a new Commonwealth together."

Early documents of the Republic emphasize strong religious commitment. Jefferson's Declaration of Independence referred to the laws of nature and of nature's God, to people as being endowed by their Creator with rights, to the Supreme Judge of the world, and to the protection of divine providence. Washington, in his first inaugural address, called upon the "Almighty Being who rules over the universe, who presides in the councils of nations, and whose providential aids can supply every defect." He spoke of the "Invisible Hand" and the "propitious smiles of Heaven." In 1789, at the request of the House and Senate, he declared that November 26 should be a public day of thanksgiving and prayer.

The God of this civil religion was not vaguely deist. He was Old Testament, stern, providentially rewarding, but also punishing. He stood for law and order more than for love and forgiveness. He was not passive but active, as Jefferson noted in his inaugural: "I shall need, too, the favor of that Being in whose hands we are, who led our fathers, as Israel of old, from their native land and planted them in a country flowing with all the necessaries and comforts of life."

That theme has been repeated in many subsequent inaugurals, most noticeably in that of President Lyndon Johnson in 1965, when he said of the colonists and founders of our country: "They came here—the exile and the stranger, brave but frightened—to find a place where a man could be his own man. They made a covenant with this land. Conceived in justice, written in liberty, bound in union, it was meant one day to inspire the hopes of all mankind. And it binds us still. If we keep its terms we shall flourish." And on March 15, 1965, speaking of the civil rights voting act, President Johnson said: "Above the pyramid on the great seal of the United States it says—in Latin—'God has favored our undertaking.' God will not favor everything that we do. It is rather our duty to divine His will. But I cannot help believing that He truly understands and that He really favors the undertaking that we begin here tonight."

Religious theme and emphasis were strong in Lincoln's second inaugural. One theologian has remarked that that address "reads like a supplement to the Bible. In it there are fourteen references to God, four quotations from Genesis, Psalms, and Matthew, and other allusions to Scriptural teaching."

Civil religion and personal religion were blended in Dwight Eisenhower's religious-political image and language.

Eisenhower was presented not only as a good man, and therefore above politics, but also as a basically religious American.

From the beginning of the 1952 campaign, Eisenhower supporters insisted that their actions and interests were nonpolitical, and that their program was to be based not on political considerations but on moral and spiritual principles. The campaign was presented under the banner of a crusade, although the cross was vague. General Eisenhower's supporters insisted that, if they were not all political novices, they were still politically innocent. They were, they said, nonprofessional, unsoiled and unspoiled, pure citizens. Their opponents, even among the Republicans, were labeled politicians. This theme was carried through the 1952 nominating convention and into the fall campaign. When Democratic candidate Adlai Stevenson suggested that the morality of public officials reflected the general level of morality in the country, his opponent rejected the suggestion and went on to ask whether individual United States citizens were responsible for the "loss of China" and the "scandal-a-day" government. The answer expected and given was an emphatic "No."

In the same campaign, when Stevenson said in a New York speech that "only men who confuse themselves with God would dare to pretend in this anguished and bloody era that they know the exact road to the Promised Land," candidate Eisenhower countered with a speech in Montana, encouraging the American people to put away uncertainty and hesitation: "Remember your own power and be not dismayed, because you can do anything."

One of the crusaders, a member of Congress, stated that the root of American failure was that Americans, acting through the previous administration, had tried to "make a settlement or an arrangement with the devil, communism, instead of spurning him as Christ did when he was tempted." The Speaker of the House of Representatives, Republican Joseph Martin, urging support for Republican candidates for Congress, said that the "future of all religious faith" hung in the balance in the 1954 elections.

As the 1952 campaign was marked by a religious and moral tone, so were the inauguration and the administration that followed. William Lee Miller wrote: "One might say that President Eisenhower, like many Americans, is a very fervent believer in a very vague religion." Eisenhower added to his first inaugural address a prayer of his own composition, written that same morning:

Almighty God, as we stand here at this moment my future associates in the executive branch of government join me in beseeching that Thou will make full and complete our dedication to the service of the people in this throng, and their fellow citizens everywhere.

Give us, we pray, the power to discern clearly right from wrong, and allow all our words and actions to be governed thereby, and by the laws of this land. Especially we pray that our concern shall be for all the people regardless of station, race or calling.

May co-operation be permitted and be the mutual aim of those who, under the concepts of our Constitution, hold to differing political faiths; so that all may work for the good of our beloved country and Thy glory. AMEN.

The civil-religion theme ran through other Eisenhower statements: that government is an attempt to translate religion into the political world; that no other nation has America's spiritual and moral strength; that America "is the mightiest power which God has yet seen fit to put upon his footstool."

The inaugural parade of January, 1953, included what was called "God's Float." The New York *Times* reported from Washington that:

> Carpenters raced against time in a remote corner of the National Guard Armory here today to complete an added starter to the procession of floats in Tuesday's Inaugural Parade. To the three men who conceived the idea it is known as "God's Float." They hope it will come to be known as such throughout the world.
>
> Last week the floats were nearing completion in the armory basement. Then it was discovered by a parade official that nowhere was there to be any representation that this was a nation whose people believed in God.
>
> Then, in keeping with the biblical precept, inaugural officials decided that this—the last float conceived—should be first in the, order of march.
>
> It will have constructed on its base a central edifice denoting a place of worship. The side aprons will carry greatly enlarged photographs of churches and other scenes of worship. In Gothic script on the sides and ends of the float will appear the legends "Freedom of Worship" and "In God We Trust."

During the Eisenhower administration, civil religion was recognized in the law. The pledge of allegiance to the flag was changed to include the words "under God." The Postmaster General issued a new red-white-and-blue postage stamp bearing the motto "In God We Trust." It was also prescribed that all American money carry the words "In God We Trust." Legislation was introduced directing the Post Office to cancel mail bearing the imprint "Pray for Peace." And President Eisenhower urged Americans to spend the first Fourth of July in his administration as a day of penance and prayer. Of that day, Elmer Davis wrote: "The greatest demonstration of the religious character of this administration came on July Fourth, which the President told us all to spend as a day of penance and prayer. Then he himself caught four fish in the morning, played eighteen holes of golf in the afternoon, and spent the evening at the bridge table."

The civic religion of the Kennedy campaign and of the Kennedy administration had a different thrust from that of Eisenhower's. Kennedy's problem was to establish, not that as one holding to a vague religion he would strongly apply religion to politics, but that as one belonging to a religion of strong beliefs and firm historical position, he would not let that religion significantly influence his activities as President of the United States. In dealing with the "Catholic Issue," Candidate Kennedy told a group of Protestant ministers in Houston, Texas, on September 12, 1960:

> Whatever issue may come before me as President if I should be elected—on birth control, divorce, censorship, gambling, or any other subject—I will make my decision in accordance . . . with what my conscience tells me to be in the national interest, and without regard to outside religious pressure or dictates. . . . But if the time should ever come—and I do not concede any conflict to be remotely possible—when my office would require me to either violate my conscience or violate the national interest, then I would resign the office. And I hope any other conscientious public servant would do likewise.

Kennedy's inauguration speech and program, however, were clearly consistent with the civil-religious themes of past inaugurations. In the opening paragraph of his address, the newly sworn President identified with the Founding Fathers in noting that he had sworn "before you and Almighty God the same solemn oath our forebears prescribed nearly a century and three quarters ago." A little farther on, in the tradition of the Declaration of Independence, he stated the belief "that the rights of man come not from the generosity of the state but from the hand of God." And he ended his address by "asking His blessing and His help, but knowing that here on earth God's work must truly be our own." Kennedy's address was part of a program which included a prayer by Richard Cardinal Cushing, the Roman Catholic Archbishop of Boston. Cardinal Cushing was followed by Archbishop Iakovos of the Greek Orthodox Church, later by a Protestant minister, the Reverend Dr. John Barclay, and (following the inaugural address) by Rabbi Dr. Nelson Glueck, who gave the benediction.

The civil religion of Richard Nixon's administration was of a somewhat different order. Religion was brought into the White House. Rather than go out to churches, the President regularly brought religious services of various denominations into the White House. The theology of this changed relationship has been described as more one of an imminent civil religion than of a transcendent one. Early in his administration, President Nixon spoke of himself, the President of the United States, as the moral leader of the country. He used the language of religion in political context, without distinguishing the words from their religious use. He used the collective "we" quite indiscriminately. The concept was vaguely incarnational, with the religious and moral life of the nation to be realized in the President. Charles Henderson observed that Nixon "appropriates the vocabulary of the church—faith, trust, hope, belief, spirit—and applies these words not to a transcendent God but to his own nation, and worse, to his personal vision of what that nation should be."

The civil religion as accepted and practiced by President Gerald Ford was more traditional. He represented himself as seeking out God's guidance. He left the White House to attend church services. In his message pardoning President Nixon, he said that he acted as God's humble servant. (I have always wondered why those who speak of themselves with some certainty as "God's servants" nearly always speak of themselves as "humble." A servant of God, it seems to me, could proceed with somewhat greater, Old Testament confidence—not arrogantly, but with quiet assurance.)

It is too early to assess the influence or significance of President Carter's religious beliefs and practices. In his inaugural ceremonies and address, he respected the traditional civil-religious requirements of chaplains, invocations, and personal recognition of God's involvement in the history of the nation. His nonofficial religion is in the line of fundamentalist Baptist tradition. He describes himself as a "born-again" Christian, an assertion no other President in modern times has made. He prays, he says, many times a day. He regularly professes his humility and his dependence on divine inspiration and support. He confesses his sins of the spirit, of pride, of lust in the heart. Before he selected his vice presidential running mate in 1976, he called upon prospective Vice Presidents to confess, at least in private to him, their faults and weaknesses. He teaches Sunday-school classes and gives reflections on the Scriptures, admonishing his listeners to heed the call of the Lord, to give up their "obsessions" and to sell what they have (or at least put it in a blind trust). He speaks of his own personal religion, and practices it, much more openly than have any recent Presidents.

The ritualistic aspects of the civil religion have come to be accepted quite uncritically. There is little or no questioning of the identification of government and politics with religion, if it is generalized enough—as demonstrated in the continuing acceptance of religious observances as a part of the ritual of government: the inaugural oath, together with the customary prayers and references to the Divinity in inaugural addresses, the chaplains' service supported by government funds for the military, the chaplains provided for the Congress and the custom of opening each session with prayer, and the rather uncritical acceptance of formal judicial statements such as that written in *Zorach v. Clauson* (1952) that Americans "are a religious people whose institutions presuppose a Supreme Being." There was also acceptance of Admiral Thomas H. Moorer's testimony in a U.S. district court that compulsory church attendance should be continued at the national military academies because religion makes good military leaders.

While Americans might disagree and quarrel over sectarian differences, the broad civil religion appears to be accepted today as it was in Tocqueville's time. It is not conceived as a substitute for other religions, but as paralleling those religions, or as a more generalized religion into which the others might be fitted. It is somewhat like dual citizenship: a generalized citizenship, such as the Romans encompassed in the *jus gentium,* and the more precise and refined citizenship, which they included under the *jus civile.*

Tocqueville, as did later religious and secular thinkers, raised the question of whether acceptance of the civil religion was good for religion. In his inquiries, he found some who thought it superficial but useful. While most Americans who were asked about religion by Tocqueville stated their belief that it was important and that it was having a great influence on the country, few were certain that the religious beliefs of individual Americans were especially profound. Some suggested that Americans took religion for granted. A Louisiana planter and lawyer said that "for the majority religion is something respected and useful rather than a proved truth. I think that in the depths of their souls they have a pretty decided indifference about dogma. One never talks about that in the churches; it is morality with which they are concerned." A Baltimore doctor said that he detected "a profound indifference beneath all religious beliefs. I imagine that the greater part of the enlightened classes have many doubts about dogma, but that they are careful not to show them; for they feel that positive religion is a moral and political institution which it is important to preserve."

Occasionally the same question is asked today, but generally by theologians and almost in passing. It may receive notice in the religious pages of popular newspapers and more detailed consideration in the religious press. For a politician to raise the question is unusual. Not only is it unusual; it is also dangerous. In a 1955 speech, Senator Matthew Neely of West Virginia made a passing reference to President Eisenhower's churchgoing and piety and observed that the President had never joined a church until he became President. Neely was immediately under attack. He became the target of editorial comment and of cartoons. His colleagues in the Congress reportedly shunned him. Religious spokesmen expressed shock. He was accused of nearly everything from having acted in "bad taste" to being guilty of a "vicious smear." How far the controversy might have gone, or what bearing on politics or religion it might have had, was never determined. For when President Eisenhower had a heart attack six months after Neely's speech, the Senator terminated his case by saying, "When God puts His hand on a man, Matthew Neely takes his away."

Nearly twenty years later, Senator Mark Hatfield of Oregon challenged the civil religion. He noted prayers at civil functions, the motto "In God We Trust" on coins, and other blurrings of the line between religion and state; he said that the trend toward civil religion had become "such a cultural thing that people aren't aware oftentimes that they're being manipulated." He went on to say: "They see a picture of Billy [Graham] speaking in a great crusade. Everything is religious in this atmosphere—

Billy speaking, Billy praying, Billy reading the Bible. Billy is one
of the most admired and respected men in our country. Billy
with the Pope, Billy with Madame Nehru, Billy with kings and
queens, Billy with the President. . . ." The next step, Senator
Hatfield observed, is made "by the Christian community more
than the secular community: 'Billy's close to God; Billy's close to
Nixon. Therefore, God must have ordained Nixon to be President and he's getting the messages through Billy.'"

Even this statement, a surprising one for a politician to have
made, was printed in the religious section of the paper.

Although civil religion seems to remain strong and largely
unchanged from what it was in 1831, the religious character of
America and the relationships of religion to politics and to government have changed significantly since 1831.

According to recent statistics, the principal religious bodies in
the United States are the Roman Catholics, with a membership
of approximately 49 million persons; the Baptists, counting about
28 million members; the Methodists, 13 million; the Lutherans, 9
million; the Jews, 6 million; the Eastern Orthodox, with 4
million; the Presbyterians, 4 million; the Episcopalians, 3 million; the Latter-Day Saints, 2 million; the members of the
Churches of Christ, 2 million. But the percentages of membership and the numbers are less significant than attitudes toward
religion and the degree of participation.

In the early 1950s, America experienced what was described
as a religious revival. It was marked by increased attendance at
church services, a building boom in church construction, an increase in religious vocations, and what was evidently a growing
interest in religion. Whereas the changes were heralded as a sign
of significant religious change by some students of religion and
social history, others questioned the significance and the depth
of change and noted that it seemed quite unrelated to theology
or to deeper moral re-evaluation.

One of the principal voices of the revival was Rev. Norman
Vincent Peale, a New York Methodist preacher whose emphasis
was on self-confidence, self-help, and American know-how,
which he presented in religious form in a book titled *The Power
of Positive Thinking*. Rev. Billy Graham, a more traditional, fundamentalist, biblical preacher, rose to fame in the same period.

With the aid of television and other electronic props, he became in terms of numbers the most popular religious spokesman. For the Catholics, Bishop Fulton J. Sheen became the television personality; his most popular book was called *Peace of Soul.*

This new popular religion was closely tied to the welfare of the country, to anticommunism, to patriotism. The symbols of religion and of politics became almost interchangeable and indistinguishable: God and country, cross and flag, religion and patriotism. Nearly every public effort, whether it was the campaign to elect General Eisenhower or a program to deal with poverty or to seek cures for disease, was presented as a "crusade."

Dr. Peale and Bishop Sheen have faded almost completely from the public scene. Billy Graham remains a most popular preacher. Along with him, there are a dozen or more popular revivalist preachers, many of whom have regular television programs. They cover the range from preaching the Bible, pure and undefiled, to faith-healing.

Most recent reports indicate that the religious revival of the fifties has faded and that overall church attendance and interest in religion are declining. More comprehensive studies, edited by Leo Rosten and published in 1975 under the title *Religions of America,* moved Rosten to conclude in his preface to the book that "our churches are forced to respond to a revolution in our moral and ethical codes." He listed random facts to be considered as supporting his conclusion. Among the facts are these:

—Roughly 75 per cent of the American people think religion is losing its influence.

—Only 50 per cent of Catholics, and only 37 per cent of Protestants, attend church during an average week.

—The birth rate among Catholics is declining and is approaching that of Protestants and of Jews.

—Of Catholic women polled, 83 per cent opposed the Vatican's ban on the use of artificial birth-control devices, and 37 per cent said that they used contraceptive pills.

—The Episcopal Church has abandoned its position which imposed excommunication on those church members who obtained divorces and then remarried without obtaining a bishop's approval.

—The Rabbinical Assembly, representing Conservative Judaism, voted to approve the inclusion of women in a *minyan* (the minimum number of adults needed for common worship). Previously only men were counted.

Rosten evaluated the data thus:

> . . . I cannot help concluding that the fortresses of faith are experiencing the most profound alterations in centuries. Church authority is being challenged on a dozen fronts. Traditional creeds are being drastically revised. Hallowed canons are being shelved. Religious practices are daily changed. Church leaders are beleaguered by new, bold, persistent demands—from their clergy no less than from their congregations.
>
> It is not hyperbole to say that we are witnessing a remarkable erosion of consensus within the citadels of belief. What prophet, what theologian, what historian or scholar could have predicted such dramatic events as those I have listed above? Or the militant participation of clergymen in civil rights marches; the reverberations of the Second Vatican Council; the presence at Catholic altars of Protestant and Jewish clergymen during marriage ceremonies; the "God is Dead" debate; the rise of desegregated congregations; the opposition of Catholics to the doctrine of Papal infallibility; the open campaign of homosexuals against anathematization; the mounting skepticism about the validity or effectiveness of church teachings; the growth of "charismatic" groups and interfaith communes; the phenomenon of "jazz Masses" and rock-and-roll music in cathedrals . . . ?

Perhaps no one could have anticipated any of these things; and no one can foretell exactly what changes and demands for change may lead to.

Along with the easing of religious commitment, there has been another movement among the churches of America. It is one toward agreement and greater unity, and away from division and conflict, especially over matters of no doctrinal importance. This movement, generally known as the ecumenical movement, now encompasses such things as common worship, exchange of theology professors between different religions, re-examination of historical differences, some common missionary efforts, and so on. Co-operation began first among Protestants; later it was expanded to include Jews and Catholics.

The social and political effects of the loss of religion (if it can be called that) and the de-emphasis of religious differences are not yet evident.

Tocqueville thought that loss of religion made people more susceptible to tyranny, that it relaxed the springs of the will and "prepares a people for bondage." He also believed that religion was most helpful in restraining the tendency toward materialism in an age of equality and that it strengthened the individual's sense of social responsibility. For, he said, "Every religion also imposes on each man some obligations toward mankind, to be performed in common with the rest of mankind, and so draws him away, from time to time, from thinking about himself. That is true even of the most false and dangerous religions." "Thus," he continued, "religious peoples are naturally strong just at the point where democratic peoples are weak. And that shows how important it is for people to keep their religion when they become equal."

On the other hand, he thought it a mistake for religions to destroy or try to destroy man's instinct for well-being. Rather, he suggested, they should purify, control, and restrain the tendency toward excessive materialism. Religions, he said, "will never succeed in preventing men from loving wealth, but they may be able to induce them to use only honest means to enrich themselves."

The record of religion in America as a force restraining materialism has not been very clear or positive. In the Calvinist tradition, worldly success was not wholly to be distinguished from spiritual perfection. The promise of the future, of eternity, was in some measure foreshadowed in the present. Poverty was not in itself a mark of perfection; in the land of opportunity it was viewed, if not as a mark of divine disfavor, then at least as one of personal failure.

The disposition of the churches has been to take care of the victims of society, rather than to challenge the society or the system which produced the needy and the defective and then cast them off. For centuries religions tolerated slavery, and men of nearly every denomination were either slave owners or dealers in slaves or passive about the existence of the institution. Even in the 1940s and 1950s, when the issue of civil rights was raised, the churches were slow to be involved. They generally accepted seg-

regation and separatism as the way of things. With the major
exception of black churches and black religious leaders, the
churches came only late and slowly to the civil rights movement.
The same was true of the anti-Vietnam War effort. Although individual clergymen of most denominations were among the early
opponents of the war, the higher church officials and the formal
church bodies remained indifferent or silent until popular opposition was strongly demonstrated.

On other, more limited political and moral issues, the religious
involvement—and even conflict between or among religions—has
been evident for many years. People may no longer believe in
their old-time religion, but many of them guard their old-time
positions. Some of the problems have been taken to the courts
for resolution. Others are fought over in the legislative chambers
at local, state, or national levels. A few have been taken to the
United Nations.

The serpentine wall still runs between the constitutional prohibition of the establishment of religion and the guarantee of freedom of worship. In most cases decided by the Supreme Court in
this area, it is best to read only the decision and not look to the
opinions, unless one is prepared to accept strained constitutional
interpretations.

The First Amendment established the separation of church as
a standard only at the national level. States were left either to establish or to disestablish churches. With the passage of time, and
following the adoption of the Fourteenth Amendment, the principle of separation reached out to include religion in the states.

Real changes came in rulings beginning about midway
through the twentieth century. In 1940 the Supreme Court held
that someone challenging a state law might appeal to the constitutional guarantee of the free exercise of religion. Also in 1940,
in *Cantwell* v. *Connecticut,* the Court found that the state, in attempting to prevent or hinder the public dissemination of religious propaganda, was in violation of the federal Constitution.
In the same year, in *Minersville School District* v. *Gobitis,* the
Supreme Court held that the children of Jehovah's Witnesses
had no constitutional right to refuse to participate in flag salutes
prescribed by the school. A few years later, in *Board of Education* v. *Barnette,* the Court reversed itself and held that the First

Amendment protection extended to freedom from coercive consent even to flag-saluting. Then, in the case of *Murdock* v. *Pennsylvania*, the Court held that a Pennsylvania municipal statute which imposed a licensing fee on canvassing or soliciting was a prior restraint of religious freedom. It said that hucksters and peddlers could be regulated, but not those who were spreading religion.

Before 1940 the Supreme Court had sustained a contract between the District of Columbia and a congressionally chartered hospital conducted by an order of Catholic nuns. It had allowed state payments for textbooks in some sectarian schools. In *Everson* v. *Board of Education* (1947), the Court held constitutional reimbursement for bus transportation costs to parents who sent their children to parochial schools. But in 1948, in *McCollum* v. *Board of Education*, the Court found unconstitutional the use of public-school buildings for released-time religious programs. Jewish spokesmen and most Baptists and Unitarians generally opposed released time, while Roman Catholics and the National Council of Churches (speaking for many Protestant churches) opposed the Court decision.

Subsequent cases have drifted between the two principles or settled into a vague intermediate position. In recent years the Court has moved to keep out that religion which was not in the public schools and also to eliminate what was already there. In *Engel* v. *Vitale* (1962), the Court supported a group of parents in their charge that a prayer recommended by a state board for recitation in public schools violated the no-establishment clause. Subsequently, the Court found Bible-reading in public schools to be contrary to the First Amendment provision barring the establishment of religion.

In another case, the Court held that a Seventh-Day Adventist, whose faith does not allow work on Saturday, could not be denied unemployment compensation if employment without Saturday work was not available. The Court has also held that a person may refuse jury duty for religious reasons.

The confusion grows with almost every Court decision. In 1971 the Court sustained a federal law granting financial aid for the building of parochial-school buildings that were used for secular purposes in higher education; but it did not allow state reimbursement of parochial-school teachers' salaries, even though they were teaching secular subjects. The major concern of the Court seems to arise where religion comes close to education, and then principally at the elementary and high school level. When separated from education, the Court tends to respect religious freedom as a positive and dominant right. But in the education cases it emphasizes the no-establishment clause and, in a reverse way, the freedom not to be religious.

Most difficult of all to explain is the traditional, Court-supported grant of exemption from military service—not because of purely rational objection, but on religious grounds alone, usually a religious commitment clearly demonstrated by the person involved or (better still) by his ancestors. Thus Richard Nixon, with a Quaker background, was eligible for exemption from service in World War II, whereas Muhammad Ali, who objected to participation in the Vietnam War because of the religious principles of his newly adopted Black Muslim religion, was not allowed exemption.

Religious controversy is not limited to the courts. The ruling on school prayers stirred a massive political response. Constitutional amendments to reverse the Court's decision and to allow school prayers have been introduced, debated, and voted on. Especially in southern states, such amendments have been raised as significant issues in congressional campaigns. Prayers have been read into the *Congressional Record*, on the theory that use in the *Record* removed them from the Court ban and that school officials or teachers who subsequently used them were exempt from any legal action.

The move toward unity of civic attitude toward religion, anticipated by Tocqueville, has not progressed very far in the school controversies.

In other areas in which there has been religious or church involvement, the controversies have been clearer, and reconciliation or accommodation easier. Prohibition was strongly supported by religious groups, but finally repealed. The birth-control controversy, once a major religious-political issue, has all but disappeared. But legalized abortion remains, along with the school controversy, as a principal center of religious-political controversy.

In the broader field of religious understanding and co-operation, the movement to ecumenism seems to have passed its high
point. Within some churches, notably the Lutheran and Catholic
churches, there is polarization into conservative and liberal
camps. On a broader front, early in 1975, a group of theologians
(including Protestants, Catholics, and Orthodox) issued the
"Hartford Appeal for Theological Affirmation," undertaking to
draw the lines of tolerable concession to the new theology.
Whether this firming of theological position will lead to political
response or identification in any significant way is doubtful.

Whereas the general beliefs that hold the civil religion together still prevail, although with some reservations, the broader
and deeper unities anticipated by Tocqueville remain unrealized
and perhaps, with the passage of time, less likely of realization.

The "nation with the soul of a church," as the United States
was described by Gilbert Chesterton, is less certain today of mission, covenant, and providential support than it was in 1831.

5

The Economy: What Is One to Expect?

The American continent at the time of Tocqueville's visit was scarcely touched. "The most extraordinary thing of all," he wrote, "is the land. . . . There are still, as on the first days of creation, rivers whose founts never run dry, green and watery solitudes, and limitless fields never yet turned by the plowshare. . . . Now, at the time of writing, thirteen million civilized Europeans are quietly spreading over these fertile wildernesses whose exact resources and extent they themselves do not yet know. Three or four thousand soldiers drive the wandering native tribes before them; behind the armed men woodcutters advance, penetrating the forests, scaring off the wild beasts, exploring the course of rivers, and preparing the triumphal progress of civilization across the wilderness."

Things were not quite as simple and pure in 1831 as Tocqueville observed them to be. Exploitation of land, of resources, and of people had begun, although the consequences were not yet serious. Agriculture was the most important economic activity, and farmers far outnumbered those engaged in other forms of economic endeavor. Agriculture was the source of most wealth, with transportation second, but only because it was necessary for the movement of agricultural products. The nation's exports, too, were principally of agricultural products, with cotton making up more than half of the total exports.

Outside the South, the small farm was the rule, and even in the South most landholdings were small. The great plantation was not typical. Most of the white farmers in the South owned no slaves at all, and the bulk of the slave owners held fewer than ten slaves.

The agriculture of the period was one of growing complexity, not just as to the operation of a single farm but also as to the general situation of agriculture in the country. There were specialized crops in some areas, such as cotton in the South, but for the most part agriculture was rather highly diversified. Livestock was bred and raised in both the North and the South. The South raised food crops as well as cash crops. Northern farmers as well as southern farmers misused and depleted the soil with equal carelessness, and those calling for soil conservation and scientific agricultural practices were heard, but more often ignored, in all regions of the country. Transportation and the opening of the lands beyond the Appalachian Mountains seriously affected northeastern agriculture, especially in states like Vermont, New Hampshire, and Maine, which fell back on sheep growing, dairying, and production of hay, fruits, vegetables, lumber, and maple sugar.

The factories drew some of the young people who might otherwise have been farmers or farmers' wives. Others went west to Ohio and Michigan where land was cheap and productive. Tocqueville gave prices for uncultivated land that ranged from $1.25 per acre near Pontiac, Michigan, to $5 or $6 per acre near Syracuse, New York. The real cost of uncultivated land, he reported, lay in clearing and preparing it for planting, which might run to as much as $10 per acre.

Joel Poinsett, undoubtedly exaggerating, told Tocqueville that in the Northwest "the land never stays in the hands of the one who clears it. When it begins to yield a crop, the pioneer sells it and plunges again into the forest. It would seem that the habit of changing place, of turning things upside down, of cutting, of destroying, has become a necessity of his existence. Very often the second owner too cannot persuade himself to stay still. When the land is in full cultivation, he sells it in his turn and goes further on to work up a newer piece of land. But the third emigrant stays; it is they who make up the population. The others are as it were the advance guard of civilization in the wilds of America."

Tocqueville seems to have accepted this as descriptive of the westward movement, for he later wrote: "It is unusual for an

American farmer to settle forever on the land he occupies; especially in the provinces of the West, fields are cleared to be sold again, not to be cultivated. A farm is built in the anticipation that . . . one will be able to sell it for a good price." There was both restlessness and stability among those who moved to the new lands.

The one worry that Tocqueville expressed about land ownership in America that has not been substantiated was his belief that because of entail and primogeniture, land holdings in America would be broken up in the name of equality of ownership to the dangerous point. He observed that "the last trace of hereditary ranks and distinctions has been destroyed; the law of inheritance has everywhere imposed its dead level."

In 1831 most of the nation's industrial goods were produced either in homes or small shops by farmers, skilled journeymen, or mechanics, rather than by mill hands or factory workers. Home manufacture was the typical method. Shoes were made by families as a supplement to agriculture or fishing in states like Massachusetts. Clothmaking, too, was a supplemental source of income to farm families.

The small shops in the towns and villages were the second source of industrial products. The organization and operation followed closely the ideal of the medieval guild with masters, journeymen, and apprentices. Gradually the system changed to one of merchant capitalism, with the masters acting as small contractors in the employ of merchant capitalists, who owned the raw material, and dealing with journeymen workers, who owned tools and equipment. Exploitation increased, and the guilds, in response, began to change and to become more like modern labor unions.

"In Philadelphia, New York, Boston, Baltimore, Newark, Pittsburgh, Cincinnati, Buffalo, Louisville, St. Louis, and New Orleans, as in small cities throughout the nation, skilled and semi-skilled workers formed their separate journeymen's societies. Shoe workers (or cordwainers as they were then known), printers and compositors, blacksmiths and whitesmiths, leathermakers, saddlers and harnessmakers, carpenters and housewrights, caulkers and coopers, bookbinders, chairmakers and cabinetmakers, gilders and carvers, bakers and soapmakers, masons and house painters, combmakers and brushmakers, tailors and hatmakers, weavers and plasterers, jewelers and machinists, ropemakers and sailmakers organized, the movement at its height claiming a membership of 300,000."

In this spirit, sixteen journeymen's societies united in Philadelphia in 1827. The first general meeting of the mechanics in New York was held in April, 1829. The meeting was called to oppose efforts to make the mechanics work over ten hours per day. The early labor efforts were largely political, and met with mixed success. They advocated such things as land reform, improved educational opportunities for the poor, abolition of imprisonment for debt, military reforms, shorter working hours, and the like.

In the middle thirties, the strike became the principal method for the expression of workingmen's protest. In consequence, by 1835, outside of New England, the ancient practice of holding men at work from sunup to sundown, in the summer more than thirteen hours, had been successfully challenged and the ten-hour day defined. Strikes and protests were successful in the same period in bringing about some increases in wages. But most of the gains registered in the strikes were all but wiped out by the Panic of 1837: wages were cut, jobs disappeared, and most of the unions disintegrated.

The factory system as a way of manufacturing industrial products was just beginning at the time of the Tocqueville visit. Apart from sawmills, gristmills, and the like, which existed throughout the country and which were more like neighborhood activities than factories, factories were concentrated in New England. Waltham, Lowell, and Chicopee were among the earliest factory towns. Cotton and woolen manufactures were the principal products of the early factories, although machinemaking and the iron industry had begun to adopt the factory system.

Factories accounted for only a small fraction of total output before 1840. But with improved transportation and communication, better financing, and an almost unending supply of immigrant labor, the factory system began its movement toward becoming the dominant form of manufacture in America. In Waltham and Lowell, the typical work force consisted of young women who lived in boardinghouses supervised by the mill owners. Rules were strict and included requirements of church attendance. Blacklists were not unknown, and wages ranged from $2 to $2.75 per week. The working day lasted about thirteen hours.

Another type of factory system, known as the Fall River type, provided no housing or paternalistic supervision. It used the labor of entire families under contract which specified hours of work (usually over 70), punishment for absences and for lateness, forefeiture of wages for violations or for failure to give notice of quitting. The wages of men dropped in the late 1830s, seldom reaching more than $4 a week. Women and children, who made up more than half of the labor force under the family system, received lower wages. For women wages ranged from $.50 per week to $2.50 to $2.75 in 1832, while children received even smaller wages. It was estimated that one fifth of the factory workers in Pennsylvania at that time were children under twelve years of age.

Tocqueville took note of the rise of the factory system and of the industrialization of America, noting that America was developing a new aristocracy—an industrial one, and he remarked as follows: "It is acknowledged that when a workman spends every day on the same detail, the finished article is produced more easily, quickly, and economically. It is likewise acknowledged that the larger the scale on which an industrial undertaking is conducted with great capital assets and extensive credit, the cheaper will its products be. People had formed some inkling of these truths long ago, but it is in our day that they have been demonstrated. They have already been applied to several very important industries, and in due turn even the smallest will take advantage of them."

Tocqueville observed that the system of mass production tended to degrade the worker, but he seemed to accept it as inevitable or as a condition of progress. He did note a kind of contradiction when he wrote: "Hence, just while the mass of the nation is turning toward democracy, that particular class which is engaged in industry becomes more aristocratic. . . . It would thus appear," he continued, "tracing things back to their source, that a natural impulse is throwing up an aristocracy out of the bosom of democracy." He saw this aristocracy as a contradiction of democratic egalitarianism in theory, but not as a real danger. For, he said, there is "no solidarity among the rich." As he saw it, "generally speaking, the manufacturing aristocracy which we see rising before our eyes is one of the hardest that have appeared on earth. But at the same time, it is one of the most restrained and least dangerous." He thought this because of three things: because the wealthy lacked solidarity, because fortunes were gained and lost rapidly, and because the business aristocracy had no great hold over its employees. Nonetheless he sounded this warning: "In any event, the friends of democracy should keep their eyes anxiously fixed in that direction. For if ever again permanent inequality of conditions and aristocracy make their way into the world, it will have been by that door that they entered."

It was a worthy warning, we realize now quite late, that he sounded when he wrote these words: "When a workman is constantly and exclusively engaged in making one object, he ends by performing this work with singular dexterity. But at the same time, he loses the general faculty of applying his mind to the way he is working. Every day he becomes more adroit and less industrious, and one may say that in his case the man is degraded as the workman improves."

"What," he asked, "is one to expect from a man who has spent twenty years of his life making heads for pins? And how can he employ that mighty human intelligence which has so often stirred the world, except in finding out the best way of making heads for pins?"

He concluded that from such work, a man's thought "is permanently fixed on the object of his daily toil; his body has contracted certain fixed habits which it can never shake off. In a word, he no longer belongs to himself, but to his chosen calling. . . . In vain are all the efforts of law and morality to break down the barriers surrounding such a man and open up a thousand different roads to fortune for him on every side. An industrial theory stronger than morality or law ties him to a trade, and often to a place, which he cannot leave."

He anticipated the worst abuses of the factory system in contrasting the paternalism of the old aristocracies with the callousness of the new business-industrial aristocracy: "The territorial aristocracy of past ages," he noted, "was obliged by law, or thought itself obliged by custom, to come to the help of its servants and relieve their distress. But the industrial aristocracy of our day, when it has impoverished and brutalized the men it uses, abandons them in time of crisis to public charity to feed them. . . ." He was writing not just of American industrial and business aristocracy, but of what he observed to be developing in Europe as well.

Recently the United Auto Workers began negotiations with the car manufacturers, seeking a contract which would provide job security to their members through a no layoff contract. In cases of cutbacks in production or increased efficiency, the reduced working time would be redistributed, without reduction in pay, among all of the qualified employees by shortening the working time. There would be no layoffs or firings. In a similar move, the United Steel Workers are seeking more comprehensive and extensive security for their members by asking for life security in their jobs and even in retirement.

The security of workers is more in legal construction and support than in traditional property claims. At the same time that organized labor is making advances of these kinds, job security is shaken by court decisions asserting the rights of minorities and of women within the labor force. This development has moved labor leaders to remind union members that, next to their union cards, seniority is their most valuable asset.

The condition of serfdom projected by Tocqueville has not been realized. Yet if we accept the testimony of the people interviewed by Studs Terkel and reported in his book *Working*, the level of frustration and unhappiness is very high and the sense of hopelessness widespread. The psychological state of workers is worse than their economic condition. In the midst of movement they feel, at least many do, trapped and immobile. There is evidence of the dehumanization projected by Tocqueville when he asked: "What is one to expect from a man who has spent twenty years of his life making heads for pins?"

Tocqueville noted that the American Government generally followed a hands-off policy toward business. It gave, he said, "no subsidies," did not "encourage trade," and did not "patronize literature or the arts." The one exception was support in building canals and main roads, although most of this support came from local or state governments.

Support for transportation by governmental units was to grow through the years. Subsidies to railroads, particularly through land grants, was the mark of the railroad-building era. The federal highway building program, with gasoline tax money as the financial support, has provided a continuing financial base for the greatest public building project in the history of mankind. Navigation of rivers and building and maintenance of harbors are largely publicly financed, in the tradition that goes back to at least 1830.

Tocqueville, without comment of any consequence, noted another important business development: the increase in charters of incorporation. At the time of his visit, ownership was largely private and personal, with partnership the prevalent form. But the corporate form was coming to be recognized. Tocqueville reports that he was impressed by observations in James Kent's *Commentaries on American Law* on the subject of corporations: "The number of charters of incorporation is increasing in the United States with a rapidity that seems to frighten Kent." He follows with what is apparently a direct quote from Kent: "We are multiplying in this country, to an unparalleled extent, the institution of corporations and giving them a flexibility and variety of purpose, unknown to the Roman or the English law."

Today, nearly 80 per cent of productive activity in the United States is controlled through corporate organizations operating under charters granted by the states.

Differences between the largest corporations and the government are more and more settled not within a framework of law, but by negotiation. Some years ago, when Du Pont was ordered under antitrust laws to divest itself of General Motors stock, existing antitrust laws and penalties were not applied. Congress passed special legislation to work out the transition. In much the same way, taxation of insurance companies and oil companies has been settled more by negotiation than by application of public judgment and law.

The dealings of the government with the steel industry in recent years demonstrate the same relationship. During the Korean War, when President Truman tried to prevent a steel strike by issuing an executive order to take over the industry, the case was taken to the Supreme Court, and the independence of the industry was sustained.

Subsequent challenges to the steel industry were handled differently. The Kennedy administration responded to major price increases not by attempting to apply existing laws or by appeals to the courts, but by public denunciation and, according to some reports, by midnight telephone calls and at least a suggestion of using the FBI.

In the Johnson administration, the presidents of steel companies were called to the White House for "jawboning sessions." The message was that prices should be kept down. It appeared that if steel executives fixed prices in the White House it was all right, but if they fixed them in Pittsburgh they might go to jail. It was as though the king had called in the barons and said to them: "If you agree to these things in my presence, they are sanctioned. But if you do them by yourselves in Wales, you are in trouble." It has been suggested that the U. S. Government seek diplomatic representation with major corporations, especially with those who are deeply involved in foreign business and finance.

What we have is a kind of corporate feudalism within America. In the feudal system, by one definition, everyone belonged to someone and everyone else belonged to the king. In modern conception, nearly every worker belongs to some corporation and everyone else belongs to the government—federal, state, or local.

Few workers in the United States own their shops or tools. Their ownership claims rest in the security they have in their jobs, either through contract or through law. The arguments given to sustain job claims more and more take on the character of those used to justify property holdings: first, priority of those who already hold jobs; and second, the argument of "stability" of society. The claims have been sustained by court decision. For example, in 1961, when Gemmer Manufacturing Company, a Detroit unit of the Ross Gear and Tool Company of Indiana, decided to move to Lebanon, Tennessee, and declined to offer transfers to the main body of its United Auto Workers employees, several workers sued. A federal district court sustained the workers' contention that their rights extended "beyond the time limitations of the collective bargaining agreement." The court said that those rights "apply to a 'plant' regardless of physical location under this contract and previous contracts." The court held that the company had "an obligation and duty to rehire on the basis of seniority" employees laid off in Detroit, even though the move to Lebanon might terminate the role of their union as their bargaining agent.

Many corporations have extended their business activities beyond the borders of the United States and have become international or multinational institutions. The growth rate of these global corporations in recent years has been spectacular. According to Barnet and Müller in *Global Reach,* a comparison of annual sales of some of the multinationals with 1973 gross national production of countries showed that General Motors is larger than Switzerland, Pakistan, and South Africa; and that Royal Dutch Shell is larger than Iran, Turkey, and Venezuela. "In the process of developing a new world," the authors pointed out, "the managers of firms like GM, IBM, Pepsico, GE, Pfizer, Shell, Volkswagen, Exxon, and a few hundred others are making daily business decisions which have more impact than those of most sovereign governments. . . ." Corporations in both their national and international operations have developed into separate centers of power. They have taken on character and strength which escape U.S. law dealing with business and financial institutions.

The form of wealth has changed in the 150 years since 1831, from ownership in real and definable property (land, shops, machinery, tools, livestock, and so forth) to legal title in mortgages, stocks, bonds, licenses, charters, union contracts, and the like. But the thinning-out of ownership to the dangerous point feared by Tocqueville has not taken place.

The small, family-owned farm persists, although the general trend has been to larger holdings. The Homestead Act of 1862 and the Reclamation Act of 1902 attempted to set 160 acres as the standard, but the standard has not been maintained. The average number of acres per farm increased from 151 in 1930 to 387 in 1975. In the same period, the total number of farms declined from 6.5 million to 2.8 million. But the rate of decline has dropped dramatically in recent years: in 1966 the number decreased 99,000 from the previous year's count; in 1970 the drop was only 45,000; in 1975, 22,000.

The distribution of personal wealth is difficult to ascertain, and at best represents a relative position of ownership and control. There is evidence that wealth in the United States has become less concentrated in the last half century; but the change has not been great. It appears to reflect temporary or unusual historical forces (the Great Depression and World War II) rather than basic economic trends. Robert J. Lampman's study of the distribution of wealth shows the highest measurable concentration of wealth in America to have been that which existed on the eve of the Great Depression. According to his report, the richest 0.5 per cent of Americans in 1929 owned 30 per cent of the net wealth held by all persons. At that time, corporate stock was the principal asset of the wealthy. The nearly 400 per cent rise in stock prices between 1921 and 1929 greatly increased the value of stock held by the rich. The collapse of the market reduced the value of stockholdings, so that by 1933 the 0.5 per cent had lost 22 per cent of their 1929 wealth. The 1939 Lampman estimate showed the top 0.5 per cent holding 28 per cent, up from 25.2 per cent in 1933. In 1945, however, he found them holding only 20.9 per cent of the nation's wealth and by 1949, only 19.3 per cent.

Studies since the end of World War II, and preceding the stock market decline of 1973–74, showed a gradual increase in the share of wealth held by the 0.5 per cent group. According to Lampman, it rose to 22.7 per cent in 1953 and to 25 per cent in 1956, at which percentage it seems to have leveled off. The one notable change in the assets held is in the decline of holdings in corporate stock: in 1953, the richest 0.5 per cent of the population held 86 per cent, by value, of all personally owned stocks; by 1969, the estimate was 44 per cent. The New York Stock Exchange census of shareholders for approximately the same period (1952–70) shows an increase of nearly 500 per cent in the number of shareholders. The share of the rich in other assets, such as noncorporate business holdings, houses, furniture, and so forth, has increased slightly but not significantly.

The trust is the special repository of the holdings of the rich. A 1976 estimate showed that about 81 per cent of the value of trusts was in the hands of the top 0.5 per cent of wealth owners, and that 90 per cent was held by the richest one per cent.

Income distribution, rather than wealth in property, is a more important indicator of economic well-being or distress for most Americans, since their security depends largely on annual income from wages or salaries, pensions, or profits from the operation of small businesses or farms. That distribution shows wide differences.

Statistics on the distribution of income leave much to be desired, but as general indicators they are quite valid. What the statistics show clearly are two facts: first, that the distribution of income is highly unequal; and second, that a substantial percentage of the population lives at income levels that most Americans consider highly inadequate. They also show that there has not been any substantial change in relative shares of the rich and of the poor in the last twenty-five years.

Recently published reports indicate that the lowest 20 per cent of American families receive about 5 per cent of the annual income and that the top 20 per cent receive about 41 per cent. In the case of unrelated individuals, the discrepancy is even greater, with the lowest 20 per cent getting 4 per cent of the annual income and the top 20 per cent getting 48 per cent. In 1976, a nonfarm family of four was defined as poor if it had an annual income of less than $5,815 per year. Within the relative definitions and standards by which statistical poverty is determined, the number of poor in America declined in recent years from 39.5 million (or 22.4 per cent of the population) in 1959 to 25 million (or 11.8 per cent) in 1976. It should be noted that the rapid decline occurred between 1962 and 1969, and that the rate has fluctuated up and down since then. The poor population contains a very high proportion of old people, of children, of blacks, and of families headed by women.

As the number and the percentage of poor has declined, it has become less and less like the population as a whole. Although there is evidence that the real income of the poor has risen, their position relative to the rest of the population has not improved in recent decades. The evidence is that a poverty class—more or less permanently fixed and distinguished by general characteristics of age, race, and sex association—has developed in the United States.

The problem of poverty is not only one of numbers, or one to be explained in economic terms. It is one of national philosophy. That philosophy is essentially today the same as it was when presented by Herbert Spencer in the nineteenth century:

> Pervading all nature we may see at work a stern discipline, which is a little cruel that it may be very kind. . . . The poverty of the incapable, the distresses that come upon the imprudent, the starvation of the idle, and those shoulderings aside of the weak by the strong . . . are the decrees of a large, far-seeing benevolence. . . . Similarly, we must call those spurious philanthropists, who, to prevent present misery, would entail greater misery upon future generations. All defenders of a poor-law must, however, be classed amongst such. . . . Blind to the fact, that under the natural order of things society is constantly excreting its unhealthy, imbecile, slow, vacillating, faithless members, these unthinking, though well-meaning, men advocate an interference which not only stops the purifying process, but even increases the vitiation . . .

According to this theory, poverty is its own cause and its own reward, rather than a consequence of other forces—economic, social, historic—which impinge on society, or a consequence of personal failings—physical or mental.

The choice of programs is between a continuation of the old type, a modification of the poor-farm approach, with the poor as dependents of the state and supplicants, and the newer approach advocated in the name of welfare rights, which quite boldly asserts that every American has a right to a decent income if working, if willing to work and without opportunity, or if unable to work because of disability or family responsibilities.

Today's political thrust is not directed toward equalizing wealth or effecting a better distribution of wealth. It is directed toward equalizing income through manipulation of income-tax rates. The original conception of the income tax as a source of revenue to meet government expenses, as a system reflecting the ability of the taxpayer to pay, and as including support for the poor, has been extended to include its use to equalize income above the poverty level. This purpose was most clearly demonstrated in the tax proposals for income redistribution presented by Senator George McGovern in his 1972 presidential campaign. It is also implicit in the negative income-tax proposals of conservative political economists and in the recent device of "tax rebates."

The political consequences of the idea of voting oneself an increase in income have not yet been assayed. It may lead to a Supreme Court test. Its acceptance and practice in England have effectively eliminated a middle class of property owners, or at least the possibility of sustaining or replacing an old property class. In a more limited way, the consequences of voting oneself an increase in income are demonstrated in the plight of New York City, which, with an inadequate tax base, voted itself subsidized transportation, subsidized medical aid, subsidized housing (especially in its rent-control program), higher pensions and salaries, and all but free college education.

President Jimmy Carter, in his inaugural address, declared that we have already achieved a high degree of individual liberty and that we are now working on equality of opportunity. This is a strange interpretation of the Declaration of Independence, which surely did not look upon liberty and equality as successive stages of development, but as conditions which should exist together—in some tension, but within a range allowing all to pursue happiness and in some measure to enjoy it.

The second indicator of failure in the operation of the American economy is the number of unemployed. Despite the fact that productivity of the American economy has more than doubled since the end of World War II, unemployment has remained high in what economists call normal periods, and has risen even higher in periods of economic decline. The most serious period of decline was the recession of 1975–76, when the rate of unemployment reached above 8 per cent and the number of unemployed in the civilian labor force rose to nearly 8 million persons.

In dealing with unemployment, as in dealing with poverty, old and fixed ideas control. The ideas and theories about unemployment do not go back to the nineteenth century, but they do go back to the New Deal period. Extended unemployment benefits, together with government-created jobs (not competitive with those which might exist in the normal operation of the economy) are offered as immediate relief for the unemployed. The more fundamental problems are approached, with the advice and counsel of Keynesian or neo-Keynesian economists, through increased federal deficits, resulting from tax cuts and high spending.

The assumption continues to be that an expanded economy will absorb the unemployed when, in fact, the historical evidence is that it will not do so. Rather, the record indicates that action must be taken to redistribute the volume of work among available workers. No such action has been taken in the United States since the late 1930s and early 1940s, when wage-and-hour legislation finally settled on the forty-hour week and the eight-hour day as the standard for most Americans. Working time should be shortened through a shortening of the working day, the working week, or the working year, in order to absorb most of those now excluded from work opportunities. There have been nearly forty years of technological progress since the working time for Americans was last set. One might expect an adjustment after the passage of that much time.

The third problem, only recently recognized by economists and by businessmen and financiers, is that of the limited potential of the American economy. In a wave of optimism, encouraged by rapid economic expansion in the United States and other nations following World War II, and especially in the period of the 1960s, economists began to project almost unlimited growth. Financiers, businessmen, and politicians accepted the optimistic view and reflected their acceptance in enthusiastic expansion. Businessmen borrowed money; banks extended credit. The government used deficit financing, even to conduct wars, on the assumption that an expanding economy would in the future take care of irresponsibility. The day, or year, of reckoning came in 1974 and 1975, quite suddenly but not surprisingly. The economy of the United States began to show the symptom of fundamental weakness: inflation together with rising unemployment. The economists could offer little more than hand-wringing, political and moral explanations, and new words like "stagflation." The real problem was that there had been overconsumption of food, fuel, and other material resources, and of money or credit.

By 1975, the American people had become the greatest consumers, if not the greatest overconsumers, in the history of the world. Making up 5 per cent of the world's population in that year, they consumed one third of the world's annual production of fuel and 40 per cent of the world production of aluminum and manganese.

In 1976, the people of the United States consumed 95 pounds of beef per person in contrast with 64 pounds per person in 1960. In addition to beef consumption, United States citizens on the average consume annually about 52 pounds of poultry, 54 pounds of pork, and 13 pounds of fish. Americans in 1971 were consuming almost two and one-half times as much of these proteins as the Japanese, who are not an underfed people. Today, 78 per cent of American grain is fed to animals. The ratio of feed protein to pound of animal protein produced, in the case of beef and veal, is 21 to 1; for pork it is 8.3 to 1; and for poultry 5.5 to 1. Thus, some 21 pounds of protein in the form of soy beans are reduced to one pound of protein nourishment if fed to a cow instead of a person.

In 1940, the average horsepower used per person in the United States was 21; by 1960 it was 62; and by 1971 it was 93. According to government reports, 28 tons of materials from mines, fields, forests, and oceans are used each year per person in the United States. The per capita consumption of material resources in the United States is more than twice that of Western Europe, four times that of Eastern Europe, and cannot even be realistically compared to consumption in other countries. The people of many countries of the world would live better on the waste of America, if it could be transported to them, than they do on their present supplies and resources. About 40 per cent of all the automobiles in the world are owned by people in the United States: there is one car for every 2 persons. Ten per cent of the material production of the country is used for the construction and maintenance of these cars, and 15 per cent of the world's annual production of petroleum is used each year to fuel them.

America was not always an overconsuming and wasteful country. Well into the twentieth century, little fuel was used for agricultural production or for transportation. Horses were a major source of workpower, and they were sustained by the produce of the land on which they worked. City workers and their families lived near their work, in contrast to the situation today when the average distance between home and work in the United States is fifteen miles.

Although there was waste of resources and overoptimism through two centuries of national existence, it was only after World War II that excessive waste became obvious. That war released a new confidence in the potential of science and technology to open the way to greater satisfaction of man's material needs. Economists were encouraged by scientists; politicians, bankers, and businessmen, by economists. The military argued, with economic justification, for preparation of all possible wars—past, present, and future. The Secretary of Defense, Robert McNamara, was moved to say that the United States could afford two wars like the one in Vietnam and still have butter. Economists began to speak of the peace increment, which was to follow the end of the war, almost as though the war were producing it. Revenue sharing was proposed as a way of sharing federal tax moneys with state and local governments.

Expanded federal budgets became the rule. The federal budget rose from approximately $110 billion in 1963 to approximately $500 billion in 1978. The federal debt in the same period rose from some $310 billion to $874 billion.

Consumer and business credit were greatly expanded. Expansion and increased production became ideals within themselves. We could produce and sell bigger cars; therefore, we should produce and sell them. Bigger and faster cars required more gasoline, more roads and highways, more garages, more parking spaces, more hospital beds to take care of those injured in automobile accidents. The oil companies were ready to provide fuel; society was ready to provide the other needs of the expanding automobile culture.

Meanwhile old buildings were torn down before their useful lives had ended, often to take advantage of special tax incentives. New buildings—many insulated against nature and dependent almost entirely on their own expensive, self-contained units for heating and cooling—replaced them.

The new consumption has both passive and active aspects. Electric toothbrushes and electric can openers are on the market, along with electric exercycles. There are television sets which give pictures the instant the sets are turned on, and with gadgets which allow the viewer to determine picture or channel selection by remote control. Powerboats replace rowboats and sailboats. Snowmobiles have taken the place of sleds, skis and snowshoes. Packaging has become a major industry, with paper and plastic wrapping cluttering urban streets and rural roadsides. Garbage disposal has become a major problem.

With planned obsolescence justified by both macroeconomics and microeconomics, American industry produces goods programed to fall apart within a given time span. Hence cars, old before their time, go, as the poet Philip Booth wrote, "to Maine" or to North Carolina or West Virginia, or are abandoned on the streets of New York and other cities of America. Throwaway cans and bottles replace bottles that can be returned and reused. Advertisers encourage "impulse buying," and the public responds.

Conspicuous waste beyond the imagination of Thorstein Veblen has become the mark of American life. As a nation we find ourselves overbuilt, if not overhoused; overfed, although millions of poor people are undernourished; overtransported in overpowered cars; and also—if we accept the estimate of experts that we have sufficient nuclear power to destroy the power and population centers of the USSR fifteen times over, and if we accept that conventional wars and conventional weapons are obsolete—overdefended or overdefensed.

Things are not desperate in the United States. The nation still has the potential to meet its economic needs. What is called for is re-examination. First, we must ask some hard questions about ourselves and about our national character.

How far have we gone down the road toward destroying ourselves as civil and social beings?

How close have we come to the state of inhumanity, described by Erich Fromm: "Man, as a cog in the production machine, becomes a thing, and ceases to be human. He spends his time doing things in which he is not interested, with people in whom he is not interested, producing things in which he is not interested; and when he is not producing, he is consuming. He is the eternal suckling with the open mouth, 'taking in,' without effort and without inner activeness, whatever the boredom-preventing (and boredom-producing) industry forces on him—cigarettes, liquor, movies, television, sports, lectures—limited only by what he can afford."

What is called for is continuing moral response; not one requiring unusual sacrifice or heroic virtues, but an acceptance of restraint within reasonable limits, of responsibility toward nature and the resources of the world.

6

The Law: Hidden at the Bottom of a Lawyer's Soul

In 1831, the time of Tocqueville's visit to America, both the practice of law and the procedures of justice were in a state of confusion and conflict. Consequently, his generalizations about law and justice in democracy have more validity than his observations about law and justice as they were practiced in 1831. When in the late 1820s the profession of law became a target, if not a victim, of Jacksonian Democracy, it had not fully recovered from its decline during and after the American Revolution.

On the eve of the Revolution, the legal profession was generally respected. In many colonies it had achieved status and distinction. By the rather rough definition of lawyer then prevailing, twenty-five of the fifty-six signers of the Declaration of Independence were lawyers. Thirty-one of the fifty-five persons who attended the Constitutional Convention were lawyers. The first Senate of the United States had ten lawyers; and the first House of Representatives had seventeen lawyers in a membership of sixty-five.

But the general effect of the Revolution had been harmful to the legal profession. Few lawyers were active in the Revolution. Many remained actively loyal to the Crown, and later fled or retired from the practice of the law. In many states lawyers who had not supported the Revolution were barred from the practice of the law either by legislative action or by court rulings. Residual strength and popular support of the profession were further eroded by the economic disorders which followed the revolutionary victory. Debt collection, foreclosures, recovery of property, displacement of tenants, and the like were the principal legal actions of the post-Revolutionary period. In the minds of most persons, the lawyers were on the side of property and of the economic oppressors.

The courts, the law, and the lawyers all came under fire. Early in the nineteenth century, some state legislatures passed laws to repress not only lawyers but also the English common law. Then came Jacksonian Democracy, giving theoretical justification for the practical and popular attacks on law, lawyers, and justice. The standards of the legal profession all but disappeared. The judiciary, reflecting the general state of the legal profession, fell into disarray. Opposition to the common law became more widespread and more virulent. It was criticized and rejected because of its English origins and because of its intricacies and technicalities. It was also criticized by more thoughtful students of the law, such as Henry Dwight Sedgwick, who deplored the American dependence on the common law and raised the valid question of

> whether these United States, or some of them, have not so increased in magnitude, whether their institutions, mode of society, tenure of property, and, in short, all their relations and their whole character, have not become so materially different from those existing in England . . . that the change and alienation . . . ought not to be formally recognized; whether we have not derived all the aid we ought to expect from the land of our ancestors; whether any further servile dependence on a foreign country does not rather tend to retard than promote our advancement; and, lastly, while we pay to England all due courtesy and respect . . . whether we should not, nevertheless, declare a final separation, not a nonintercourse, but an independence in jurisprudence, as really and nominally absolute, as it has long been in point of political sovereignty?

The more common and popular attacks were like that of Robert Rantoul, a member of the Massachusetts bar during the 1830–40 period. He described the English common law as "sprung from the Dark Ages." He said that it had "its beginnings in the time of ignorance . . . in folly, barbarism, and feudality" and "sheds no light but rather darkness." In this spirit, the Pennsylvania legislature in 1810 passed a law forbidding the citation of any English decision handed down after July 4, 1776. The Kentucky legislature at about the same time considered the prohibition of citations or references to English decisions or authorities of any time—a position subsequently modified to apply only to decisions which took place after the day the Declaration of Independence was signed.

Both the legal profession and the judicial system tended to disintegrate, to become ill-trained and primitive. Lawyers, especially on the frontier, had little legal training. Some had read in law offices or had learned something of the law by attending and studying court proceedings. But after 1830, even the requirement of reading with a lawyer as a condition to practicing law was widely ignored. Men were allowed to practice law if a judge accepted that they knew some law.

Legal fees reflected the quality of the lawyers, and the deprofessionalization of the law. In 1910 one American reported that his father, who practiced in upstate New York in the late 1820s, had earned $217 during his first year of practice and $670 in his third year. Mr. Redin, a lawyer in the District of Columbia about 1835, was reported to be so hard-up that he walked to Rockville, Maryland (a distance of twelve miles) and back again to save expenses. Philip Barbour, a Virginia lawyer, was making less than $7,000 a year at about the same time. And William Wirt reported that $6,000 to $8,000 a year was considered to be a good income for lawyers in New York. In 1838 Alphonso Taft, practicing in Cincinnati, Ohio, estimated that a lawyer could make from $3,000 to $5,000 a year in that city. For handling an estate involving $100,000, Abraham Lincoln charged $5. For writing pleadings and participating in a jury trial in the case of *Nolan* v. *Hunter,* he again received $5. For collecting a debt of $600, he charged $3.50. For arguing a case before the Illinois Supreme Court, he was paid $5 or $10.

Earlier in the century, the practice of the law apparently was more profitable—at least for some lawyers. William Pinkney of Maryland, for example, in 1816 had an income well over $20,000. And in 1814 Alexander James Dallas of Philadelphia earned approximately $20,000.

The courts reflected the informal and primitive conditions prevailing in that era. Frontiersmen believed that justice should be popular and egalitarian, and that experience was the best teacher. Many judges were untrained, even uneducated. Often they were wealthy farmers, merchants, or landlords.

Lawyers and those interested in the law, either out of self-interest, or social and professional concern, did not fully surrender to the popular pressures. Individually and through organizations they had begun to fight back in the post-Revolutionary period. Following some setbacks, those efforts continued despite the challenge of the frontier and of Jacksonian Democracy. David Hoffman, opening a series of lectures on the law at the University of Maryland in 1823, spoke of the special responsibility of the lawyer as one "who does justice to his profession, and to the important station he holds in life." And Justice Joseph Story of the U. S. Supreme Court described lawyers who appeared before that tribunal as "sentinels upon the outposts of the Constitution." Story added that "no nobler end can be proposed for their ambition or patriotism, than to stand as faithful guardians of the Constitution. . . ."

Under criticism, without full public support or respect, the practice of law was pursued. The University of Virginia Law School was established in 1826 by Thomas Jefferson, to teach "the common and statute law, that of the Chancery, the laws Feudal, Civil, Mercatorial, Maritime and of Nature and Nations, and also the Principles of Government and Political Economy." In February of 1826, when Jefferson was involved in the selection of a professor of law, he wrote to James Madison:

> We must be vigorously attentive to his political principles. You will recollect that before the Revolution, Coke Littleton was the universal elementary book of law students, and a sounder Whig never wrote, nor of profounder learning in the orthodox doctrines of the British constitution, or in what were called English liberties. You remember also that our lawyers were then all Whigs. But when his black-letter text, and uncouth but cunning learning got out of fashion, and the honeyed Mansfieldism of Blackstone became the students' hornbook, from that moment, that profession (the nursery of our Congress) began to slide into Toryism, and nearly all the young brood of lawyers now are of that hue. They suppose themselves, indeed, to be Whigs, because they no

longer know what Whigism or republicanism means. It is in our
seminary that that vestal flame is to be kept alive; it is thence it
is to spread anew over our own and the sister States.

In 1826 Yale opened its new law school. In 1829 Harvard Law
was reorganized. In 1834 Judge John Reed established at Car-
lisle, Pennsylvania, a law school which later became connected
with Dickinson College.

Young men of good or better eastern families began to go
West. Some of them laid the foundations for family fame and
fortunes through practice of the law. Alphonso Taft established
the beginnings of what was to become the Taft dynasty in Ohio.
After finishing his legal studies, he left Connecticut in 1838 and
in that same year settled in Cincinnati, Ohio. Others who went
West to practice law left their mark not only on their own careers, but also in the careers of their descendants—in law, politics, and other professions. And they left their names in foundations, in cities, and in companies such as Kimball and Parker in
Wisconsin. James Whitcomb, a native of Vermont, practiced law
in Bloomington, Indiana; his name was carried by the Hoosier
poet, James Whitcomb Riley.

The frontier in this period began to produce its own lawyers in
its own way. As New York and Philadelphia had in earlier times
developed reputations as states in which the legal profession was
superior, so too western and frontier states came to be distinguished by the quality of their lawyers. Early in the nineteenth
century, Indiana lawyers were considered to be the best educated in the Northwest Territory; consequently, they dominated
the legal and political life of the Territory and later of the state.
Tennessee also had a reputation as a state which produced great
lawyers. Included among the Tennessee professionals were men
like Andrew Jackson, John Bell, and James K. Polk. Tennessee
also produced lawyers who became famous in other states—notably Sam Houston, who went to Texas, and Thomas Hart Benton,
who migrated to Missouri.

Despite confusion, conflict, and some regression, the years before and after the visit of Tocqueville were years in which the
basis for an American-made common law was established. It was
a time during which great lawyers and great judges—through arguments, decisions, and opinions—shaped the law that was to

come. The great lawyers included Luther Martin, William Pinkney, Jeremiah Mason, Daniel Webster, Horace Binnery, and Re-
verdy Johnson. The great judges included John Marshall, James
Kent, Joseph Story, John B. Gibson, and Thomas Ruffin.

Trained as he was in French law, Tocqueville found the common law as followed in America less precise and less rational
than that of his own country. Nevertheless, he thought it right
for America. He saw it as a force for conservatism and a protector of liberty. "Born among the Barbarians," he wrote, "the
Common Law is, like the civilization that brought it forth, defective, but it breathes the spirit of independence of the centuries in
which it began to flourish."

He noted the contradictions in American law and its inadequacy in some areas. Laws as passed, he wrote, "are often defective or incomplete; they sometimes violate acquired rights or
sanction dangerous ones; even if they were good, their frequent
changes would be a great evil." Yet he saw the benefits of
localism, observing that diverse municipal laws appeared to di-
vert citizens' passions, which might be harmful to the state, to
the problems of the township or parish. His overall conclusion
was that the American system of law was good and that it was
likely to get better. Americans, he thought, had time to make
mistakes and to learn from them. "In general," he observed, "the
laws of a democracy tend toward the good of the greatest number, for they spring from the majority of all the citizens, which
may be mistaken but which cannot have an interest contrary to
its own." He might have endorsed the idea that "that government is best which governs least," and he believed, in some
measure, that the natural man and society of Rousseau were
being realized in America. He seemed little disturbed by the
Quaker who explained why Negroes in Philadelphia were
harassed when they tried to vote: "The law with us is nothing
when it is not supported by public opinion." And he observed:
"In the new states of the Southwest the citizens almost always
take justice into their own hands, and murders are of frequent
occurrence." He noted that "duels are still preferred to lawsuits
there."

Tocqueville saw Americans as generally law-abiding, since
they could vote and thus share in the making of the laws. He

believed that they obeyed the law, "not only because it is their work but also because they can change it if by any chance it does injure them; they submit to it primarily as a self-imposed evil, and secondly as a passing one." The participation of many sustained popular support of the law, according to his theory. "In the United States," he observed, "except for slaves, servants, and paupers fed by the township [he did not include women], no one is without a vote and, hence, an indirect share in law-making."

If the Americans had this disposition to accept the law and abide by it, they had, according to Tocqueville, an even deeper and less questioning commitment to court decisions. The latter acceptance seems to be most likely for court decisions following passage of law or arising from interpretation and extension of past decisions. The clearest case of the people's not accepting a law was the response to Prohibition. But even in this case, whereas the prohibition amendment generally was not accepted, the court decisions were honored. Those who contributed to the violation of the law, principally consumers of illegal liquor, seemed undisturbed by the harsh penalties imposed on those who made, transported, or distributed the liquor.

Confidence in the courts, or the need for such confidence, rests on two facts. First, as Tocqueville noted, "There is hardly a political question in the United States which does not sooner or later turn into a judicial one." Second, he observed that the Supreme Court was the most powerful tribunal of any nation in the world, with the ultimate right to pass on the constitutionality of laws. In addition to its jurisdiction over treaties, federal law, and international law, the Supreme Court, he wrote, "may be said to summon sovereigns to its bar. When the court crier, mounting the steps of the tribunal, pronounces these few words: 'The state of New York versus the state of Ohio,' one feels that this is no ordinary court of justice. And when one considers that one of these parties represents a million men and the other two million, one is amazed at the responsibility weighing on the seven men whose decision will please or grieve so many of their fellow citizens." He continued: "The peace, prosperity, and very existence of the Union rest continually in the hands of these seven federal judges. Without them the Constitution would be a

dead letter . . ." He noted that it was vital that the justices of
the Supreme Court be men of great integrity and ability. He
warned that "if ever the Supreme Court came to be composed of
rash or corrupt men, the confederation would be threatened by
anarchy or civil war."

Americans seem to have sensed the importance of preserving
the integrity of the Supreme Court, its independence of political
interference, and its stability. Most noteworthy was the resistance to Franklin Roosevelt's effort to "pack the Court." At the
height of Roosevelt's popularity, and at a time when his political
proposals generally received wide popular appeal, the people
rejected his court-packing effort, which was wholly within constitutional limits. His plan even involved a concession to the
existing court, since he proposed to add new justices, when sitting justices reached the age of seventy, without forcing the in-
cumbents to resign.

In Tocqueville's judgment, the Court was—as it remains today
—the last and greatest protector of liberty. He thought it would
grow in importance as democracy became more egalitarian. For,
as he saw it, "Private rights and interests are, then, always in
danger unless the power of the courts grows and extends com-
mensurately with the increase of equality of conditions." Today
court action often involves demands for equality. The lot of the
courts is not easy in a time of tension, when equality or the
demand for it impinges upon liberty and upon the inequalities
that are a condition of liberty and a consequence of it.

The drafters of the Constitution were apprehensive of democracy and of equality. Either with arrogance or with wise foresight, they provided that the Constitution which they had
drafted could not be amended except by proposal of an amendment by two thirds of both houses of Congress or by constitutional convention and approval by legislatures or conventions
of three fourths of the states. They may have been too modest in
their effort to preserve from change the Constitution as they had
written it. Had they been less trusting of democracy, the momentum to amend the Constitution, which has been the mark especially of this century, might well have been slowed. There were
only four amendments to the Constitution in the whole of the
nineteenth century. Three of those—the Thirteenth, Fourteenth,

and Fifteenth—were corrective of the Constitution following the Civil War.

In the twentieth century, beginning with the adoption of the Sixteenth Amendment (some forty years after the adoption of the last preceding one), the disposition to amend the Constitution has grown stronger. The use of the amendment route to achieve substantial political objectives, rather than to correct procedures or clarify basic rights, has become much more common. The Sixteenth Amendment, for example, was more one of legislative substance than of change in constitutional principle. But its adoption—inevitably, because of the way in which income taxes must be imposed and taxpayers checked for conformity— has been followed by weakening of the constitutional guarantees of due process and privacy. The Seventeenth, providing for the direct election of senators, reflected a national trend to a more direct electoral system. It nationalized a practice which had already been adopted in many states or was on the way to adoption. It was an amendment which was truly radical, as it bore upon the constitutional principle of representative government exercised through varying procedures for choice of representatives. It also ran contrary to the conception of senators accepted when the Constitution was adopted. Then they were viewed as representatives of the states in a somewhat formal and detached way, almost as though they were ambassadors.

The Eighteenth Amendment (the Prohibition Amendment) marked a new step: use of the amendment route to achieve a specific social change or a reform of manners and morals. Although it was repealed thirteen years after it went into effect, the precedent of its failure has not deterred efforts to achieve other moral and social, even religious, commitments by constitutional amendment. The most recent, strong effort has been one to amend the Constitution so as to reverse or change the Supreme Court's ruling that matters relating to abortion are not to be seriously or significantly controlled by legislative action. Another proposed amendment, receiving less popular support but advocated by some politicians in and out of office, is one which would allow prayer in public schools—again in contradiction of a Supreme Court decision. This has become an issue in national elections, although not of the seriousness and scope of the anti-abortion amendment.

Significantly, there has been an increase in the number of amendments, both those adopted and those proposed, which bear upon decisions of the Supreme Court or which anticipate such decisions. Of those adopted in this century, the Sixteenth (income tax), the Eighteenth (Prohibition), and the Twenty-fourth (poll tax) are clear examples. The fact of their adoption indicates a change in respect for the Constitution—at least as interpreted by the Supreme Court. At the same time, respect for the Court (popular support, that is) remains high. And there is a general belief that membership on the Court affects the character of judges for the better. Since the Roosevelt experience, few politicians have dared to propose any serious tampering with the Supreme Court. And the thesis that the office changes the man has been used as justification for less-than-full examination of those proposed for the Court.

Respect for the office is also demonstrated in the ready criticism of Presidents who use the Court or its members for political activities or other services. President Truman was criticized severely for assigning Justice Robert Jackson to the Nuremberg trials. President Johnson, similarly, was criticized for appointing Chief Justice Earl Warren to head the commission to investigate the assassination of President Kennedy—as he was criticized for using men in other high offices, especially congressional leaders, in nonjudicial and nonlegislative proceedings.

The general attitude toward lower courts and their judges is markedly different from that demonstrated toward the Supreme Court. This, if Tocqueville's judgment was accurate, indicates a change of attitude, for he noted a general respect for judges and wrote that a judge's influence reached far beyond the courts. He wrote that "the American judge is constantly surrounded by men accustomed to respect his intelligence as superior to their own, whether he is at some private entertainment or in the turmoil of politics, in the marketplace, or in one of the legislatures; and apart from its use in deciding cases, his authority influences the habits of mind and even the very soul of all who have co-operated with him in judging them." It appears that Tocqueville talked about judges largely with lawyers; and they are loath to speak badly of sitting judges. Albert Gallatin explained in part why judges were so respected. "Our judges," he told Tocqueville, "are held in very high esteem. Being entirely dependent on public opinion, they need to make continual efforts to keep this esteem. Their integrity is unquestioned. I look on the judges, *supported as they always are by the lawyers* as a body, as the regulators of the irregular movements of our democracy, and as those who maintain the equilibrium of the system."

Lack of respect for judges reflects distrust of politics and suspicion of politics. Judges generally do not get to the bench without some political support or involvement. Appointees to the federal bench are nominated by the President and confirmed by the Senate. In twenty-two states judges are appointed either by the governor or the legislature; some are first appointed and then must run for election on their own. In fourteen states judges are elected without party affiliation, and in another twelve states they are elected with partisan identification. Practices as to term of office show comparable variation.

Distrust of the courts and concern over their operation have deeper causes than the political elements that go into the appointment or election of judges. It was not until after the end of World War II and the historic civil rights decisions that the nation began to move toward one system of justice for all Americans. Previously—that is, at least since the compromises that ended the Reconstruction Era—justice as reflected in judicial appointments was regional. There was one set of standards for judges in the Northwest, a somewhat different standard for those in the Midwest and the North, another for the Southwest, and still another for the South. Regional differences, as reflected in the views of senators from the area, bore heavily on nominations for the federal bench made by the President. Within the fellowship of the Senate, the recommendations of senators from the regions in which the judges were to serve were accepted almost without question.

The first challenge to regionalism came at the level of circuit-court appointments. Senators from within and from without the affected areas became concerned as civil rights became a national issue and as the greater mobility of industry, business, and persons left no state in isolation. The concern for one system of

justice has finally reached appointments at the level of federal
district courts, on the proper assumption that a standard system
of justice for the country should be established at the district
level. It should not, in most cases, have to wait for review at the
circuit level or for decisions of the Supreme Court.

The Supreme Court should not be the last line of defense; nor
should it be the only line. If American society were moving toward greater liberty and freedom, one would expect that the
Supreme Court would be performing its constitutional role by
restricting movement beyond the prescribed limits of liberty as
set by the Constitution. This would be its defensive role. But, in
fact, the Supreme Court is more often called upon to stand
against challenges to the freedoms guaranteed by the Bill of
Rights than it is called upon to stand against the extension of liberty.

Changing the physical shape of the bench in the Supreme
Court chambers from a straight line to a shallow semicircle was
one of the early recommendations of Warren Burger after he became Chief Justice. (He reasoned that such a change would
make it easier for the justices to see which one of them was talking. We have long thought that justice was blind, and not deaf.)
There are more fundamental concerns and difficulties in the operation of justice than the matter of judges' deafness.

One should first ask: Why do so many matters go to court for
settlement?

One reason is that social, economic, and political institutions in
the United States are not operating effectively. They are not accepted as they have been traditionally, almost without question
or criticism. Old relationships no longer hold, and no longer are
given public support. What were once accepted as reasonable
rules of compromise and accommodation are no longer looked
upon as reasonable. Institutional relationships which formerly
settled conflicts between individuals and institutions are no
longer acknowledged. Stockholders who formerly waited pas-
sively for their dividends are now suing the directors of corporations. Patients who formerly loved and revered their doctors are
suing them for malpractice, and doctors are testifying against
other doctors. Universities are sued by students. Churches are in
court as dissident members raise the issue of who, as a true

believer in the old-time religion, properly owns the church. The Little League was taken to court to force it to include girls on its player rosters.

A second reason is that the complexity of life in America today calls for a redefinition of the basic liberties guaranteed by the Bill of Rights. Definition and law have not caught up with technology and practice. Freedom of speech and of the press are now something quite different from what they were in the early days of our Republic. The one meant little more than the right to say something in a public square; the other, to publish a pamphlet or newspaper. Now freedom of speech and freedom of the press involve complicated questions of monopoly control of the press; of government-licensed television and radio stations; and of the government's right to release or withhold information when it has become a principal source of the information that is carried by the news media. Freedom of assembly once defined little more than the right of people to have meetings. Now it must include demonstrations, protest marches, and looser forms of organization, held together by no more than verbal communication—some touching on conspiracy. When the Bill of Rights was adopted, the right of privacy was exercised by insisting that search warrants be presented before private property could be examined and by not allowing the government to quarter troops in privately owned homes. Today the right is challenged by complicated technological devices for spying on people. Many of these problems do not lend themselves easily to legislative distinction, and consequently become a burden on the courts.

A third reason for the burden is the failure of other institutions of government to meet their basic responsibilities. When Congress and the President failed to take the initiative on civil rights, the courts were forced to act. This was especially evident in the issue of "one man, one vote," and later in the effort to desegregate schools by busing students. The failure of the Congress and of the executive branch to act meant that there was little or no administrative machinery, procedural rules, or money to carry out the court decisions.

A fourth reason the courts are overburdened is that the Congress and the Executive have failed to bring old laws up to date, and have passed others which are little more than good intentions and are almost impossible to. administer. Federal drug laws, for example, are outdated. The penalties for marijuana use are absurd; yet the courts are expected to enforce the unenforceable and the ridiculous. Much of our antitrust legislation has no significant reference to current problems.

Some confusion and conflict in the administration of justice must be expected in a system which is committed to equal justice under the law for all. The question, to be fairly asked, is whether the progress toward equality is in the range of what should have been achieved. It is difficult to give a very certain answer. It is not difficult to observe failures to achieve the ideal. The record on liberty and equal justice indicates that we have a long way to go. The ancient Romans were more honest, or more objective, than we are. They admitted that they had two systems of justice: one for Roman citizens, a second for the other peoples of the empire. We insist that we have but one; but in fact we have at least four different systems of justice.

First, there is the ideal one, the one in which we properly take pride. This is the constitutional one in which rights are recognized; due process is not just an abstract right but a reality. This is the system in which we believe. It does exist and operate for many Americans. They must have status, money, and one or two other qualifications.

There is a second system of justice for the poor, for the members of racial minorities, for the young people of the nation, for those who challenge established positions. This is the system which allows for wiretapping and bugging. This is the system within which the FBI infiltrated and harassed the Socialist Workers Party and other anti-establishment groups. Within this system, constitutional rights are defined differently.

There is a third system, for the members of the military. It has in it many of the same contradictions and inequities that are found in the lesser orders of justice in the civilian society. It is a system which was allowed to grow on its own, and which received little attention until the cruelties of war and the injustices within the military were brought home through the Vietnam War. In the aftermath of that war, a lieutenant was punished for the My Lai Massacre, while a general who had conducted unauthorized bombing raids in Vietnam was allowed to retire without even a court-martial, suffering a slight reduction of rank and being granted full retirement pay. At the same time, the Commander-in-Chief was campaigning for re-election as President of the United States, promising that he would make young draft evaders "pay a price" for their action.

The fourth system applies to those who administer justice in the other systems. The operating principle is that those who act in the name of the state are subject to different rules of process and punishment. This exceptional and limited system was demonstrated in its purest form in the treatment of the highest political figures, the President and the Vice President, in the Nixon administration.

There are proposals and efforts to bring about greater order, consistency, and justice. One body of proposals is for change of procedure: to speed up court proceedings, to redefine the use of the jury, to limit appeals, to modify grand jury proceedings, to appoint more judges, to define jurisdiction more clearly, to control pretrial or prejudgment publicity, and so on. Other proposals bear on the improvement of the officers who interpret and apply the law—to improve the qualities of lawyers and judges.

Many of the old controversies and questions remain. Is the jury system effective as an instrument for insuring that justice will be done? In the time of Tocqueville, the jury system was questioned. An Alabama lawyer mentioned to Tocqueville the problem of pretrial publicity. "The jurors," he said, "know about the matter before it is argued. It is judged before it is heard and judged in a tavern." Some jury verdicts, he reported, had to be quashed because of errors in law or (less frequently) errors of fact. Tocqueville expressed doubt overall as to the jury's value, and even as to its bearing on justice, especially in civil cases. But he saw the jury as a political institution, and said it was from that point of view that it must always be judged. It should be, he wrote, "regarded as one form of the sovereignty of the people." He believed that juries spread respect for judicial decisions, teach citizens about equity, teach them to accept responsibility for their own acts, and show them their obligations to society. "I think," he remarked, "that the main reason for the practical intelligence and the political good sense of the Americans is their long experience with juries in civil cases." And he added, "I do not know whether a jury is useful to the litigants, but I am sure it is very good for those who have to decide the case. I regard it as one of the most effective means of popular education at society's disposal."

Although jury duty is the lot of few citizens today, and although the direct educational benefit which Tocqueville observed in jury experience is not clearly demonstrable, his general observations and conclusions hold today. The jury is looked upon as a form through which popular sovereignty can be expressed, even though the measure of that sovereignty is in fact very limited. In some cases the court can overrule the jury; but in many the jury verdict is determining. And the jury is looked upon as a check on the power of the written law and of judicial application of the law.

Lawyers today perform the same functions their predecessors did in the pre-Civil War era. They occupy or claim about the same place in society. They continue to have influence on American politics far beyond their numbers, although the lawyer-statesman of the pre-Civil War period has disappeared. Their mark and influence today is quantitative rather than qualitative. About 55 per cent of the Congress of the United States are lawyers. Of the last four men to occupy the White House, two have been lawyers, although better-known for their political careers than for careers in the law.

Tocqueville's observation that the lawyers at the time of his visit were generally conservative does not clearly apply to lawyers in politics today. It is more applicable to those lawyers who practice law rather than politics and to those who have mixed the two professions. Excepting lawyers whose interest is in the practice of criminal law, and the new breed of public defenders and those who are involved in public law and class actions, the normal association of lawyers is with property interests. It may not be true that the study of the law leads to conservative tastes and to a sense of belonging to a privileged and superior intellectual class, as Tocqueville observed, or that "hidden at the bottom of a lawyer's soul one finds some of the tastes and habits of an aristocracy" or that lawyers share an aristocracy's "instinctive preference for order and its natural love of formalities; like it, they conceive a great distaste for the behavior of the multitude and secretly scorn the government of the people." But it is true that practice of the law moves many lawyers well within the orbit of established wealth and of those who control the economic power of the nation.

The late Senator Wayne Morse argued that there is no such thing as the private practice of the law; he believed that every lawyer (by his profession and oath) is a servant of the court, of the law, of justice, and of society. The Morse conception is well served by attorneys who donate their time and talent to defend the poor, the unpopular, and the dissidents of American society. To use but one recent example, in 1976–77, volunteer lawyers won eighteen cases establishing the right of fair ballot access for independent candidates.

In reality, however, much of the practice of the law is private. In such cases, the order of the lawyer's interest apparently is first, himself; second, his client; third, his profession; fourth, the law itself; and finally, the public interest. The corporation lawyer and the salaried lawyer, whether paid by private industry or by the government, are relatively modern inventions—ones which raise more questions about the legal profession than the profession itself has been willing to raise or to answer.

Conflicts in society lead to conflicts in the conception and practice of the law. In a democratic society, although the time of change may be long, the law must eventually become common law. The intervention of constitutional protections or barriers and the slowness of the legal process can delay change, but not prevent it. There is a special and current pressure on the legal profession today. In some respects, this is misdirected and even unfair, since the basic responsibility is on politicians and legislators. The new style of reform that began in the 1960s, one that demanded changes more far-reaching than in previous reforms, and even different in character, increased the pressure on the legal system. Law became not personal and particular, but social. Civil rights, opposition to the Vietnam War, the challenges to poverty, to environmental waste and to pollution—all of these quickly took on a social character and a momentum that could not be put off to await legislative action. The immediate burden and challenge were placed on the courts and on the legal profession. A new breed of lawyers and of law professors, even a new kind of law school, were necessary. The new lawyers have been found, professors have emerged, and most law schools have given recognition to the new trends and demands of society.

There is growing evidence that America is about to challenge, seriously, the self-regulation of the profession by bar associations and the general control over legal education exercised by the law schools. State legislatures are passing laws requiring lawyers already in practice to take refresher courses or additional studies as a condition to continuing their practice of law. The Chief Justice of the Supreme Court has suggested significant changes in the manner in which lawyers are prepared for the practice of the law. The special, protected sources of lawyer's income—title guarantees, title searches, fees for handling even routine, probate-court matters—have been challenged. More specialized and personalized actions, having the potential of large fees for lawyers, are now being subjected to legislative examination and at least partial control. No-fault automobile insurance has been approved in a number of states, and there are suggestions for no-fault divorce proceedings. There are moves to set limits on the amount of damages, and incidentally the lawyers' fees, in medical malpractice suits. It has been suggested that there should be a distinction between the private or corporate or government practitioners of law and those who are public practitioners, comparable to the distinction made in England between solicitors and barristers. The bar associations are becoming more strict in passing judgment on the behavior of their members. A former President and a former Vice President have lost their bar memberships, and there has been a rise of malpractice complaints against lawyers.

The confusion in the practice of law, and in the law itself, is a reflection—concentrated and also simplified—of the confusion, the conflict, and the changes in American life. It is evident that, for a long time to come, one Tocqueville observation will be accurate: namely, that everything in America is justiciable. Everything may well be taken to court for settlement, even though that settlement may at best be temporary, lasting only until the composition of the Supreme Court changes. Only when American society becomes stable will American law and the practice of law reflect stability and order. None of these conditions is likely to be reached soon.

7

The Media: And That's the Way It Is

The principal means of public communication at the time of Tocqueville's visit to America was the newspaper. It was supplemented by private letters and by word-of-mouth communication.

There are conflicting estimates as to the number of American newspapers published in the early 1830s. The conservative count is about 700 to 800; the liberal count, about 1,000. Of some 700 papers covered in one study, 650 were weeklies and 65 were dailies. There were a few papers that were published two or three times a week, and also a few Sunday papers. But strict religious observance of that day generally discouraged Sunday reading, and hence also Sunday publication.

Many of the 1830 publications were essentially commercial in nature. A commercial or "mercantile" paper often had the word *Advertiser* as part of its name: for example, the Boston *Daily Advertiser* and the Rochester *Daily Advertiser*. Advertisements took up half or more of most commercial papers. In most cases the advertising type was the same as, or only slightly larger than, that used for regular news reports. In terms of space taken by advertising, the proportion taken in the 1830s is less than that taken by advertising displays in most metropolitan papers today. Today's papers come closer to Tocqueville's somewhat exaggerated report that advertising in the 1830s took up three quarters of most newspapers.

In addition to advertisements and mercantile reports, the commercial papers carried international and local news and news from other states. Some carried a significant amount of national political news; others did not. The general-interest papers had fewer ads and more national and international news as a rule. The special or limited-interest papers included religious papers, agricultural papers—some printed in foreign languages (mostly German), a few labor papers, and the beginnings of the antislavery press.

Individual newspaper circulation, by today's standards, was low. Top circulation of the largest city papers was about 4,000. Papers were not sold on the streets, but only by subscription. The subscription price for a daily ranged from six to ten dollars a year. (Two or three dailies in New England, using less paper than others, sold for only four dollars a year.) Subscriptions to weeklies and semi-weeklies, of course, were cheaper.

Since eastern papers generally insisted on advance payment of subscriptions, workingmen could not afford papers. The large city papers were written mainly for businessmen, professionals, and the educated. It was some time after Tocqueville's visit that penny-papers caught on and became available to workingmen in the cities.

Western papers were more flexible about subscriptions, prices, and payments. Their rates probably were lower on the average than those of the eastern papers. Some of them accepted subscription payments at the end of the subscription year at slightly higher prices than those charged for prepaid subscriptions. In areas where cash was scarce, western papers resorted to barter. Editors and publishers sometimes accepted firewood, candles, or other goods in place of cash for subscriptions. The system did not always work smoothly. A Michigan Territory paper ran the following notice in the winter of 1835: "Subscribers who have engaged to furnish us with Fire Wood are informed that we are freezing."

Advertising was an important source of revenue for the early publishers. The papers ran an incredible variety of ads. They ranged from notices about stray horses and cows, to notices of slaves for sale and slaves who had run away, to announcements about steamboat, stagecoach, and canal-barge services, to ads for patent medicines. Commercial advertisers often placed one ad and let it run without change for many months or for a year or more. Rates for these long-term ads were low; at least one historian has suggested that the commercial papers actually undercharged on advertising.

Job printing was a major source of revenue, especially for papers or printers in small towns and rural areas, as it is today. And as papers today compete for legal notices, especially in county-seat towns, so too in 1830 there was competition for patronage printing. In the era of Jefferson and Hamilton, national politicians subsidized papers directly. By Jackson's time, however, politics had become somewhat more sophisticated, and friendly papers were given government printing jobs. Printing jobs for the Congress and for the Executive departments could be profitable.

There was some federal patronage available to papers outside Washington. Several times a year, for example, local post offices would print lists of the unclaimed letters they were holding. This printing job evidently went to favored papers; an anti-Jackson paper in Massachusetts lost business after Jackson came to power.

State, county, and local governments also favored "right thinking" newspapers with official printing contracts.

Most of the papers of the 1830s were about the same size as today's papers, although a few tabloid-size papers were published then. The usual format was four pages, with each page divided into six columns. The customary type was agate (five and one-half points). The Boston *Transcript* in 1833 changed its advertising type to diamond (four and one-half points) to save space and thereby print more advertising. The size of paper and of type, as well as the general format, were in large part the result of technical problems and paper supply. Flatbed presses were commonly used. A four-page paper consisted of a sheet that was run through on one side of the sheet for the first and fourth pages, and then run through on the other side for the second and third pages. The side with the first and fourth pages was customarily run first; these pages, therefore, carried ads and other material that could be typeset well in advance of press time. The inside pages were kept largely for news, editorial comment, and late-arriving advertisements.

The advertising columns provided the only pictures in the

paper, and these pictures were standardized, essentially no more than symbols. A small picture of a house was used to mark house-for-sale ads; a steamboat or stagecoach was used to designate travel notices; and so on. Larger, display-type ads were not used, for a number of reasons. Some publishers thought they were a waste of space. Some thought them unfair to the small-space daily advertisers. There were also technical problems in breaking columns. The surge in advertising would come some twenty-five years later.

Subscription counts in the 1830s were not a measure of circulation or readership. Tocqueville noted the wide circulation of papers even in remote areas such as Michigan, which at the time of his visit was still a territory. "In America," he wrote, "one of the first things done in a new State is to make the post go there; in the forests of Michigan there is no cabin so isolated, no valley so wild but that letters and newspapers arrive at least once a week. . . ." After reporting that the living conditions and character of the inhabitants of Kentucky and Tennessee left much to be desired, he went on to note that, no matter how mean the cabins might be, they often had books "and almost always a newspaper." And after commenting on the laziness of the frontiersmen, he remarked that "these men nonetheless belong to one of the most civilized and rational peoples in the world. . . . The philosophic and argumentative spirit of the English is found there as in all America. There is an astonishing circulation of letters and newspapers among these savage woods. . . . I do not think that in the most enlightened rural districts of France there is intellectual movement either so rapid or on such a scale as in this wilderness."

This widespread circulation was not accidental. Colonial postal policy had allowed exchange copies of newspapers to go through the mails without charge. This policy was continued into the nineteenth century, and it produced an exchange of news somewhat like that provided by today's wire services. Reprints of news and editorials were commonly made and circulated. A paper reprinting an item often did not note the date of the original printing. Evidently readers, having some knowledge of travel or delivery time, were expected to make their own estimate.

About six weeks after Tocqueville and Beaumont arrived in

America, the Detroit *Courier* carried an undated news report that read as follows:

> PRISON DISCIPLINE. Two French gentlemen, commissioned by the King of the French, have arrived in this country, to visit prisons, and become acquainted with the system of discipline. They have spent two weeks at Westchester, New York, and pronounce the institution there superior in many of its branches, to any they had inspected in Europe.

Newspapers generally did not summarize or interpret official documents except in their editorials. They did not, as the New York *Times* and other papers do today, run a news story in a prominent place and then run a reprint of a speech or document at some other place in the paper. The reprint itself constituted the news—without instant analysis either before or after the printing.

Reprints or summaries of news from foreign newspapers were common. And national news was well covered. Often it was presented in the form of letters between prominent officeholders: for example, President Jackson and various officials. Presidential messages were reprinted, as were excerpts from speeches in Congress. Two Washington papers ran detailed and extensive accounts of congressional proceedings, providing roughly the same service that the *Congressional Record* does today.

State politics was also well covered, especially in papers located in the state capitals. The *Ohio State Journal and Columbus Gazette* ran minutes of the state legislature's meetings and long reports on state problems.

Local news often received less attention than foreign, national, or state news. This may have resulted from the fact that the average editor put the paper together on his own, occasionally with help from his family or an apprentice. The professional reporter was unknown. A report on the Springfield *Republican* (Massachusetts) holds that insofar as local news was concerned, "the editor took it for granted that everybody knew it anyway. He devoted himself to informing his public of that which it had no means of knowing. One finds in the early issues of the *Republican* news about pretty much everything but the life of Springfield itself."

Although the papers generally allocated certain sections to advertising and others to news, within the general scheme there was a bewildering variety of both advertising and news. This was true especially of the inside pages, which might carry, in no particular order, reprints of letters between the President of the United States and his cabinet, reprints of foreign news, the paper's own editorials, and items that today might be called filler material, but were in fact intended to fulfill an educational role. The March 30, 1827, issue of *Freedom's Journal*, published in New York, carried on one page the "Memoirs of Capt. Paul Cuffee," an excerpt to be continued, a commentary on "People of Colour," and a treatise on the "Cure for Drunkenness." One newspaper historian has suggested that editors gave no special attention to placement of items because they assumed that readers would read the entire paper in any case.

The early nineteenth-century papers did not carry advice on how to play cards. There were no columnists, comic strips, gossip columns, horoscopes, lonely-hearts columns, sports pages, or society pages. There were few obituaries. Cartoons, especially political ones, were common in magazines or handbills, but not in newspapers.

Poets and poetry appear to have received more attention and respect in newspapers than they do today. Poetry was sometimes printed on the front page, sometimes anonymously, sometimes with the author's name or a pseudonym. John Greenleaf Whittier's early poetry was published in a newspaper. He also wrote prose for papers and became an editor, as did William Cullen Bryant, who edited the New York *Evening Post*. Shortly after Tocqueville's visit, a boy of thirteen, Walt Whitman, became a printer's devil. He spent a good part of his adult life in journalism, as both writer and editor.

Evidently poets, especially if they were politicians, were reticent about publishing poetry over their own names. The most famous example was Abraham Lincoln. In 1846–47 Lincoln corresponded several times with Andrew Johnston of Illinois, a friend who shared his interest in poetry. Lincoln sent a few of his poems to his friend, and Johnston offered to try to have the poems published. Lincoln agreed on the condition that they be published anonymously. "To say the least," he wrote, "I am not at

all displeased with your proposal to publish the poetry, or dog-
gerel, or whatever else it may be called, which I sent you . . .
but let names be suppressed by all means. I have not sufficient
hope of the verses attracting any favorable notice to tempt me to
risk being ridiculed for having written them." Two of the poems,
"My Childhood's Home" and "The Maniac," were published
anonymously in the Quincy *Whig*.

The press of the 1830s had its critics. Tocqueville interviewed
many of them and evidently agreed with much that they had to
say. "Generally," he wrote, "American journalists have a low social status, their education is only sketchy . . ." Certainly in the
Northeast there were a number of college-educated editors. In
the smaller towns and on the frontier, his judgment may well
have applied. But the general evidence is that even in those
places, the editors and publishers were accepted as respectable
businessmen if not as literary or intellectual powers.

The style and content of the early American newspapers, as
Tocqueville viewed them, reflected the lack of education and
culture of the editors. In comparing American newspapers with
the French press, he said that there was much more advertising
in the American papers than there was serious news or commentary. "In America," he wrote, "three quarters of the bulky newspaper put before you will be full of advertisements and the rest
will usually contain political news or just anecdotes; only at long
intervals and in some obscure corner will one find one of those
burning arguments which for us are the readers' daily food."

He expressed great dismay over the standards of taste and integrity of the American press. "It is pitiful to see what a deluge
of coarse insults, what petty slander and what gross calumnies,
fill the newspapers that serve as organs for the parties, and with
what shameful disregard of social decencies they daily drag before the tribunal of public opinion the honor of families and the
secrets of the domestic hearth."

"The hallmark of the American journalist," he wrote, "is a direct and coarse attack, without any subtleties, on the passions of
his readers; he disregards principles to seize on people, following
them into their private lives and laying bare their weaknesses
and their vices."

Tocqueville's observations may have been strongly influenced by the persistent attacks on President Jackson's politics. Editorial and newspaper policies varied in style and degree of vehemence. Many of the political papers did have strong editorials for or against Jackson and his administration. But the press as a whole did not show the "destructive tastes" or "violence" of which Tocqueville complained. Nor was there widespread reporting on the private lives of public officials.

The case of Peggy O'Neale Timberlake Eaton was in the news, or at least in the gossip, during Tocqueville's visit. Fifteen years earlier, an attractive and flirtatious young Washington woman, Peggy O'Neale, had married a Navy man named Timberlake. While he was away on long cruises, Peggy remained in her father's Washington home. Jackson's good friend, Senator John Eaton of Tennessee, boarded in that home for years. Washington gossip held that Mrs. Timberlake and Senator Eaton were having an affair while poor Timberlake was at sea. Timberlake died in 1828; Mrs. Timberlake married Senator Eaton less than a year later. Shortly after their marriage, Jackson made Eaton his Secretary of War. The wives of several other Jackson cabinet members, shocked by Peggy Eaton's reputation, refused to call upon her. Although a Calhoun-Van Buren power struggle was partly behind the social war that ensued, personal gossip took over. Jackson's own marriage to a divorcée had been the subject of much gossip throughout his career; because of this and loyalty to his friend, he sided strongly with the Eatons.

It is possible that Tocqueville came across nasty comments on Jackson's marriage, as well as references to the Peggy Eaton affair, and that these limited observations led him to his rather sweeping generalizations about the malicious character of the American press.

Newspapers had an important influence on politics in the second quarter of the nineteenth century, or at least politicians believed they had such an influence. One of the complaints against President Jackson was that he had corrupted the press by giving government jobs to editors who supported him. Friendly editors today find favor with Presidents and are often rewarded with commission memberships, ambassadorships, and other government positions.

Dissatisfied with a Washington paper, Jackson encouraged the establishment of a new paper, the Washington *Globe*. The *Globe* received much government printing, and Jackson appointees and supporters were encouraged to subscribe to the newspaper. In return the newspaper became the administration's mouthpiece and faithfully supported the President. And Jackson, a close personal and political friend of Francis P. Blair, the editor of the *Globe*, is reported to have told people with problems, "Take it to Blair." Or, "Give it to Frank Blair—he knows everything."

Presidents today in their conflict with the press are less direct than was Jackson. In President Kennedy's administration, the fact that one newspaper had been dropped from the White House reading list was made public. And the President remarked that he was "reading more and enjoying it less." President Nixon, at a reception honoring Alice Roosevelt Longworth on her ninetieth birthday in 1974, credited her longevity, at least in part, to her not having read too much of the Washington *Post* or the Washington *Star*.

The early American press was quite free and easy. There was little danger of monopoly, the economics of newspapers being such that starting a newspaper was easy. "Anybody may take to it," Tocqueville said, "but competition prevents any newspaper from hoping for large profits, and that discourages anybody with great business ability from bothering with such undertakings."

A New York lawyer explained American libel law to Tocqueville, saying that the expression of opinion was perfectly free but that when a paper published libelous facts, when "it gratuitously suggests culpable motives, then it is prosecuted and generally punished with a heavy fine." The lawyer told of his own recent prosecution of a man who had written an article suggesting that a jury had reached a verdict because of political motivation.

Whereas Tocqueville repeatedly stressed the importance of the free press in America and in a democracy, he had grave reservations about how the free press was in fact operating and about the influence it had. He did not believe that it was creating an open-minded society, or one with flexible opinions. Quite the contrary, he wrote: "Once the American people have got an idea into their head, be it correct or unreasonable, nothing is harder than to get it out again." He believed that this condition was largely due to the free press. "It has been noted that in ages of religious fervor men sometimes changed their beliefs, whereas in skeptical centuries each man held obstinately to his own faith. In politics the same thing happens under the reign of a free press. All social theories having been contested and opposed in turn, people who fixed on one of them stick to it, not because they are sure it is good but because they are not sure that there is a better one." Nonetheless, and with these reservations, Tocqueville saw the free press as essential to democracy and to the protection of the individual. In a democracy, he wrote, "an oppressed citizen has only one means of defense: he can appeal to the nation as a whole, and if it is deaf, to humanity at large. The press provides his only means of doing this. For this reason freedom of the press is infinitely more precious in a democracy than in any other nation."

He saw no middle ground between freedom and despotism. "To cull," he said, "the inestimable benefits assured by freedom of the press, it is necessary to put up with the inevitable evils springing therefrom. The wish to enjoy the former and avoid the latter is to indulge in one of those illusions with which sick nations soothe themselves. . . ." Or as one cynical observer said of Spiro Agnew's attacks on the press: He agreed with everything Agnew said, but denied Agnew's right to say it.

Although the same theoretical judgments seem valid today, the media (to include radio and television) are quite different in structure and in operation from what the press was 150 years ago.

In 1830 there were about 65 daily papers, with a probable circulation of less than 300,000. In 1977 there were 1,762 daily papers in America. They had a combined circulation of about 61 million. In the total current population of roughly 216 million, there is one paper for each 122,000 persons.

Whereas someone aspiring to publish a paper in the 1830s could get started with very little capital, it now takes millions of dollars to start a major daily paper. Individual ownership of large papers is all but impossible for nearly everyone except the very rich.

Newspaper chains now own about 60 per cent of the daily papers in the country; and chain dailies have roughly 70 per cent of the national circulation. The Gannett Company has about seventy dailies; the Scripps League Newspapers about twenty; New-house about thirty; Scripps-Howard fifteen; and so on. Some of the chains, interested principally in the commercial potential of their holdings, allow local editors a great measure of autonomy. Other owner-managers, corporate or private, exercise tight control over editorial and news policies.

Concentration of ownership and control is not limited to the newspapers. It includes in many instances ownership and control of radio and television stations and even networks, of book publishing companies, and of magazines.

CBS, Inc., owns over twenty magazines and the publishing house of Holt, Rinehart and Winston—or did until recently. It is difficult to report accurately, since in the world of conglomerates, sales and exchanges occur every day.

The RCA Corporation owns Random House as well as the National Broadcasting Company.

Dow Jones and Company publishes the *Wall Street Journal* and *Barron's National Business and Financial Weekly*. It publishes Dow Jones books and is involved in two overseas financial news services. It also publishes a dozen local newspapers in the United States.

The Washington Post Company owns the Washington *Post*, the Trenton *Times, Newsweek*, one radio and four television stations. It owns a joint news service with the Los Angeles *Times*.

Australian publisher Rupert Murdoch, a one-man conglomerate, now controls *New York* and *New West* magazines, the *National Star*, two Texas newspapers, the New York *Post*, and the *Village Voice*.

The New York Times Company publishes the New York *Times, Family Circle, Us*, a tennis magazine, two golf magazines, three North Carolina newspapers, and ten Florida newspapers. It also owns Arno Press, Cambridge Book Company, and Quadrangle/NYT Book Company.

Many American cities today have no competition between separately owned morning papers, or between *any* separately owned papers. According to a recent report, readers in fewer than forty cities may choose between separately owned dailies. Those forty cities represent less than 3 per cent of all cities with dailies.

What effect this concentration has had on public information and public education is difficult to determine. In most chains one can detect a similarity of editorial attitude and news coverage. The same is true of many non-chain papers that depend chiefly on wire services as their source of news and on nationally syndicated columnists for editorial commentaries.

The columnist is a relatively new development in the American press and one whose value has not yet been proved. The use of columnists is a sign of surrender on the part of editors and publishers and, to a degree, an offense to readers. John Kenneth Galbraith explained the problem: "For one thing," he wrote, "the volume of political comment substantially exceeds the available truth. So men who must produce columns once or several times a week run out of truth and must resort to imagination, which is often a wayward thing. . . .

"Another old problem is that nearly all of our political comment originates in Washington. Washington politicians, after talking things over with each other, relay misinformation to Washington journalists who, after further intramural discussion, print it where it is thoughtfully read by the same politicians. It is the only completely successful closed system for the recycling of garbage that has yet been devised."

Nearly every civilization, at least every primitive one, has institutionalized the rash judgment. In some societies, the makers of rash judgments are, or were, the witch doctors; in others the soothsayers, the oracles, the augurs; in others the high priests. In our case they seem to be the newspaper columnists, although there is some competition from members of the United States Senate.

Today's papers are different from those of the 1830s in several other ways. The format has changed, especially in the makeup of advertising. Special news sections have been added and set apart from the rest of the paper. Gossip columns, women's pages or style sections, and horoscopes are an essential part of most daily papers. They may be distractions, but their inclusion does not bear significantly on the question of whether the press is fulfilling its responsibility to educate and inform the public.

The right of freedom of speech and of the press exists only as the counterpart of the right to the truth. Since truth cannot be defined in advance, the only practical approach is to allow free speaking and writing and the dissemination of what is spoken and written. With concentration of control over the press, there is growing concern, by the press and by the public, about whether the press is publicizing the facts it should publicize and whether it is presenting alternatives in matters where there is difference of opinion.

Some papers have assigned the task of critical evaluation to their own editors or reporters. A few regional journalism review boards, made up of newspaper persons, have been set up; and there is now a national board. Most newspaper spokesmen have declared forcefully against acceptance of any review organization which includes any persons outside of the newspaper profession. This seems a sound position—although it conflicts with their willingness to accept awards of various kinds for best reporting, best editorials, and so forth from organizations or persons who are not of the newspaper fraternity. Why not accept continuing judgments on the good and bad of the press from the same persons, or persons like them?

In response to criticism of prejudiced or one-sided editorial policy, there is a growing disposition on the part of papers to water down editorial comment, to strive for what is called a balanced editorial page, and, in some cases, to avoid editorial comment.

In the early 1970s the Los Angeles *Times,* long a voice of conservative Republicanism, announced that it would no longer endorse candidates for major offices, and also that the drawings of its controversial cartoonist would no longer appear on the editorial page but on the page opposite. *Newsday,* the Long Island paper which is owned by the Los Angeles *Times,* announced in 1972 that it would not endorse political candidates at any level of government. The New York *Times,* in the interest of balance, has opened its op-ed page to a variety of writers and hired an admitted and acknowledged conservative columnist, William L. Safire, a former Nixon White House aide. The Washington *Post* has its letters-to-the-editor column. Lesser papers, trying to establish their fairness or balance, carry the syndicated columns of both liberal and conservative writers, especially in the field of politics.

Studies indicate that only a small percentage of the people of the United States read either editorials or columns. How the public mind is formed is something of a mystery; but all evidence points to the influence of news stories—the slanting of news, the intentional or unintentional editorializing in the news columns—as having more influence than the thoughtful commentaries of the editorial pages.

And then there is television. Radio came so gently into the range of communications that it provoked few social changes that were identifiable or that could be analyzed by the sociologists and psychologists. The radio message was much like reading aloud, and it still is. There are some political analysts who say that the voice of Franklin Roosevelt, heard on radio broadcasts, contributed much to his political success. And there are others who say that, without television, Richard Nixon would have been elected in 1960. Perhaps. The one certainty is that the addition of radio communication to the printed word did not result in a radical change of response. People were used to listening to readings. The written word and the spoken word were not very different. But the word with sound, and then with personality and with the pictures and lighting effects of television, is different, especially if that word is not the result of direct observation of an event, but a "production."

Very young children, looking at television for the first time, sometimes go around behind the set to see the people who are on the screen. One family whose everyday life was filmed for TV reached a point, according to some analysts, where they were not sure whether they were a real family or a group of actors on television. Jay Meek, in one of his poems, described President Nixon in these words:

> Grey-jawed, barricaded in the White House,
> the President has been watching television,
> an avid fan, tuned to the whack of players
> deployed in random patterns on the grid;
> he takes the stance of a gentleman pugilist.
> "Socko, socko," he says. He is schooled
> in calculating the appropriate response,
> and suddenly there comes from his mouth:
> "Gentlemen, let me say that . . ." He stops.

He has been watching himself too long.
His eyes click and roll like fruits
in the windows of a gambling machine. . . .

Television news, as Edward Jay Epstein notes in his book
News from Nowhere, is shaped and constrained by certain
structures imposed from without: government regulation of
broadcasting, the economic realities of networks, certain uniform
procedures for filtering and evaluating information and reaching
decisions, and certain practices of recruiting reporters and producers who hold or accept values that are consistent with organizational needs.

Personalities of newscasters take on added importance. Walter
Cronkite is regularly rated high in national polls as a man to be
trusted. One must ask, Why? Is it because he can read a tele-
prompter without looking furtive? Is it because people like his
voice or believe that he presents a balanced news program? Is
his program of news any better balanced than those presented
on other networks? Is it better produced? Do people feel reas-
sured when, at the end of the program, he says: "And that's the
way it is . . ."

Richard Salant, president of CBS News, evidently to establish
objectivity, once said: "Our reporters do not cover stories from
their point of view. They are presenting them from *nobody's*
point of view."

Rather than "nobody's" point of view, the news is more likely
to become a projection of a corporate or organizational point of
view. This can lead to produced news. It can tempt some reporters and producers to aid revolutions for the sake of television
coverage (early and under controlled circumstances) or to have
their own children or the children of friends hitchhike in order to
get good interviews. It can also move Presidents of the United
States to repeat the swearing-in ceremonies of government
officials for cameramen who miss the first and official act. One
can assume that there can be only one official oath-taking.

A second mark of television news is its dependency on government because of government licensing and regulation of stations and networks—a fact noted by a network news president
when he said that: "The newspaper or magazine journalist is
influenced in reporting the news primarily by the traditional

canons of American journalism . . . The broadcast journalist . . . must also keep in mind that he is working in a medium that, unlike print, operates under federal regulation that has an impact upon what is disseminated."

The networks, especially, operate from fear: fear of a drop in ratings, fear of losing station licenses, fear of further regulation. The contrast between television and the writing press is most evident in the response of the separate media to presidential addresses. The President of the United States, in effect, advises the networks to stop their regular programs because he wants to go on during prime time. Regularly they do, and allow him as much time as he wishes, using his own producers and editors. The writing press, if it were to respond in a similar way, would give the President its front page, allow him to write the headlines and make up the page, and give him whatever other space he might demand. In practice, of course, the writing press does not yield to presidential wishes in this way.

In 1960 the television networks sought suspension of the equal-time provisions of federal communications law so that they might present the Kennedy–Nixon debates.

In 1976 two of the networks offered free time to the candidates of the Democratic and Republican parties, on condition that the Democrats and Republicans suspend the law so that candidates of other parties could not claim equal time. These proposals were superseded by the League of Women Voters' plan for presidential debates. The Federal Communications Commission held that, since the League would be sponsoring the debates (they had never before sponsored presidential debates), the debates would be news events, and that the networks could cover them as such and not be subject to equal-time provisions. The FCC thereby frustrated or avoided the intent of the equal-time provisions.

The result of the debates was that the writing press became practically insignificant as a force in the campaign, being left little more than the role of television commentators, and resorting to such devices as having debate judges score the presidential debates to establish a basis for headlines and news stories.

Television is forbidden to carry cigarette and hard-liquor ads, although allowed to portray smoking and drinking in their noncommercial programs. Television stations, and to a lesser degree radio stations, are regulated in a number of other ways.

The argument usually given to justify government intervention in communications is that television stations and radio stations are licensed by the government and that, consequently, the constitutional guarantee of freedom of expression does not apply. It is a questionable argument. A better one would be protection of privacy, since television and radio programs are in one's house before one has time to evaluate what they are likely to be.

But control of news and educational programs, beyond allocation of time, raises serious questions of censorship. Certainly if there is to be regulation and control, it should be direct and open rather than indirect, through threat of loss of licenses. And until we know about the effect of television beyond its power to distract, the chances should be taken on the side of freedom in programing; or else, if the danger is as clear, as it has been determined to be in the advertising of cigarettes and hard liquor, to exclude news and commentary altogether; or to exclude news and commentary in those areas where they may have most serious consequences—religion and politics.

In the meantime, station owners should have greater security in their licenses; and chances should be taken on the side of multiplicity of news sources and commentary.

It is easy to deplore the realities, easy to describe the ideal, but difficult to prescribe what ought to be done to insure full and impartial, opinion-free news reporting and balanced editorial comment.

Who is to determine who is to speak and write, since not everyone can speak or write?

Who is to determine what is to be written or spoken, since not everything can be spoken or written?

Who is to select what is to be recorded or transmitted, since not everything can be transmitted or recorded?

The best hope is in multiplicity of publications, multiplicity of ownership or control, and greater professionalism within the newspaper and television world. The tensions, the conflicts, and the contradictions that go along with a free press are risks of a free society.

Winston Churchill suggested that democracy is the worst form of government, except all those other forms that have been tried from time to time. The same can be said of the free press. It is certainly the worst kind of press, until you consider the alternatives.

8

Voluntary Associations: The Most Natural Right of Man

Freedom of association, in the opinion of Tocqueville, was "the most natural right of man, after that of acting on his own." "Therefore," he wrote, "the right of association seems to me by nature almost as inalienable as individual liberty." He observed that better use was made of association in America than anywhere else in the world, and for a multitude of purposes. "To make festivities grander and more orderly" was at one end of the scale; and "to combat exclusively moral troubles" (such as intemperance), at the other.

"If some obstacle," he wrote, "blocks the public road, halting the circulation of traffic, the neighbors at once form a deliberative body; this improvised assembly produces an executive authority which remedies the trouble before anyone has thought of the possibility of some previously constituted authority beyond that of those concerned."

In this disposition to organize, and to form associations for almost any purpose, America has not changed very much within the last one hundred and fifty years. Almost as popular as the saying "There ought to be a law against it" (whatever it may be) is another—namely, "Let's organize."

Organizations are legion in America, and they continue to come thick and fast. The range of their objectives covers the whole spectrum of American interests and conflicts. The following are some of the many organizations listed in the 1977 edition of the *Encyclopedia of Associations:*

Trade, Business and Commercial Organizations
Brand Names Foundation
Cheese Importers Association of America
Mailing List Brokers Professional Association
Helicopter Association of America
Fertilizer Institute
Bow Tie Manufacturers Association
Asphalt Institute
The Moles (social club of men presently or formerly engaged in tunnel, subway, sewer, foundation, marine, subaqueous, or other heavy construction work)

Agricultural Organizations and Commodity Exchanges
International Flying Farmers
National Buffalo Association
National Christmas Tree Association
Flax Institute of the United States
American Alligator Council
Beaver Defenders
Friends of the Sea Otter
Prairie Chicken Foundation
American Cranberry Growers' Association
North American Blueberry Council
National Peanut Council
National Pork Producers Council

Legal, Governmental, Public Administration and Military Organizations
National Conference of Bankruptcy Judges
Conference of Funeral Service Examining Boards of the United States
American Academy of Matrimonial Lawyers
National Conference of State Liquor Administrators
Chief Petty Officers Association

Scientific, Engineering and Technical Organizations
American Society of Bakery Engineers
Herb Society of America
American Meteor Society
Society of Soft Drink Technologists

Cultural Organizations
National Society for the Preservation of Covered Bridges
Society for the Preservation of Old Mills

Edgar Allan Poe Society of Baltimore
Horatio Alger Society
American Canal Society
Society for Creative Anachronism (medievalists)
American Guild of English Handbell Ringers
Midwest Old Settlers and Threshers Association
Titanic Historical Society (formerly Titanic Enthusiasts of America)
Aaron Burr Association
Millard Fillmore National Society
Richard III Society

Fraternal Groups
Native Sons of the Golden West
Honorable Order of the Blue Goose
International Order of Hoo-Hoo

Hobby and Avocational Organizations
Horseless Carriage Club of America
American Cat Fanciers Association
Beer Can Collectors of America
American Begonia Society

Representative government is not trusted. Even before elections are held, organizations to influence government are already in existence. These organizations are commonly labeled "lobbies." Some represent important national interests and well-organized groups. The National Association of Manufacturers has lobbyists who try to influence government policy. So do the AFL-CIO, the American Petroleum Institute, the Association of American Railroads, and nearly every major industrial, labor, and financial interest in the nation. The so-called "little people" also have lobbyists.

Representation may be by a large and well-financed staff, or by a single person. Some lobbyists are well paid; some receive little more than expense money, if even that. Some operate directly on government officials, either in the executive branch or in the Congress. Some operate indirectly through appeals to constituents or to voters. Some are lawyers, some professional lobbyists; some are not lawyers and are less than professional. Some spend a great deal of money; some spend little or none. Some seek public recognition through charters, licenses, special tax status, and other official marks of recognition. Others choose to be independent and free of all but minimal legal recognition.

There are five or six different organizations of war veterans; the principal ones are the American Legion and the Veterans of Foreign Wars. The others include the Disabled American Veterans, the Catholic War Veterans, and the Jewish War Veterans. After World War II, the American Veterans Committee was organized; during the Vietnam War, there was a Vietnam Veterans Against the War.

Moral objectives still inspire organization. The prohibitionists have never given up. There are organizations to promote abortion and organizations to make abortion illegal. Farmers are organized into three major national organizations, each claiming that it speaks best for American farmers: the National Farmers Union, the American Farm Bureau Federation, and the National Farmers Organization. A fourth farm organization, with older credentials, is the National Grange.

Recent interest in environmental protection has produced a multitude of organizations—some concerned with outer space, some with inner space, some concentrating their attention on industrial pollution, some on protecting nature and preserving mountains, rivers, oceans, and lakes not only from pollution but from habitation and use. Others are concerned with endangered species, both plants and animals, including wolves and coyotes. The Bicentennial celebration caused a proliferation of groups working to preserve and restore historic sites and buildings.

Mutual protection through insurance has spawned a great number of benevolent and fraternal societies, with a strong or tenuous point of common interest. Most benevolent and fraternal societies have adopted symbolic representations. The Woodmen of the World is a benevolent society, as is the Catholic Order of Foresters. So are the Elks and the Moose. The Masons thrive, as do the Knights of Columbus.

The business community is organized into Chambers of Commerce, Junior Chambers of Commerce, Rotarians, Kiwanians, Lions, Civitans, and so forth. There is in most cities a women's organization called the Junior League, although there is no Senior League.

Fraternal societies have special social and legal privileges. A liquor license often goes with a charter, allowing sale of liquor at times and places not allowed to the nonorganized. Some organizations are tax-exempt; that is, they can retain all of their earnings and spend them in keeping with their charter or license. Some have achieved a status that allows contributors to obtain tax deductions for their donations. Escape from the generally applicable laws is a mark of distinction for organizations. Thus, whereas state and city statutes commonly classify bingo as gambling, and therefore ban the game, exceptions are made for three organizations: churches (most of them Roman Catholic, although some of the less puritan Protestant churches also take advantage of the exception); veterans organizations; and volunteer fire departments with their affiliates, the rescue squads.

The volunteer fire department is a remarkable example of the American will and capacity to organize which Tocqueville noted. There are about 22,000 fire departments in America today. Of these, only about 1,800 are fully paid. The other 20,200 are wholly or partly served by unpaid volunteers. Whereas volunteer fire departments are as old as the United States, the great increase in numbers took place following World War II. In that period, also, their organization became more formal, and they began to assume many social and quasi-political roles beyond the limited objective of fire-fighting and fire control.

Although the growth of volunteer fire departments would not have surprised Tocqueville, he might have been greatly surprised by the growth and influence of two other organizations: the consumer-protection movement, inspired and led by Ralph Nader; and Common Cause, founded by John Gardner and designated as a public-interest lobby.

Consumer-protection efforts and organizations are not new to America; but none of them has ever become a national force in any way comparable to what is generally called the Nader movement. Designed, as its founder says, to protect the "public interest" against what he calls the "private or special interests," the complex of Nader organizations has challenged government agencies such as the Food and Drug Administration, the Federal Trade Commission, the Interstate Commerce Commission, and others. In the nongovernmental field, its special target has been corporate power generally, and the automobile industry more particularly. The automobile industry, in large part because of the Nader pressures, has taken on wholly new responsibilities for automobile safety, for performance, for quality, and for pollution control. The least successful Nader movement was a kind of consumer-protection report on Members of Congress. For a number of reasons—the complexity of American politics, the force of personality in politics, and other considerations—this undertaking proved to be too much for the objective, analytical approach of Nader's research and reporting.

Another major effort is John Gardner's Common Cause, which is concerned almost exclusively with politics and government. Its principal emphasis has been on the political process, on campaign financing and spending, on the activities of lobbies and lobbyists, and on more open conduct of governmental affairs. Common Cause represents itself as the voice of the people and as their observer and critic of government. It calls on the people to trust itself rather than to trust their elected officials and the government conducted by those officials. It also takes upon itself, as critic and reporter, a share of the burden traditionally assigned to the press. To see a group assume these roles and carry them out with reasonable success, as Common Cause has, with a membership of some 250,000 persons in a nation of over 200 million, would surprise Tocqueville. He might be more surprised to note its success in pressing Congress to pass the 1974 Federal Election Campaign Act, and the President to sign it, despite charges that the law was unconstitutional in at least two or three major respects (charges later sustained by the Supreme Court), with reference to its violation of freedom of speech and the separation of powers. In 1977 Common Cause met a major defeat when its effort to extend public financing to congressional campaigns was stopped by a Republican filibuster in the Senate.

Beyond organizations, there is in America another manifestation of public expression sometimes related to organization, sometimes only a personal expression of opinion or position. This is the common practice of wearing buttons. Surely Tocqueville would have marveled at this custom, as did the Russian poet Andrei Voznesensky, who expressed his response in a poem entitled "The Buttons of New York":

Buttons, buttons, flashing; buttons
shouting at the tops of their lungs,
"People are monkeys' ancestors."
"The governor is a lesbian."
"Print the unprintable."
"If it moves, fondle it."
"Ban, banning."

"God lives at #18, Pasteur Street, Rear Entrance Please."

I worship Greenwich Village
with its buttons and their sarcasm.
Who's that, that shaggy fellow
like a brush wearing dark glasses?

It's Allen, Allen, Allen.
leaping over the mortal carnival,
Allen, in nothing but your underpants.
Irony is the God today.
"Power to the People" sounds
like a holy slogan from the Bible.

Hooligans? Yes, Hooligans.
Its better to stick your fingers in your mouth
and whistle; better to blow raspberries.
than to be a silent bourgeois,
Button stars of Bethlehem
tremble on everybody's bottom
Mini-skirts up to the navel

A wild girl
It's Selma, Selma, Selma
winks from a doorway and calls out
"Make love, not war."

Irony is the God of the day
The buttons glow over the yawns.
The funnier they are, the more terrifying
And like bull's-eyes waiting for bullets.

"God has moved to #43, Avenue of Peace, Ring Twice."

And above the hippies, above the whirlwinds
like an ironic cyclops

Time flashes its button, installed
as a glittering eyeball.
Ah, Time.
will I be able to read what's written in your eye,
rushing at me,
growing bigger and bigger, like a headlight?

Can I interpret your antics?

O, Autumn, round aspen leaves, late dawdling
on the tree
Eight plates, tossed up by a juggler
and instantly frozen in the air.
As if a giraffe had run away
and left its spots behind.

The giraffe withdraws wearing
buttons like sacred toadstools
and on its rear end, one saying
"Make love not war."

Similar to button-wearing is the widespread practice of putting stickers on automobile bumpers or on other parts of cars,
trucks, and trailers. Like the button, the bumper sticker is a continuing public assertion of purpose, commitment, association,
some kind of identification. The sticker is not quite as personal
as the button, since it is offered from the more defensive and
safer position of the automobile. There are no reported cases
of persons' crashing into other automobiles because of disagreement with bumper stickers. There have been assaults provoked by buttons.

Stickers, like buttons, cover the whole range of personal and
social concern. They are especially popular in political campaigns. Political experts give thought to how a candidate's name
will look on a sticker and also to what colors are best. Red-
white-and-blue is a popular political color. It was generally
believed that in 1976 Carter–Mondale looked better on a sticker,
and that it sounded better than Ford–Dole, and that in 1972
Nixon had a better ring than McGovern–Shriver.

Conservationists have taken strongly to stickers to "Save the
Redwoods," "Save the Rappahannock," "Save the Snail-Darter,"

and so forth. Stickers also give warning such as, "We Brake for Animals." Beethoven and Bach are remembered. Religious affirmations are also popular.

If there is a significant mark of distinction between the associations described by Tocqueville and associations today, it is in the negative or defensive thrust of many, if not most, modern organizations. Whereas most of the groupings described by Tocqueville had positive purposes, such as building roads, building churches or schools, organizing a community, many organizations today are set up to prevent, to stop, or to reverse something which is already organized or which has organized support. These are associations today whose purpose is to stop the building of roads or dams, to prevent cutting of trees, to keep airplanes from landing, to prevent the building of electric-power plants and transmission lines, to stop what used to be called "progress."

9

Politics: A Sort of Tumult

Tocqueville was greatly impressed by the concern of Americans over government and by the extent of their involvement in politics. "To take a hand in the government of society," he wrote of the American citizen, "and to talk about it is his most important business and, so to say, the only pleasure he knows. . . ." "But if," he continued, "an American should be reduced to occupying himself with his own affairs, at that moment half his existence would be snatched from him; he would feel it as a vast void in his life and would become incredibly unhappy."

"Taxation without representation is tyranny" was one of the rallying cries of the Revolution. This commitment to self-government evidently persisted at least into the fourth decade of the nineteenth century, even though there were severe limits on the right to vote. Most states restricted it to white males over the age of twenty-one. Some states gave free black men the legal right to vote, but this right was not always honored in practice. Property requirements for voting were common. Tocqueville listed fifteen states out of the existing twenty-four as requiring property, military service, or tax payment as prerequisites for voting. His information was not quite accurate and did not reflect the somewhat contradictory trends of the 1820–40 period, under which property restrictions on voting were reduced, while voting by Negroes was banned in more and more states. There was no move to extend suffrage to women.

While there were serious restrictions on suffrage, those who

had the right to vote did so often and in large numbers. Many
states held annual elections for members of the lower houses of
state legislatures. Some held annual elections of governors.
Nathaniel Macon, a Jeffersonian, is credited with the slogan
"Tyranny begins where annual elections end."

Most states held their state elections in the late summer or fall,
when the major agricultural work of the year had been finished,
and their presidential elections in November. A few states allowed two or three days for voting because of the distance rural
voters had to travel to reach the polls. The protracted voting was
discontinued as travel became easier and communications improved, partly because the longer voting period had encouraged
voting fraud.

The secret ballot, as we know it, was not in use. States did not
provide official ballots; rather, somewhat like "sticker candidates" today, each party or slate provided its own. With a little
skill in noting which ballot was taken or from whom it was
taken, observers could tell how a man would vote. Rhode Island
required voters to sign their ballots, and three states had voice
voting.

Possible embarrassment or intimidation did not seem to deter
voters, especially when the competition was strong and the race
close. For the 1828 Adams–Jackson election, the turnout, as calculated by Richard McCormick, was over 75 per cent in New
Hampshire, 70 per cent in New York, about 72 per cent in New
Jersey, 76 per cent in Ohio, almost 70 per cent in Indiana.

Tocqueville did not attempt to sort out the varieties of electoral processes. He did note their complexity and intensity. "No
sooner," he wrote in *Democracy*, "do you set foot on American
soil than you find yourself in a sort of tumult; a confused clamor
rises on every side, and a thousand voices are heard at once,
each expressing some social requirements." He found citizens active in planning churches, roads, schools, in choosing their representatives, in supporting or opposing the government, and even,
to his surprise, in fighting alcoholism through temperance societies.

He concluded that this active participation in politics and in
community decisions was good for America, especially in its indirect effect of training the people in self-government, and that

the enlightenment that would come from it encouraged industrial expansion and improved the general welfare of the people. He was less enthusiastic about what he saw as the direct effects of political agitation, especially that associated with presidential elections.

"As the election draws near, intrigues grow more active and agitation is more lively and wider spread. The citizens divide up into several camps, each of which takes its name from its candidate. The whole nation gets into a feverish state, the election is the daily theme of comment in the newspapers and private conversation, the object of every action and the subject of every thought, and the sole interest for the moment."

Tocqueville also remarked: "The President, for his part, is absorbed in the task of defending himself. He no longer rules in the interest of the state, but in that of his own re-election; he prostrates himself before the majority, and often, instead of resisting their passions as duty requires, he hastens to anticipate their caprices."

President Nixon agreed to a 20 per cent increase in social security payments just before the 1972 election, after he had advocated an increase of only 5 per cent and had threatened to veto any increase in excess of that. He later justified an increase in milk price supports on the grounds that the political pressure from Congress was too great. Both actions seemed to prove Tocqueville's observation about presidential motivation during a re-election campaign.

Tocqueville observed and seemed to accept the personalization of politics, for he wrote that "in the United States as elsewhere, parties feel the need to rally around one man in order more easily to make themselves understood by the crowd. Generally, therefore, they use the presidential candidate's name as a symbol; in him they personify their theories."

American politics at the time of Tocqueville's visit were in a rapidly changing and generally confusing state. Federalists seemed to be giving up their traditional identity and joining or forming new factions. Followers of both Andrew Jackson and Henry Clay claimed to be the true heirs of the old Republican party of Thomas Jefferson and continued to use the Republican label. It was, they thought, a good name.

The old Republicans had dominated national politics from 1800 through 1824 with the "Virginia Dynasty" of Thomas Jefferson, James Madison, and James Monroe. Jefferson and Madison each served two terms and then passed the presidency on to the Secretary of State via a Republican congressional caucus and the electoral college. Monroe also served two terms, but when his second term ended he did not pass the office on to a chosen successor. He abstained from any strong role in choosing his successor, just at the time when the congressional caucus as a device for selecting the party's presidential nominee was coming under serious challenge. Consequently, Monroe's Secretary of State, John Quincy Adams, had to fight for the office in 1824. Or more precisely, his supporters had to fight for it; for under the circumstances in which presidential choices were then made, it was considered improper for a candidate to campaign actively for the office. A vestige of this practice remains in the accepted practice that at national conventions of major parties today, candidates for the presidential nomination do not appear on the convention floor or address the convention.

The Federalist party, which had roots in the Constitutional Convention, reached the peak of its influence in John Adams' administration. After that, it did not go far beyond being the party of opposition. It was never very well organized, and its aristocratic outlook certainly did not attract the growing numbers of small farmers and workingmen in the body politic. The Federalists lost their greatest leader, Alexander Hamilton, when he was killed in a duel with Aaron Burr in 1804. Federalist opposition to the War of 1812 added to the unpopularity of the party. Moreover, old Federalist programs such as the protective tariff and a strong peacetime military force had been taken over by some Republicans.

Although there were Federalists in Congress through 1824, and in some legislatures even beyond that year, the Federalists as a political party and political force were all but dead by 1824. Because of their decline and Monroe's inaction, the 1824 presidential election was a four-way contest among members of the old Republican party. In the contest were John Quincy Adams, Monroe's Secretary of State; Andrew Jackson, U. S. Senator and the hero of New Orleans; William Crawford, Monroe's Secretary of the Treasury; and Henry Clay, Speaker of the House.

Since no candidate received a majority in the Electoral College, the election was "thrown" into the House of Representatives. (Why the word *thrown* is used is not clear. It carries a connotation of desperate, last-minute, nearly irrational action—like throwing the cargo overboard to keep the ship from sinking or throwing in one's cards.)

Henry Clay of Kentucky had come in fourth in the Electoral College balloting and hence was eliminated from consideration in the House vote. Although Clay was considered to be from the West by the standards of the time, he gave his support to New England's John Quincy Adams. Adams won in the House vote and soon named Clay his Secretary of State. Jacksonians attacked what they called the "corrupt bargain" and vowed to avenge the shabby treatment of their hero. Jackson expressed his private feeling about Clay in these words: "So you see the *Judas* of the West has closed the contract and will receive the thirty pieces of silver. His end will be the same. Was there ever witnessed such a bare-faced corruption in any country before?"

The 1828 campaign began immediately after the 1824 election of Adams by the House of Representatives. Adams never recovered from the bad start of his election and the "corrupt bargain" charge. He was the last of the colonial line of Presidents. The Tennessee legislature nominated Jackson for the presidency in the fall of 1825. In Congress the Crawford men, known as radicals, joined the Jackson men in opposition to Adams. Jackson's campaign was essentially an anti-Adams campaign, and his victory personal rather than ideological or programmatic. Jackson was presented as a man of the people and Adams as an aloof aristocrat. Jackson won, and was in office at the time of the Tocqueville visit, having been elected with 56 per cent of the popular vote and with 178 electoral votes to Adams's 83.

The Jackson Era was marked by the presence of a number of new minor parties. One developed from the Anti-Masonic movement, which had started in New York in 1827 with the strange disappearance of William Morgan, a Mason who had decided to reveal Masonic secrets. It was alleged that he had been killed by fellow Masons before he could do so. In 1828 the Anti-Masons showed some strength in western New York and in parts of Pennsylvania and Ohio; and in 1832 their presidential candidate won 8 per cent of the popular vote. In addition to the Anti-Masons, there were a number of workingmen's parties (some called People's party, Farmers' and Mechanics' Society, and so forth). The first Workingmen's party was established in Philadelphia in 1828. Another was started in New York City in 1829, and one in Boston in 1830. Workingmen's parties followed in towns or cities of Connecticut, Delaware, Maine, New Hampshire, New Jersey, Ohio, and Vermont. These parties stressed local issues for the most part. They called for such things as universal public education, mechanics' lien laws, abolition of imprisonment for debt, tax reform, and electoral reform.

This was the confused and changing political scene which Tocqueville found in America, and the one which he tried to interpret. There is little wonder that he came up somewhat short. Most of those whom he interviewed, or with whom he discussed politics, were of the colonial, quasi-aristocratic tradition. The concern and complaints of this class were primarily about universal suffrage—really the extension of suffrage—and about President Jackson. They remembered what they considered to be better days, when government and politics were more stable and presidential succession involved changes of persons rather than policy.

"America has had great parties; now they no longer exist. This has been a great gain in happiness but not in morality," Tocqueville wrote in *Democracy*. He apparently looked back to the days of the Federalist party and the early Republican (Jeffersonian) party as the times of the great parties. He observed that it was only natural that the Federalists were a minority, since America was a democracy. Yet he noted that the Federalists had been able to control the government in the early years of the nation for two reasons: first, because most of the great men of the Revolution were Federalists, and their influence was great; and second, because the failure of the Articles of Confederation had made the people wary of anarchy.

In any case, Tocqueville thought that there were no great parties in America at the time of his visit. He was sustained in this judgment by the opinions of Americans whom he consulted. A

Baltimore lawyer, for example, told Tocqueville that when the Jeffersonians came into power, "they managed things in almost all respects in the same way as their adversaries would have done. . . . Oppositions never can govern with the principles that have brought them to power. Now, to put the matter truthfully, there are no parties in the United States; everything turns on questions of personalities. There are those who have got power and those who want to have it; the 'ins' and 'outs.'" Other Americans, like Nicholas Biddle, President of the Bank of the United States, and Peter Schermerhorn, whom Tocqueville had met on the Atlantic crossing, made similar comments.

Tocqueville also charged that the parties, as he observed them, tended to opportunism and to North-South division on the tariff issue. After a conversation with Joel Poinsett of South Carolina, he noted: "Tariff oppressive in some respects, but imaginary cause of real passions."

"Lacking great parties, the United States is creeping with small ones and public opinion is broken up ad infinitum about questions of detail," said Tocqueville. He apparently believed that there were no major political issues involving religion, class, or economic conditions, for these divisive forces were scarcely evident at the time of his visit. He observed that "the ambitious are bound to create parties, for it is difficult to turn the man in power out simply for the reason that one would like to take his place. Hence all the skill of politicians consists in forming parties; in the United States a politician first tries to see what his own interest is and who have analogous interests which can be grouped around his own; he is next concerned to discover whether by chance there may not be somewhere in the world a doctrine or a principle that could conveniently be placed at the head of the new association. . . ."

Tocqueville did not think highly of political parties, especially of the small ones. He acknowledged that parties "are an evil inherent in free governments." "Small parties," he wrote, "are generally without political faith. As they are not elevated and sustained by lofty purposes, the selfishness of their character is openly displayed in all their actions. They glow with a factitious zeal; their language is violent, but their progress is timid and uncertain. The means they employ are as disreputable as the aim sought." There were, he said of American political parties, "men of integrity in almost all parties, but there is no party of integrity. . . . I cannot," he continued, "conceive a more wretched sight in the world than that presented by the different coteries (they do not deserve the name of parties) which now divide the Union. In broad daylight one sees in their breasts the excitement of all the little shameful passions which ordinarily are careful to keep themselves hidden at the bottom of the human heart."

Despite a good word for a few officeholders, Tocqueville's overall view was that the quality of officeholders in the United States was very low. He seemed to agree with the more aristocratic Americans with whom he spoke in attributing this to universal suffrage. He accepted their general view that Jackson was not qualified to be President. And he reported the words of a Mr. Livingston who said that public offices generally "are held by men whose abilities and characters put them in the second rank. Such places do not carry sufficient pay, social consideration or power to attract men of distinction. But that was not so in the first years of Independence. Now we have no great men in politics. They use their energy and their resources in other careers."

Tocqueville and Beaumont did have a social visit with President Jackson. Although routine and peaceful, the visit did nothing to change Tocqueville's view that Jackson "is a man of violent character and middling capacities; nothing in the whole of his career indicated him to have the qualities needed for governing a free people; moreover, a majority of the enlightened classes in the Union have always been against him." Tocqueville thought that good qualities were "common among the governed but rare among the rulers" and that outstanding Americans were "seldom summoned to public office."

He believed that the Senate was far superior to the House in the quality of its members and that it had "eloquent advocates, distinguished generals, wise magistrates, and noted statesmen." The House, he thought, was made up of mediocrities. The difference he attributed to the fact that the senators were chosen by state legislatures, while members of the House were chosen directly by the people. He singled out one congressman as an example of "how low the people's choice can descend and how far it can be mistaken. . . . Two years ago," he wrote, "the inhabitants of the district of which Memphis [Tennessee] is the capital sent to the House of Representatives of Congress an individual called David Crockett, who had received no education, could read only with difficulty, had no property, no fixed dwelling, but spent his time hunting, selling his game for a living, and spending his whole life in the woods."

Tocqueville believed that wealth was a disadvantage in running for public office and that the wealthy generally avoided becoming candidates because they did not wish to engage "in an often unequal struggle against the poorest of their fellow citizens."

Tocqueville was not impressed by party discipline in democracies; he thought it especially lax in the matter of oratory. His generalizations on these matters seemed to be drawn as much from his general reflections on democracy as a form of political organization as they were from his observations of democracy in action in America. In any case, he stated his opinion that parties in a democracy "show themselves obedient only when the danger is very great. Even then, though in those circumstances the leaders' authority may be enough to make them act and speak, it is hardly ever sufficient to make them keep quiet." Tocqueville blamed this failing on vanity and on constituent pressure. The latter, he said, "drives to despair those honest mediocrities who, knowing their limitations, would never willingly have stepped forward. Thus goaded, the deputy gets up to speak, to the great distress of his friends, and rashly bursting in among the most celebrated orators, he confuses the debate and bores the assembly." He noted that the consequences were that congressional debates "are frequently vague and perplexed, seeming to be dragged, rather than to march, to the intended goal."

On a more resigned note, he accepted the rhetorical state of affairs as one that could not be overcome. Americans, he wrote, seemed to accept the matter and "they bear witness to their long experience of parliamentary practice not by refraining from dull speeches but by summoning their courage to listen to them. They are resigned to them, as to an evil that they know by experience cannot be cured."

Tocqueville did not himself observe national elections. But he included election reports of at least two Americans, one a

Marylander who had run for the state legislature as an anti-Jacksonian. The Maryland man described his campaign experience as follows: "My opponent happened to be one of my best friends. We went together two days before the election to Washington Square where a platform had been erected for speakers at the town meeting. I got up first and began to explain to the audience —there were at least 10,000—the mistakes which General Jackson and the present administration had committed since they came to power, whereas my opponent made the case for the government. When I say we did that, we tried to do so; for the boos of the opposing party continually drowned the speaker's voice. Several men came to fisticuffs. There were several broken limbs and finally everyone went to bed. The next day my adversary and I went off to tour the different parts of the county. We traveled in the same carriage, ate at the same table, lodged at the same inns and then appeared as adversaries on the same hustings." This sounds like something of a put-on, especially the numbers reported to have attended.

The second report came from Ohio, where Tocqueville was told that "in the West a candidate must go and harangue his partisans in the public places, and drink with them in the taverns." Tocqueville accepted this story and wrote later in his notes that to gain votes candidates "must descend to maneuvres that disgust men of distinction. One must haunt the taverns, drink and argue with the mob; that is what is called *Electioneering* in America."

Although the use of patronage in the national government did not seem to disturb him, he reported the complaint of a young lawyer named Timothy Walker. According to Walker, when Jackson came to power he "dismissed 1,200 officials for no other reason than that he wanted to put his partisans in their place. . . . Places have served to pay for services to him personally. That is what I blame him for most; he has introduced corruption into the central government and his example will be followed. All the journalists who worked for him have been given places. For appointments even up to the Supreme Court he has picked among his friends."

Tocqueville made no reference to campaign financing other than the reward after the act noted above. Certainly patronage was used as a reward and a subsidy to friends. Pro-administration papers were given government printing contracts, and some editors received government jobs that required little time but carried helpful salaries.

Government officials and contractors were asked for campaign contributions. Congressmen used the franking privilege to send out party newspapers and campaign material, apparently with more freedom than is allowed today. Political dinners were used in part for fund-raising, although their principal purpose seems to have been to glorify the party and keep up party morale. Delegates to state conventions were sometimes charged a fee.

It is assumed that much of the money raised by Daniel Webster for the National Republicans in 1828 came from business interests. There are allegations that money from the Bank of the United States was used against Jackson in the 1832 election, although the best evidence indicates that Bank participation was indirect. The Bank, in the second half of 1832, spent about $17,000 to print and distribute some 30,000 copies of Jackson's message vetoing the bill that would have renewed the Bank's charter, copies of pro-Bank speeches, and other propaganda.

There is no evidence to show that fund-raising for politics had become anything like the science it is today. Neither did candidates have sophisticated campaign staffs, chartered trains, or airplanes. In many ways, however, the presidential campaigns of 1828 and 1832 foreshadowed modern campaigns. They were much more lively and exciting than previous presidential campaigns had been. Jackson's election was not a happy accident; for Martin Van Buren and others were crafty campaign managers. Jackson and his men did not invent new techniques, but they perfected the old ones and used them with great skill.

Jackson himself played an active managerial role. He was supported by effective state machines in states like New York, Virginia, and New Hampshire. A Central Committee, established in Nashville, Tennessee, in 1827, kept in touch with committees in other states and answered attacks on the General. Another Central Committee in Washington, D.C., distributed campaign material. A Jackson congressional group was established, and Jackson organizers were sent around the country. Jackson Committees and Hickory Clubs were organized on the local level. The Jack-

son people also had what may have been the earliest form of the
"advance man": "To whip up enthusiasm prior to a public meeting, local committees frequently sent out squads of men on horseback 'with labels on their hats' to identify their party and their
candidate. In the Baltimore 12th Ward these riders threw small
coins among the crowds that gathered, and called to the boys 'to
huzza for Jackson' as they rode by. . . ."

There was a campaign biography of Jackson. There were Jackson buttons of sorts. Actually, the button was a medal with his
portrait on one side, a slogan on the back, and a hole so that the
medal could be attached by ribbon or string to a man's lapel.

The ethnic vote was searched out. Campaign literature printed
in German was distributed in the large German community in
Pennsylvania. Jackson was presented to the Irish immigrants as
Irish (he was Scotch-Irish) and to the religious as very pious.
The Jacksonians also had good Election Day operations. In some
areas party workers took voters to the polls, marching them in
large groups behind Jackson banners.

The 1832 election year marked the establishment of the national convention. The Federalists had held a national convention of sorts in 1808, but had not used conventions to nominate
anyone thereafter. The Republicans had regularly used a congressional caucus to nominate their presidential candidates. In
the confused politics of the 1820s, state legislatures and even
mass meetings made nominations. But all three parties competing in the 1832 campaign used national conventions.

The Anti-Masons led off with a convention in Baltimore in
September 1831, nominating William Wirt, a former Attorney
General, for the presidency.

The National Republicans followed with a convention in the
same city in December 1831 and nominated Henry Clay as
their candidate.

The Democrats held their convention in May 1832, also in Baltimore. Since there was no question of who their presidential
candidate would be, the principal business of the convention was
the selection of the vice-presidential candidate. Jackson wanted
to dump John Calhoun and take on Martin Van Buren, and the
convention followed his wishes. This first Democratic party convention used a two-thirds rule for the nominating process and a

rule allowing states to vote as a unit. The first practice prevailed for about 100 years, and the second for almost 140 years.

Overall, the Tocqueville observations on American politics of the 1830s were quite accurate. He was in error in saying that rich men avoided public office. If he had said "old wealth," he would have been closer to the truth. There were many self-made, wealthy men (including Andrew Jackson) in office at the time of Tocqueville's visit. In fact, even the relatively radical Workingmen's parties supported wealthy candidates. They did not demand that their candidates be workers, only that they be in sympathy with basic Workingmen goals. This reality confirmed Alexander Hamilton in his argument at the Constitutional Convention against proportional representation in the House of Representatives: he said that the workers, the less educated, would prefer to vote for someone better qualified.

Tocqueville seemed to underestimate the quality of public officials of the day. The list included men like John Quincy Adams, Thomas Hart Benton, John Calhoun, Henry Clay, Sam Houston, James Polk, Roger Brooke Taney, Martin Van Buren, and Daniel Webster. Even Davy Crockett, whose character, to some extent, and whose cap came to be the marks of the Estes Kefauver campaigns for the presidency in 1952 and 1956, was not as bad as Tocqueville thought.

What is the political situation in the United States approximately 150 years after the Tocqueville visit? At first glance, perhaps even at second or third, one might say not very different or, if anything, worse.

The quality and character of members of Congress and other officeholders remain a matter of concern today, as they were in 1831. It is popularly held that members of the House are, on the average, inferior to members of the Senate. However, about one fifth of the senators are former House members. Old politicians, historians, and columnists talk and write of the giants of the past, as did the men who spoke with Tocqueville during his visit. Whether the ability and moral character of officeholders are better or worse than they were in the past is beyond accurate determination. Sufficient for the day are the inadequacy and the evil thereof. Peter Odegard, writing on political corruption in the 1937 edition of the *Encyclopaedia of the Social Sciences*, observed that among the great modern nations the United States had the least enviable record with regard to public morality. Watergate and related incidents suggest that not much has changed since he made his judgment forty years ago.

There are at least three forces that bear quite directly on political morality. First are the general level and standards of morality prevailing in the country; second, the level of morality in business, in the legal profession, and in other professions that bear directly on politics and government; and third, the accepted ideals and traditions of political responsibility.

Obviously a society's general level of morality will be reflected in the conduct of public officials who are chosen or selected from that society. I will not attempt a judgment on the general level of morality in the United States, except to say that it could be higher.

Of more immediate concern, and also of easier determination, is the level of morality accepted in the business and professional world that touches most directly on government. It is significant that in most cases in which accused public officials try to defend themselves, they argue that their actions are within the bounds of accepted practices in the outside world from which they have come. There, dealers in influence, high-pressure artists, public-relations men (some of them following the philosophy of one who explained that his work was simply to find doubt and expand it) often sit, if not at the head of the table, at least on the right hand. And the transfer of the adversary relationship, acceptable under the restraints of legal and court procedures, to other areas of social exchange can undermine mutual trust and confidence.

A third cause for the unsatisfactory standards of morality in government is the lack of a strong tradition of the special responsibility and honor of public office. When in the beginning of our national existence we cut ourselves away from the aristocratic traditions of the Old World and adopted an egalitarian political system, every citizen was given a share in political power. In transferring this power we somehow failed to transfer a corresponding sense of political responsibility which the old traditions and institutions had, with some success, imposed upon the ruling elite. We failed to develop new institutions and new traditions directly attaching responsibility to office as a substitute for the system which attached responsibility to birth and class.

While basic conditions and attitudes remain unchanged, or at best change very slowly, there are many proposals to improve the quality of officeholders and to make political and government operations more honest and effective. Periodically the salaries of members of Congress and other officeholders are raised. Usually a sustaining argument for the increase is that higher salaries will attract better candidates. There is no evidence that salary increases in the past have accomplished this purpose.

Members of Congress are now required to make public reports as to the amount and sources of outside income and assets. Voluntary financial disclosure was fairly common in the past: sometimes it was done freely, sometimes under pressure of challenges from the opposition. Whether disclosure has any effect on elections or conduct in office is not clear.

The presidential election of 1976 was unique in that it was the first presidential election in the history of the nation conducted under the Federal Election Campaign Act, which provides government financing for presidential campaigns. It was an unusual election, in that both political parties were showing signs of strain and confusion unmatched since the Adams-Clay-Jackson period of 1824–32, with the possible exception of the pre-Civil War period, when the Whig party was disintegrating and the Republican party had not yet been formed. In the interim Abolitionists, Free Soilers, Independent Democrats, Conscience Whigs, Barn-burners, Know-nothings, and even Prohibitionists were all active.

The Republicans came into the 1976 campaign with a stand-in President as their candidate, following the resignation of the President and of the Vice President they had elected in 1972. Republicans were kept busy in the campaign defending the Watergate complex of criminal or near-criminal activities, along with trying to explain the general failures of the government and of the country in dealing with such problems as unemployment, poverty, inflation, oil shortages, and the like.

The Democrats were divided among themselves, if not against themselves. In the early primaries they had a great variety of candidates, ranging from Fred Harris, a self-defined populist, to George Wallace, a press-defined populist. They finally nominated and then elected Jimmy Carter, who had made his way along the nomination trail by submitting that he was slightly more or less than his immediate opponent—less extreme than Governor George Wallace, militaristic but not quite as militaristic as Senator Henry Jackson, less liberal than Congressman Morris Udall, younger than Senator Hubert Humphrey, older than Governor Jerry Brown of California.

A secondary issue in the campaign was the viability of what has come to be called the "two-party system." Another was the constitutional issue of whether politics in the United States should, by practice and by law, be confined in effect to two political parties, a conception which was basic to the federal election act. That act effectively restricted government financing of campaigns to the candidates of the Republican and Democratic parties. It not only denied public funding to independent and third-party candidates, but also made it difficult for them to organize and to collect money with which to pay campaign expenses.

The concept of two-party politics as essential to the working of American democracy was not developed or contemplated at the convention which wrote the Constitution of the United States. On the contrary, the prospect of partisan politics, and especially of two-party politics, was a matter of concern at that convention. John Adams, in 1780, said that the worst political arrangement, under a constitution similar to that which was adopted for the nation, would be to have politics controlled and conducted by two strong political parties. He suggested that such an arrangement was a prescription for irresponsible politics and for bad government. The Constitution was designed partly to protect the country from government by faction, from party control of the government. It was designed to avoid the instability of the parliamentary system, and did not anticipate that expressions like "party loyalty" or the "loyal opposition" would ever have any bearing upon the conduct of government affairs. Even the institution of the party whip, now employed in both the House and the Senate, would have been looked upon by the Founding Fathers as a perversion of the constitutional system.

The acceptance of the idea of two-party politics happened without any special notice or event. Political philosophers like Elihu Root suggested that the two-party system was a sign of political maturity and then, making improper comparisons with governments organized on parliamentary principles, noted that countries with politics concentrated in two parties had stable and good government. (The example usually cited was England. England still has two-party politics, but their performance is not cited as an encouraging example of what comes of a two-party political system. The bad example used to be France.) Political scientists began to teach courses in "The Two Party System." It was a convenient frame for analysis, even though invalid. The two-party system had the appearance of balance, somewhat like Newtonian physics. It could be diagramed.

Politicians accepted the idea. Democrats and Republicans in state after state moved to give their parties special advantages and to preclude third parties and independents from effective participation. The two-party system became a matter of belief. When Gerald Ford expressed his belief in the two-party system, he spoke with reverence, as though he were reciting part of a religious creed or swearing by the Constitution.

Actually, the two-party system, apart from the theoretical unsoundness of the conception, has not worked very well in practice.

Two-party politics in the nineteenth century demonstrated that it was unable to deal with the slavery problem and, after the Civil War, unable to deal with the problems of reconstruction. In the twentieth century, the two-party system dominated American politics, as we experienced the great Depression and later became deeply involved in the Vietnam War. It still controls American politics and government as we acknowledge the realities of unemployment, inflation, and the disintegration of major American cities, among other problems.

Despite all of this on record, the same two parties in control of the federal government passed a federal law giving themselves special position and advantages over any other political movements. When the law was first tested in the Supreme Court, in 1976, the Court held that it clearly violated basic constitutional rights and provisions in two major areas—one, the right to free-

dom of speech and, two, the constitutional principle of separation of powers. The Court also indicated that it would be prepared, after experience with the law in action, to examine that
experience for demonstration of interference with other constitutionally guaranteed rights, such as privacy and freedom of assembly for political purposes.

I am sure that if Tocqueville were to visit America today, he
would be puzzled, if not shocked, to note the rather easy way in
which a country born of a revolution based on the right to organize for political purposes, with self-government as its ultimate
purpose, has accepted a law under which the politics of the
country are determined largely by the government itself, which
government in turn is determined by the controlled political system. He might describe the politics of the country as "Politics of
the government, by the government, and for the government."

10

The Presidency: Make the Gentleman in the White House Take Down His Flag

Andrew Jackson was serving his first term as President of the United States at the time of Tocqueville's visit. He had been elected in 1828 and was preparing, as was the country, for his campaign for re-election. Tocqueville's view of Jackson was significantly colored by the attitudes of those to whom he spoke. His own experience was a very limited meeting with the President, a social call that involved no serious conversation. The more conservative and established professionals and businessmen who spoke to Tocqueville of Jackson were inclined to downgrade him, as a man and a military leader and a President.

A more accurate report would have portrayed Jackson's presidency as the result of his character and personality, both of which were forceful to say the least. Jackson was decisive and brave, if not rash. The record shows that, once decided upon a course, he seemed capable of facing any kind of personal, military, or political opposition—from whatever quarter—without flinching. He had great physical courage, a trait that appealed to Americans generally, but especially to frontiersmen, who lived with danger nearly every day. He was stoical in bearing physical pain. When first elected to the presidency, he still carried a bullet near his heart, a reminder of a duel he had fought some twenty years earlier. Doctors, limited in skill and without adequate anesthetics, apparently thought it better to leave the bullet alone. Another bullet, from a gunfight, had been in his arm for fifteen years. Jackson was often sick during his presidency, and reportedly close to death two or three times. Yet he was an active President, carrying on almost as though he had no health problems.

A more personal picture of Jackson shows that he had a classical sense of honor, that he was politely reserved with strangers, and that he had the manners traditionally attributed to southern gentlemen. If we accept reports as accurate, the third trait surprised and pleased political opponents who were cultured and established.

Jackson generally was a good judge of the men he dealt with, though at times his loyalty to friends (a quality which is not all bad in politicians) and his stubbornness led to blunders. The most conspicuous of such incidents was the Peggy Eaton affair, in which he made the social status of a cabinet wife a major political issue. Among the persons whose political talents he recognized were Martin Van Buren, Roger Brooke Taney, Amos Kendall, and others.

Personality and character alone cannot explain Jackson's popularity with the Americans of his day. He had a habit of winning most of the contests in which he was engaged. A winner is seldom unpopular, no matter what faults he might have. Questions about character, whether that of Andrew Jackson or Lyndon Johnson or Richard Nixon, generally are considered of secondary political importance in the midst of political success. Jackson's victory in the Battle of New Orleans was one of the few clear victories in the War of 1812. Evidently it boosted national morale and helped distract attention from the stalemated conclusion of that war. Tocqueville, however, thought it a light victory. In one of his notebooks he wrote: "How can one be in doubt about the pernicious influence of military glory in a republic? What determines the people's choice in favor of General Jackson who, as it would seem, is a very mediocre man? What still guarantees him the votes of the people in spite of the opposition of the enlightened classes? The Battle of New Orleans. And yet that battle was a very ordinary feat of arms, and the people who so allows itself to be captivated is the most antimilitary, the most prosaic and the least emotional that there is on earth." Similar questions were asked in 1952, when General Dwight Eisenhower ran for the presidency.

There was a Jackson cult, similar to the Eisenhower cult, which began long before Jackson's presidency. It was consciously used by his managers to help win the 1828 election, and it was continued throughout his life and beyond. The January Eighth dinners celebrating Jackson's victory at New Orleans were made into major patriotic observances, but they also celebrated Jackson as a person. In the 1828 political campaign, his managers encouraged the use of the dinner to exalt Jackson, the presidential candidate, and to help his campaign. (Democrats still honor Jackson in what were until recently called Jefferson–Jackson Day dinners, but which now include other Presidents' names in the list of those to be honored.)

In a later time, the physical disabilities of Franklin Roosevelt kept him from becoming the physical, personal representation of the American military position. Instead, Americans identified with Winston Churchill, standing amidst the ruins of London, visiting the war front, and the like. They also identified with General Eisenhower, who personified our military presence and achievements in Western Europe. And in a limited way, they identified with General Douglas MacArthur, Admiral William Halsey, and General Curtis LeMay, two of whom later ran for national office.

In honor of Jackson's nickname of "Old Hickory," there were hickory tree plantings, hickory pole raisings, and hickory clubs. Perhaps the strongest political testimonial is an attempt to transfer a hero's name and reputation to other politicians. Some years later, James Polk's supporters called their candidate "Young Hickory."

Jackson and his administration were not, of course, universally approved. The disapproval included that of men who told Tocqueville that the President was not very competent, that of political opponents who accused him of being tyrannical, and that of cartoonists who labeled him "King Andrew I." His supporters were fiercely loyal, even in his late years at the Hermitage when, as one Jackson biographer reported:

> As in bygone times, a stream of callers flowed to and fro. Democrats came to pledge allegiance, Whigs to confess their sins and beg absolution; and all to cut hickory canes. A hickory cane was the badge of a Jackson man, a hickory cane cut at the Hermitage the badge of a Jackson man who had been to Mecca. . . .

Basic to all of this approval and criticism was the fact that Jackson had two successful administrations. He won most of his political battles. He all but retired the national debt, then considered an important achievement. He was successful in his Indian removal policy; he won the fight against the Second Bank of the United States. He successfully collected a large debt owed to the United States by France. He defeated the nullifiers of South Carolina. These were the major achievements of Andrew Jackson. The conditions, political and personal, in which he occupied the presidential office and exercised its power set his administration apart from previous administrations. His presidency was more personal, more flamboyant, one might say more democratic, since it incorporated something of the spirit and character of the new, west-moving America.

Jackson, like Thomas Jefferson many years before, walked from his lodgings to his first inauguration. He was escorted by old soldiers of the Revolutionary War, who acted as ceremonial escorts, not as bodyguards. After he was sworn in, Jackson rode on horseback to the White House, in triumph, followed by a great crowd of supporters. Polite society was shocked when supporters without formal invitation invaded the inaugural reception.

The White House of Jackson's time was, as Beaumont reported, like a fine private residence—impressive by American standards, but apparently not by French standards. "Its interior," wrote Beaumont, "is decorated with taste but simply, the *salon* in which [the President] receives is infinitely less brilliant than those of our ministers. He has no guards watching at the door, and if he has courtiers they are not very attentive to him, for when we entered the *salon* he was alone, though it was the day of public reception; and during our whole visit but two or three persons entered . . ."

There were eighteen White House servants, apparently paid by Jackson or kept as his slaves. The President received a salary of $25,000 a year. This enabled him to entertain friends and White House visitors. During his second administration Jackson had to cut back on entertaining because his son, who was managing the family's Tennessee estate, the Hermitage, did not do well. In fact, his son incurred so many personal debts that Jackson had to dip into his presidential salary to pay them.

John Quincy Adams, Jackson's predecessor, often walked around Washington while he was President. Jackson preferred to go about on horseback. There were no Secret Service agents in Jackson's day, and apparently no regular bodyguards, even though Jackson received a number of assassination threats during his presidency. One attempt on his life was made at the Capitol in 1835. The assailant's pistols did not fire properly, so Jackson was unharmed. Jackson went on the attack, with his cane as his only weapon; but the man was captured by an Army officer before the President reached him.

The government did not provide funds for presidential staff assistants. Jackson's nephew, Andrew Jackson Donelson, served as private secretary to the President, helping with paperwork and answering letters. Donelson held a nominal position as clerk in the Land Office; that position provided a salary, but demanded little work. This practice, an obvious subterfuge, did not extend very far or include many persons. Departmental clerks might be borrowed for special work, such as making copies of the annual presidential messages (in that pre-Xerox, pre-mimeograph, and pre-quick-printing age), but they were not given long-term assignments at the White House. One or two members of Jackson's "Kitchen Cabinet" held departmental jobs, but apparently ones that demanded genuine work and time commitments.

Jackson, like other Presidents of the time, was burdened with a great deal of routine work and was without assistants for speech-writing, congressional liaison, departmental liaison, political operations, and other essential functions. Jackson's "Kitchen Cabinet" was developed as a way of taking care of some of these needs. The men of the Kitchen Cabinet were used as advisers, operators, speech writers, and political handymen—performing many of the tasks carried out in recent years by White House staff members such as Theodore Sorensen, Lawrence O'Brien, and Richard Goodwin of the Kennedy administration; H. R. Haldeman, John Ehrlichman, John Dean, and Patrick Buchanan of the Nixon administration; Jody Powell and Hamilton Jordan of the Carter administration.

Andrew Jackson had only six cabinet members: Secretary of State, Secretary of the Treasury, Secretary of War, Secretary of the Navy, Attorney General, and Postmaster General. The Secretary of War was roughly equivalent to today's Secretary of the Army. There was no overall Secretary of Defense, since the President held and exercised direct authority over the military establishment. Jackson changed cabinet members often. He arranged for the retirement of almost the entire Cabinet in 1831 because of dissent within the ranks over the social status of Peggy Eaton, wife of Jackson's Secretary of War. During his second term, he fired a Secretary of the Treasury who refused to remove government deposits from the Second Bank of the United States. It was argued that by law the Secretary of the Treasury had authority to make the decision. But Jackson took the position that this was an executive policy decision which properly belonged to the President and that, consequently, he had the right to dismiss the cabinet member. His decision was not seriously challenged, at least not to the point of being taken to the Supreme Court.

Jackson did not altogether dominate his Cabinet. He kept some of them on longer than he really wanted to. For the most part, his relationship with cabinet members was in the tradition of successful Presidents. He consulted cabinet members on major problems, but did not feel bound by their advice. His informal Kitchen Cabinet competed with the formal Cabinet for attention; and in some areas, Jackson's reliance on it was greater than his reliance on the regular, constitutional Cabinet.

The executive branch of the government headed by Jackson and his men was small by modern standards. In 1831 the Government had only 11,491 civilian employees. Of these, only 666 worked in Washington. The greatest number of federal workers (over 8,000) worked for the Post Office Department. Fewer than 400 civilians worked for the War and Navy departments.

In 1831, the federal government had receipts of roughly $28 million, expenditures of about $15 million, and a surplus of about $13 million. Financing the federal government was relatively easy and politically noncontroversial. The greatest part of federal revenue came from customs collections. The second largest source of revenue was the sale of public lands. Domestic taxes were third, but in 1831 provided only $7,000 for the federal budget. Jackson's fiscal record was conservative. He balanced the budget every year that he was in office. He also reduced the public debt to its lowest point since before the Constitution was adopted. When his first term started in 1829, the debt stood at about $58 million; by the end of 1834, the debt was down to $38,000.

The Panic of 1837, an economic crisis and largely a fiscal one, followed Jackson's administration and has been blamed on Jacksonian policies, including his attack on the Bank of the United States. Economic historians now hold that this is not the case. They believe that the panic resulted from a combination of forces over which Jackson and his economic advisers had little or no control, and which they could not have been expected to understand. Large capital imports from England and a change in the Chinese attitude toward silver together produced a rapid increase in the quantity of silver in the United States. The banks' specie reserves increased significantly; and in the banking theory and practice of the time, an increase in specie reserves almost automatically led to expansion of money and credit supply. Significant is the fact that fiscal and economic policy, rather than agricultural versus industrial policy, came to be a dominant political issue.

Jacksonians controlled the House of Representatives through both of Jackson's terms as President. For the most part, the House supported Jackson, although there was some dissent in the Bank fight and some murmuring against Jackson's expansion of presidential power. In June of 1834, for example, Representative David Crockett assailed Jackson with these words:

> Sir, of what use are your laws, while he walks over your laws, and your Constitution, too, with impunity? Sir, I do not consider it good sense to be sitting here passing laws for Andrew Jackson to laugh at; it is not even good nonsense. Sir, what does he care for your laws or the Constitution? He is the Government, and his will is the law of the land. . . . and out of those that the President has got about him, I have never seen but one honest countenance since I have been here, and he has just resigned. . . . Let us all go home, and let the people live one year on glory, and it will bring them to their senses; and they will send us back here and teach us to make the gentleman in the White House take

down his flag. Sir, the people will let him know that he is not the Government. I hope to live to see better times.

Somewhat more restrained was an attack on President Jimmy Carter by House Minority Leader John J. Rhodes in 1977, when he said that the Carter White House had demonstrated "uncertainty and ineptitude, compounded by moral blindness and a lack of understanding of the processes of government." Rhodes declared that:

> Nothing really has been accomplished and one of the reasons it hasn't been accomplished, I think, is because the administration started out not knowing a thing about Congress, not knowing a thing about the government, and apparently proudly so, with the idea that anything that happened prior to Jan. 20 [Carter's inauguration] had to be wrong . . ."

Jackson did not dominate the Senate, which was more closely divided over his policies than was the House. It also contained men like Daniel Webster, Henry Clay, and John Calhoun, who were effective in the opposition. The Senate voted to censure the President over his removal of federal deposits from the Bank of the United States. Toward the end of Jackson's second term, however, the resolution of censure was formally expunged from the record of the Senate.

In addition to the Bank controversy, the major domestic issues during Jackson's presidency were over "internal improvements" (road building and other public works) and Indian removal. His handling of these issues sustained Tocqueville's point that Jackson had great personal power. Jackson generally had his way on domestic issues, partly because on some (such as Indian removal) he represented public opinion, and partly because he was willing to use the veto power and to assert other presidential powers which his predecessors had not used.

Jackson's foreign policy was generally successful and was carried out within the bounds of the Constitution. His achievements included the reopening of trade with the British West Indies (trade that had been closed off for most of the years since the American Revolution) and his settlement of claims against the French for merchant ships seized by the French during the Napoleonic Wars.

Jackson's significant difference with the Supreme Court occurred in 1832, when he refused to enforce a Supreme Court decision favorable to the Cherokee Indians of Georgia. Jackson reportedly said of that case: "Well: John Marshall has made his decision: *now let him enforce it!*" By refusing to assert federal power on behalf of the Cherokees, Jackson inadvertently encouraged the nullifiers of South Carolina, who were challenging federal policy on tariffs. But Jackson contained the nullifiers with a show of military force and a compromise on the tariff issue.

American military forces in 1831 consisted of about 11,000 men, about the same as the number of civilian government employees. Of this number, the Army had about 6,000 men; the Navy had over 4,000; and the Marines, about 800. The Army Corps of Engineers was already in existence, with authority over U.S. seaports and inland waterways. Most civil engineers in America had been trained at West Point, so some of them were used for civilian work. John Quincy Adams, for example, had lent Army officers to help build the Baltimore and Ohio Railroad. During the Jackson Era, the Army was between wars and was chiefly engaged in exploring, engineering, and sporadic Indian fighting.

Although the military establishment was small, military thinking was not. The Commander-in-Chief was a military man who had shown little concern for the niceties of civilian control when, long before his presidency, he had invaded Florida in 1818. Jackson's policy of Indian removal depended on the threat of using force. In 1834 Jackson sent federal troops to Maryland after pitched battles had broken out between competing groups of Irish laborers working on the Chesapeake and Ohio Canal.

Jackson was land-minded rather than sea-minded. He called upon Congress to support the building of shore installations and forts for coastal defense. He also asked for more warships, but the shore installations provided more jobs than did shipbuilding. They also received quicker and more enthusiastic support from the Congress, this despite the fact that the Navy was doing good work. Jackson used it to protect American commerce on the high seas, especially in the Pacific, where New England whaling ships were active. After the *Friendship* of Salem was attacked and part of her crew slaughtered at Quallah Battoo on the coast of

Sumatra, Jackson sent the U.S. frigate *Potomac* to retaliate. The mission was judged to be successful. In similar fashion the sloop of war *Lexington* sailed to the Falklands to protect the interests of Connecticut seal hunters. There were at least two cruises lending prestige to the Navy and to the United States. In 1826–30 the sloop of war *Vincennes* made the first round-the-world voyage of any American warship. On a later cruise, the same ship stopped at the Fijis, the Marquesas, and Tahiti; rescued American seamen held in the Palaus; and burned at least one Samoan village in which American whalers had been murdered. Jackson also used Navy ships to threaten Charleston when South Carolina declared federal tariff law null and void and threatened secession. South Carolina soon backed down. Despite this record, the Navy remained small. At the end of 1831, Secretary of the Navy Levi Woodbury reported to Congress:

> The naval force in commission has consisted of five frigates, eleven sloops, and seven schooners; but, of these, four small schooners, purchased, and temporarily used in guarding our live oak, and in making surveys of the coast, can hardly be considered as a permanent portion of the establishment . . .
>
> Our force abroad has been divided between the Mediterranean, the West Indies, Brazil, and the Pacific. . . .

Tocqueville's observations and reflections on the presidency were not based on his view of the Jacksonian presidency, which he looked upon as something of an aberration. Rather, they were based on his study of the presidency as defined in the Constitution, on what was said by contemporary commentators, and on the history of the office up to the time of Jackson. Putting all of these together, Tocqueville concluded that the presidency was not an office of great power or of glory. He made the obvious comment that, in the conduct of foreign policy, the President was significantly dependent on the Senate. For, he wrote, "the Senate supervises him in his relations with foreign powers and in his appointments to offices so that he can neither corrupt nor be corrupted." At the same time, however, he noted that the power of the Senate is limited, for "it cannot force him [the President] to act or share executive power with him." He also observed that the Congress could encroach on presidential power by indirect action, which he saw as one of the inherent weaknesses—vices he said—of republican constitutions. Tocqueville credited the drafters of the Constitution with having at least curbed this vice by providing for the presidential veto. He believed the veto to be helpful in sustaining presidential power, although he qualified that opinion by the further judgment that a persistent Congress could always override a veto.

The office of the presidency has changed significantly since the time of Jackson. The power exercised from it, the sweep of executive responsibilities, and the incidental perquisites and ceremonies attached to the office have all grown.

It has been a long time since an American President has walked to his inauguration. President Carter did walk away from his; but he was, of course, surrounded by Secret Service agents. That Service will not say how many agents are assigned to guard the President; but the estimates run over 100 men. In addition, special officers guard the White House and its grounds.

A presidential inauguration is no longer a simple ceremony. Special stands are built, at great expense, on the east front of the Capitol. There is an elaborate parade in which all of the states are expected to participate. The parade also features representation of other national institutions, particularly the military.

The White House itself has changed in many ways since Jackson's time. If the General were to revisit it today, he might be surprised to learn that a bomb shelter has been constructed in the basement; that an East Wing and a West Wing of offices have been added; and that a huge building next door is also used for executive offices. A pre-Carter survey showed 75 domestic servants, paid by the government, staffing the White House. In addition, 21 gardeners and maintenance workers were taking care of the building and grounds. About 65 Army men were assigned as chauffeurs for the White House fleet of cars.

Even after cuts ordered by President Carter, the White House still has 17 cars, 19 trucks and service vehicles, 7 Boeing 707 jets, 6 Lockheed JetStars, 3 DC-9s, 14 Sabreliners, and 13 helicopters. Moreover, special aircraft are available to carry the President, other high-ranking officials, and a large "battle staff" in the event that imminent nuclear war forces a hasty evacuation.

The President's salary is $200,000 a year, with an additional

$50,000 expense account. A former President receives an annual pension of $60,000, a generous allocation for payment of staff and office expenses, and Secret Service protection until death.

In contrast with the limited Jacksonian staff and the Kitchen Cabinet, the office staff at the White House now numbers about 350. At the end of 1973, there were 14 military officers assigned to the White House. These included an Air Force major general, who served as physician to the President, a Navy rear admiral who served as assistant physician to the President, and an Army colonel who also served as assistant physician to the President. The three major services plus the Marines each provided a military aide to the President. Two officers were assigned to the National Security Council, and an Army colonel even served as Associate Director of the Domestic Council. In the late and difficult days of the Nixon administration, General Alexander Haig was given major responsibilities in the midst of the crisis.

Presidential advisers, both civilian and military, have special powers and influence. They are a kind of fifth estate in government. Their role is marked by three special conditions: First, they compete with cabinet members, who are distracted by administrative responsibilities, in policy-making. Second, they are largely independent of the Congress, for they are not confirmed by the Senate, as are regular cabinet members, and they are not accountable to the Congress in the clear and direct and formal way that cabinet members are held accountable. White House staff members claim "executive privilege." Third—and this may be their greatest advantage and most distinctive mark—they control the political and governmental environment of the President. As George Reedy noted:

> Of all the factors which tend to isolate Presidents from the normal stream of human experience, none plays so direct a role as the White House assistants. They are virtually his environment—the people whom he sees every day; the people upon whom he depends for his needs; the people through whom is filtered all information about problems he must face. Whether he intends it or not, they become the testing ground for his views on standards of normal behavior. It is a very poor testing ground because it gives a President nothing but a reflection of himself—a dangerous guide for any political leader.

Reedy observed that staff do not generally give false information to a President, for "the Presidential position is generally too awe-inspiring for people to tell him lies. But it does mean that what he knows will come to him without the adversary overtones that are so essential when the political leader of a democracy tries to understand how people react." Reedy continued:

> That is why it was so difficult for Lyndon Johnson to judge the true depths of the opposition to his policies on Vietnam. To him, the "real" young people were the neat, carefully combed, eager young faces in the White House. To him, the "real" intellectuals were the well-tailored Ph.D.s on his staff, with their computerized victory levels on the "kill ratio" in Southeast Asia. The deep currents that were swelling on the outside could not penetrate those human walls, and he kept counting on reserves of popular support that simply were not there.

The Cabinet, which was somewhat downgraded by Jackson's setting up the Kitchen Cabinet, has been further weakened and downgraded—by the growth of the presidential advisers and by other changes. For example, the establishment of the National Security Council, the Domestic Council, and a host of independent agencies has reduced the power of the Cabinet.

The number of cabinet members has doubled since Jackson's day; there are now twelve cabinet members. The policy seems to be: when in doubt or under pressure in dealing with a difficult problem, establish a new department, appoint a new cabinet member, and hope for the best. Recent additions to the Cabinet include a number that Jackson almost certainly would have opposed on constitutional grounds: the Secretary of Transportation and the Secretary of Housing and Urban Development, for example.

Meanwhile, the number of federal civilian employees has grown from roughly 11,000 in Jackson's time to about 3 million. The Post Office Department had the largest number of civilian employees in the 1830s. Today the Pentagon has the largest number, about 35 per cent of the total. The federal budget has grown from $15 million in the year 1831 to approximately $500 billion in the current fiscal year. Deficit financing and a large public debt have become part of the American Government's fiscal way.

The public debt today is approximately $874 billion—in contrast with the $38 thousand of 144 years ago.

Whereas most tax revenue in Jackson's time came from customs receipts, and domestic taxes were a relatively unimportant source of income for the government, today personal income taxes are the largest source of revenue. Social Security taxes are the second most important source; corporate income taxes are third. Customs receipts contribute only a minimal amount to the federal treasury.

Perhaps the greatest change, in terms of power and measurable, quantitative change has been in the growth of military power. The 23-ship navy of 1831 has grown into a navy of over 300 ships, including 13 aircraft carriers and 70 nuclear attack submarines. The military establishment has 1,054 intercontinental missiles armed with nuclear bombs, 656 Polaris-Poseidon missiles (also carrying nuclear bombs), and 24 squadrons of B-52s armed with nuclear bombs.

The United States military capacity—which in 1831 did not go much beyond a capacity to harass Indians, put down labor insurrections, and deal with pirates—is now sufficient to kill nearly everyone in the world. There are over two million men and women in the armed services today, supported by more than one million civilian employees—in contrast with the eleven thousand members of the armed forces in 1831. The military budget hovers around $120 billion a year. There are American military bases and military personnel on, or adjacent to, every continent.

While American foreign-policy commitments in Jackson's time were very limited, today they are almost without limits.

Along with the increase in power, there has been in the last twenty to twenty-four years a progressive personalization of the office of the President, beginning with the Eisenhower administration. President Eisenhower did not personalize the office by abuse of power or by usurpation, but rather by failure to exercise the powers of the office and by excessive delegation of powers, especially to his Secretary of State, John Foster Dulles, and through him to the Central Intelligence Agency. As President he was inattentive to the growth of the military-industrial complex, although he warned the country of its existence in his farewell address.

The subsequent Kennedy administration was personalized, first in style, and then in substance. Cabinet appointments were made largely without regard for precedent or party identification. Family identification with the office of the presidency was cultivated. Practices initiated or followed by the Eisenhower administration, especially in the use of the CIA, were continued. CIA programs, some of which were extra-legal, if not illegal and unconstitutional, were continued. Thus, the invasion of Cuba, planned without congressional approval or participation, was carried forward. The 800 advisers placed in Vietnam by the Eisenhower administration were given the added support of about 16,000 troops—a quantitative change which altered the nature of our commitment in that country.

President Johnson, especially after his overwhelming victory of 1964, carried personalization a few steps farther. He expanded the war, with questionable legal and constitutional authority. He showed little respect for the integrity of other offices of the executive branch, using officeholders for purposes other than those for which their offices were intended, either by law or Constitution. Thus he chose the Chief Justice to head the investigation of the assassination of President Kennedy, the American Ambassador to the United Nations to settle an opera strike, and a justice of the Supreme Court as his personal adviser. He treated the Senate as though it were the House of Representatives, and the House of Representatives as though it had the constitutional powers of the Senate. There is evidence that he used both the FBI and the CIA with a rather free hand.

President Nixon carried personalization to a more advanced stage. He invaded Cambodia without even the cover of a resolution similar to the Tonkin Gulf Resolution. He impounded moneys authorized and appropriated. He misused and abused his power over the FBI and the CIA, not only in their service within the government, but in a political campaign as well.

The character of the Carter administration is not entirely clear. President Carter has put aside some of the trappings of the presidency, but there is little evidence that he contemplates a depersonalization of the office, or that he has a very clear understanding of its constitutional limits. One of the first things he did, almost immediately after being inaugurated, was to establish his domination over the Vice President by sending him on a visit to foreign capitals (not one of the constitutionally defined responsibilities of the Vice President). Mr. Carter then personalized or "familized" his own office by sending his number-two son Chip to China, his mother Lillian to represent him at the funeral of the President of India, and his wife on a diplomatic mission to Latin America.

President Carter has also taken to himself the role of moral spokesman—not only for the country, but to it. This role was partially claimed by President Nixon when he said that, as President, he was the moral leader of the country. Carter's approach to the moral leadership role is somewhat less direct. He speaks often of presidential and personal compassion and of forgiveness. He preferred to pardon draft resisters rather than to grant amnesty.

President Carter has also spoken of taking personal responsibility for the CIA. That is what President Nixon did. Mr. Carter would have been closer to the mark if he had said that he would take presidential responsibility for it.

Personalization of the presidency is not simply a result of individual presidential character or even of historical conditions, although historical events like wars do result in at least temporary transfer of power to Presidents. The trend to personalization is sustained by more consistent political and governmental procedures.

Three principles were included in the constitutional procedures for electing members of the Congress and the President. The House was to be chosen by popular vote, district by district, throughout the country. The two senators from each state originally were to be chosen by the state legislatures rather than by popular election; thus they were to be a step removed from popular choice. The President was to be chosen in the Electoral College by presidential electors who had been chosen within each state. He was not to be chosen by direct popular vote. Though unit rule was not required by the Constitution, almost every state eventually decided to award all electoral votes to the presidential candidate who carried the state.

The Electoral College, of which Tocqueville approved, is under fire today for several reasons. There are some who argue for direct election of the President on a national basis, with the person who wins a majority or plurality becoming the President. This proposal would eliminate the current practice of giving all of the votes of one state to the candidate who wins the election within that state; and it would eliminate the "undemocratic institution" of the Electoral College.

Curiously, the argument for change comes when the character, ability, and political competence that are needed in the President are more complicated and more difficult to determine than ever before. They come when a strong argument can be made for refinement and perfection of the electoral process, so that the ultimate choice would be made, not by popular judgment, but by those who may be popularly chosen to make the decision. This system would approach a modified parliamentary government. The electors would be held responsible for their decision— either personally or as representatives of political parties.

Winner-take-all primaries, which provide a form of unit rule, have been either modified or abolished after serious challenge. A similar challenge is being raised against the Electoral College as it now operates. The traditional justification of having each state vote as a unit was that the cultural, economic, and political differences among the states were best represented in the choice of the President if brought to bear in blocs. Whether this was sound judgment in the nineteenth century is open to question. But sound or not then, it is difficult to justify today. The differences within most states are greater than the differences between states or regions of the nation. The differences between New York City and congressional districts in upper New York, for example, are greater than the generalized differences between the state of New York and the state of Wisconsin. Milwaukee has many of the same problems that exist in New York City. Yet electoral votes, instead of representing differences within a state, only indirectly and sometimes quite inadequately reflect those differences in the unit vote which is cast for President.

If one assumes that a representative procedure is desirable (namely, that an elector should be chosen who then makes a responsible choice) and also that the final choice should be made after the democratic process has run to reasonable limits, the case for having electors chosen on a district-by-district basis across the country becomes a very strong one. And if compromises are to be made, it would be better to make them in a meeting of the Electoral College than in the conventions of the two major political parties, after which two compromises are offered as the choices of the people.

Tocqueville approved the procedures of the Electoral College, but he thought it a mistake to allow a President to be re-elected. "Intrigue and corruption," he wrote, "are natural vices of elective governments; but when the head of state can be re-elected, these vices spread beyond bounds and compromise the very existence of the country. When a simple candidate forces himself forward by intrigue, his maneuvers can only take place within a restricted sphere. But when the head of state himself is in the lists, he can borrow all the power of the government for his private use." So that, he continued: "In the first case it is a question of a man with feeble resources; in the second, it is the state itself with all its immense resources which intrigues and which corrupts."

The application to the Watergate affair is startling. In that affair and in related misdeeds, the Nixon men used the immense resources of the state to harass political enemies, to raise funds for the President's re-election, and finally to obstruct criminal prosecutions.

Yet Watergate is not directly attributable to the constitutional provision allowing two presidential terms. A President concluding his second term might have done all that was done by the Nixon administration to insure the succession of his party in power—although that is unlikely.

A one-term limit would be, I believe, preferable to the present two-term limit, which appears to be the worst of all possible arrangements. It is a prescription for a carefully hedged first administration, which is pointed toward re-election, and for a second administration which can become irresponsible. If there were no limit on the number of terms a President might serve, in the second term he would have to be concerned about re-election to a third term or about the disgrace of rejection by his party or defeat in the general election. Removing the limit would also reduce the pressure to be carefully political in the first term, in anticipation of the grand fling of the second.

Tocqueville also reflected on the constitutional provisions for removal of a President. He noted that, since the only penalty upon conviction is removal from office, the process "is much more an administrative measure than a judicial act." The constitutional reference to impeachment for "high crimes" supports his judgment. High crimes are generally beyond ordinary judicial reach, since they can be committed only by certain persons. In the case of the United States, this might mean the President in his conduct of foreign policy or as Commander-in-Chief.

Until the Nixon administration, impeachment action against Presidents was restricted to what Tocqueville defined as "administrative" measures. The intrusion into the area of "crimes" as defined by statute, in the Nixon presidency, raised new problems with reference to impeachment. Most of them have not yet been resolved. Tocqueville thought that definitions of impeachable offenses were too vague. He also believed that the relative mildness of the penalty, removal from office, was so mild as to make convictions likely.

His additional comments run into confusion, if not contradiction. He evidently anticipated impeachments as being readily pronounced on Presidents, unless the Presidents were intimidated by the prospect and therefore became timid in office. "Great criminals," he wrote, "would no doubt brave its vain rigors" and act boldly in the face of possible impeachment. But lesser men would not do so because, in his opinion, "ordinary men see it [impeachment] as a decree which destroys their status, stains their honor, and condemns them to a disgraceful leisure worse than death." It was lesser men who he thought had been elected to the office and who might be elected in the future. For, he noted: "No one has yet come forward willing to risk his honor and his life in order to become President of the United States. . . . Fortune must put a huge prize at stake if such desperate players are to present themselves in the lists. So far no candidate has been able to arouse ardent sympathies and dangerous popular passions in his favor. The reason for this is simple: when he gets to the head of the government, he has little power or wealth or glory to distribute among his friends, and his influence in the state is too small for any faction to feel that its success or its ruin depends on his elevation to power."

This was one hundred and fifty years ago. Since then four Presidents have been assassinated, and attempts have been made upon the lives of several others. Power in the presidency has greatly increased. Yet the impeachment procedures remain unchanged. Except for the political effort made against Andrew Johnson, they were untested until the challenge to Richard Nixon. Even then, the test was stopped short by his resignation. The original constitutional provisions and procedures for impeachment proved inadequate.

So did the terms of the Twenty-fifth Amendment to the Constitution. As the Twenty-second Amendment was drafted after the act—namely, after the four elections of Franklin Roosevelt to the presidency—so too was the Twenty-fifth Amendment adopted by a Congress reacting to what it judged to have been critical conditions. Those conditions were the uncertainty of presidential power during two illnesses of Dwight Eisenhower and the absence of a Vice President while Lyndon Johnson completed John Kennedy's term. Whereas the principal goal of the Twenty-fifth Amendment was to deal with the presidency during presidential illness or incapacity, the provisions of the amendment were invoked when Vice President Spiro Agnew resigned under threat of indictment.

Six possible solutions to the problems of presidential succession should be considered:

1. The office of Vice President should be eliminated. It confuses elections through the device of the balanced ticket as well as in other ways. It puts men in line to become President who would otherwise not be chosen. It is, if we are to believe former Vice Presidents and some commentators, a frustrating office and one in which great talent is wasted.

2. The Twenty-second Amendment should be repealed, and Presidents be permitted to run for as many four-year terms as they choose. The constitutional limit of two four-year terms is a prescription for two irresponsible, and possibly contradictory, terms: the first one carefully calculated to assure the second, and the second lacking the restraint that the anticipation of a third election or rejection by one's own party might bring to it.

3. The Twenty-fifth Amendment should be repealed. The determination of presidential disability should not be left to the Vice President, the Cabinet, and the Congress but should, I believe, be vested in the Supreme Court. Presidents should not be allowed to resign, either temporarily or permanently, without congressional approval.

4. By statute or by constitutional amendment, procedures for the appointment of an interim President in the case of death, disability, or displacement of the President should be provided; preferably the interim President should not be drawn from the Congress, but from the executive branch. Almost any cabinet member would do.

5. By statute or by constitutional amendment, two procedures for filling a presidential vacancy should be provided: one to be used in the event of death or disability (I suggest a simple reconvening of the same Electoral College which had chosen the President); and a second to be used following impeachment and conviction or resignation (accepted by Congress) because of failure in office. Under these conditions, the House of Representatives should be made the body of choice, in the manner provided for the election of a President when no candidate receives the majority vote of the Electoral College.

6. Procedures for changing presidential policies, short of impeachment or the cutting off of funds, should be provided.

The essential strength of the presidency should rest in the office itself—not in the person who occupies it at a given time. The power of the presidency is great, but it is clearly limited by the Constitution. The limits of power should be defined as carefully as possible, and honored in practice. When unconstitutional use of presidential power is not checked in time, there is clear and demonstrated danger that the Congress, in reaction, and sometimes in an effort to cover for congressional neglect and failures, will abuse the presidential office and hamper Presidents in the proper exercise of their constitutional powers. Overreactions of this kind, demonstrated in the post-Vietnam and post-Watergate periods, lead not only to unconstitutional government, but also to less effective government.

11

Democracy in America: An Overview

Tocqueville wrote of two Americas: the one which he saw and which was described to him; and the one which he projected for the future. Much of what he foresaw, or predicted, both good and bad, has occurred. Other things which he expected, both good and bad, have not happened. Many problems, institutions, and ideas remain almost unchanged. The race problem is still with us. We have made little progress either in understanding or in dealing with criminals. Demagoguery is a threat. On the other hand, the tyranny of the majority has not yet become a reality, nor has the movement toward equality, which he thought dangerous and inevitable, reached the critical point. American individualism has not brought about social disintegration, although, as Tocqueville anticipated, more and more matters of controversy are not settled by social practice or precedent or within institutional relationships, but by the courts.

A new judgment of America in the mode of Tocqueville requires recognition of five major institutional changes, no one of which was clearly anticipated when the Constitution was adopted, or even when Tocqueville looked at American democracy and its principles and institutions.

The first such change is in the power of the presidency. Tocqueville recognized that the President necessarily would have great influence on foreign affairs, for "a negotiation cannot be initiated and brought to a fruitful conclusion except by one man." He thought that under some conditions, which did not exist in his time, and which he did not foresee for America, the election of the chief executive could pose dangers to the nation because a change in leadership might interrupt foreign policy, which he saw as needing continuity and stability. But he saw the elections of the President as posing no such danger to the United States in his day. For, he wrote: "American policy toward the world at large is simple; one might almost say that no one needs them, and they do not need anybody. Their independence is never threatened." He quoted with approval parts of George Washington's Farewell Address, which recommended neutrality as a general policy for the United States, with temporary alliances to be used in event of extraordinary emergencies. Tocqueville remarked that Washington and Jefferson had set the direction of American foreign policy. That policy, he said, "consists much more in abstaining than in doing."

This was just as well, apparently, in the judgment of Tocqueville, who believed that a government of the aristocracy was far superior in the conduct of foreign policy to the government of democracy. Democratic governments, he thought, find it "difficult to co-ordinate the details of a great undertaking and to fix on some plan and carry it through with determination in spite of obstacles." For democracy, he believed, "has little capacity for combining measures in secret and waiting patiently for the result." Moreover, he thought that the people of a democracy tended to rely too much on their feelings. This was shown, he said, at the time of the French Revolution, when only Washington's great influence prevented America from going to war with England on the side of France.

The reality of international relations today includes the existing power of the Soviet Union and the growing power of China; the spread of nuclear weapons to smaller countries; the newly found economic and political strength of the raw-material-supplying nations, especially those that produce oil; and extensive American treaty obligations around the world.

The problem is not only one of substance, but also one of form and process. It is quite likely that, if the men who drafted the Constitution had anticipated a time when foreign policy would be so major a part of the government's responsibility, an argument would have been made at the Constitutional Convention for a parliamentary, or quasi-parliamentary system—rather than the prescribed one of Senate ratification of treaties and confirmation of the Secretary of State and of foreign ambassadors, and the rather vague provision that foreign policy should be made and conducted with the advice and consent of the Senate.

At the time the Constitution was written, treaties involved specific and limited commitments. This is not the case today. Now we have sweeping treaty agreements, executive agreements, and continuing commitments involving great sums of money. The House of Representatives has become more involved in foreign policy as financial support has become a major aspect of that policy.

During the 1960s, in particular, the Senate became more and more isolated from decisions on foreign policy. At the same time, there was growing arrogance on the part of administrations in the conduct of foreign policy. Presidents Lyndon Johnson and Richard Nixon exercised virtual monopoly in that field. Their theoretical statements about presidential power in foreign affairs were accepted uncritically by many Americans until the Vietnam War forced another look at the Constitution. Even after Vietnam, there was a tendency to accept and applaud the private diplomacy of Henry Kissinger, instead of insisting upon genuine participation by the Senate in making foreign policy.

Critics of the Nixon-Kissinger policies failed to note the importance of procedure. In the 1972 presidential campaign, for example, Senator George McGovern proposed a major reduction of American troop strength in Europe. Although this would have been a significant change in the American commitment there, Senator McGovern did not suggest that as President he would consult with the Senate on the matter.

Even those who challenge independent, presidential foreign policy do so only with reference to positive or aggressive action. At the same time, they would allow the President to make independent decisions about withdrawal of support or reduction of strength which could bear significantly upon treaty obligations and accepted policies. During the Eisenhower administration, Secretary of State John Foster Dulles withdrew support from the building of Egypt's Aswan Dam, to which the government (with congressional support) was obligated. His policy decision went unchallenged. President Carter speaks quite freely of changing foreign policy.

The second significant institutional change is the rise of the military. The question is not one of whether we need a military establishment, but whether the one we have had to develop in the way it did and whether it should be subject to better direction and control. Is a military establishment of such magnitude compatible with a free, democratic society? Or does it inevitably become a separate force of excessive influence?

Tocqueville did not give much space to the President's role as Commander-in-Chief. He apparently did not think it very important either in the structure of the Constitution or in the context of the early nineteenth century. The President does command the Army, he noted, but "that Army consists of six thousand soldiers; he commands the Navy, but the Navy has only a few ships; he conducts the Union's relations with foreign nations, but the Union has no neighbors. Separated by the ocean from the rest of the world, still too weak to want to rule the sea, it has no enemies and its interests are seldom in contact with those of the other nations of the globe."

Tocqueville did speculate at length, however, upon the possible future military role of the United States, upon the relationship of the military establishment to democratic government and society, and upon democracy and war.

If involvement in a great war were to come for America, he thought it would come at the point where the United States touched Mexico. But Mexico's poverty and backwardness, he believed, would long prevent its having a high place among the nations. In the meantime, the United States was fortunate in its isolation: "How wonderful is the position of the New World," he reflected, "where man has as yet no enemies but himself. To be happy and to be free, it is enough to will it to be so." War with Mexico was to come within twenty years; but it was not to be a great war, and Mexico has remained weak and backward.

Tocqueville predicted that, because of its natural advantages and aptitude for trade, the United States would one day "become the leading naval power on the globe." Americans, he said, "are born to rule the seas, as the Romans were to conquer the world." Americans were great sailors, great shipbuilders, and great traders throughout the nineteenth century; but American dominance of the sea with fighting ships did not come until World War II. The significance of that dominance was reduced almost immediately after that war, by the development of nuclear weapons and by the rise of the Soviet Union as a naval power.

Of more importance than Tocqueville's specific predictions were his theoretical reflections on military power, war, and democracy. Tocqueville thought that the army of a democracy continuously posed the threat of war or of revolution. "For armies," he wrote, "are much more impatient of peace when once they have tasted war. . . . I foresee that all the great wartime leaders who may arise in the major democratic nations will find it easier to conquer with the aid of their armies than to make their armies live at peace after conquest. There are two things that will always be very difficult for a democratic nation: to start a war and to end it."

The American experience does not wholly support Tocqueville's theories. On the other hand, it does not wholly disprove them. Following all of our major wars, there has been an immediate move to reduce drastically the size of our military forces. This was true after World War II, although a number of things interrupted the process: the Berlin Blockade, the Korean War, the Cold War, and the development of the concept of containment. After the Korean War, there was no drastic reduction of military strength, but rather the beginning of a trend to increased military power and more expensive armaments. By 1960, the last year of the Eisenhower administration, the military budget had reached about $45 billion. In his farewell address, one for which he was much praised, President Eisenhower warned the nation against the danger of the military-industrial complex in these words:

> In the councils of government, we must guard against the acquisition of unwarranted influence, whether sought or unsought, by the military-industrial complex. . . . We must never let the weight of this combination endanger our liberties or democratic processes.

In the campaign of 1960, the Democratic candidate charged

that the Eisenhower administration had slipped into a position of relative disadvantage against the Russians. "Missile gap" was the campaign cry. When after the election it was found that there was no such gap, military deficiencies of other kinds became the concern of militarists and of the military-industrial complex. The Secretary of Defense announced that it was national policy to be prepared for two and one-half wars: nuclear war; "conventional war" (defined as a war like the last one fought by the country); and a new half-war, a sophisticated guerilla war. Subsequent administrations have advanced this concept of preparedness to the point where the competition is not clearly one with potential enemies, but rather with the military level achieved by the previous administration.

Wartime leaders as defined by Tocqueville, or military leaders in times of peace, have not been as ready to involve the country in war as Tocqueville anticipated they might be. Some, after finishing their military commands, or even before retirement, have entered politics. The tradition began with the election of General George Washington as the first President. It was given support in the election of Andrew Jackson in 1828; for Jackson had been the chief military hero of the War of 1812. The tradition was strongly sustained after the Civil War with the election of Ulysses S. Grant, the victorious Union general. There was a small boom for Admiral George Dewey for President after the Spanish-American War, and for General John Pershing after World War I. Yet peace came so quickly after each of those wars that gratitude and respect for military leadership did not carry over into politics very strongly.

This was not the case after World War II, for peace did not come. Generals turned to politics or were drafted into it. General Douglas MacArthur sought the Republican nomination as early as 1948. General Dwight Eisenhower, sought by both Republicans and Democrats in 1948, accepted the Republican nomination in 1952 and was elected and then re-elected in 1956. The Air Force, in which heroic leaders are more difficult to identify, and which has a shorter tradition of both war and politics, offered one marginal candidate in 1968 when General Curtis LeMay was the vice-presidential running mate of George Wallace on the American Independent party ticket.

The Vietnam War resulted in military promotions. The war it-self, however, was so unpopular that military advancement was not easily translated into civilian political advantage. General William Westmoreland, the most political of the Vietnam War generals, was used as a spokesman for the war by President Johnson. Westmoreland's best political effort came in 1974, when he sought the Republican nomination for Governor of South Carolina, but was defeated in the primary.

The military establishment of the United States after World War II was such that it provided opportunity for satisfying nonmilitary service, for promotions in service, and for security after retirement. Whereas peace was not good for promotions, it did not preclude them. Military men of the United States did not "ardently long for war," as Tocqueville judged they would, "be-cause war makes vacancies available and at last allows violations of the rule of seniority, which is the one privilege natural to a democracy." For the military became what Tocqueville de-scribed as "a little nation apart," a nation with political, eco-nomic, and cultural institutions comparable to those existing in civilian society. Military missions to foreign countries were quasi-diplomatic. Military institutions in some cases duplicated civilian schools. Less directly, military grants for study and re-search resulted in the development within the military of an educational structure for the administration of GI educational programs. For military personnel, there was a separate retire-ment program, a nearly total medical-aid program (including death benefits), and a continuation of wartime life insurance into the peacetime years that followed. For those men whose calling to the military had drawn them away from wholesaling and re-tailing, the military offered a comparable opportunity in the run-ning of the post exchanges. The military went so far as to make preliminary studies on the possibility of unifying the religions of the armed services, so as to make unnecessary separate chaplains for the different faiths. The purpose was to establish a GI reli-gion which would satisfactorily serve the needs of all members of the military.

An example of the extension of military power into civilian life is the Corps of Engineers. The Army Corps of Engineers, origi-nally set up in 1802 to direct military construction and engineering, was later given jurisdiction over navigational construction, not only on the seacoast but also over inland waterways. With an annual budget of roughly $2 billion, it provides opportunities for work quite unrelated to military needs or military action. Concentration on flood control and navigation has given the Corps influence and power, as well as personnel and opportunity for promotion within the Army, far beyond what would have been possible if Corps activities had been limited to military construction. Their power to approve or disapprove navigational and flood-control projects gives them great political influence with the Congress, as members compete for approval of public works.

The Corps has been slow to shift to environmental engineering, but there are signs of awareness and response. Environmental control, contour engineering, and the restoration of lands following strip mining will open great fields of action, careers, and influence to the Corps of Engineers if they gain jurisdiction. The same would have been true of military scientists if they had gained the control which they sought over atomic and nuclear power.

During the critical days before the resignation of Richard Nixon, the military—not surprisingly—thought about what it might do in the event of political crisis. It would be too much to expect the military to operate in a vacuum of policy or of politics. Any institution as powerful as the military establishment of the United States is inevitably somewhat political and somewhat concerned about national policy. It is not altogether surprising that in 1965 the Army contracted with Douglas Aircraft for a study of what would be required to impose order upon the world. The name initially given to the study was "Pax Americana." It was perhaps not so surprising, moreover, that Army intelligence gathered information and kept files, not just on potential foreign enemies or just on military personnel, but also on civilians.

Whereas war undoubtedly opens the way to quicker and perhaps easier (although more dangerous) ways to promotions, opportunity to rise in a military establishment as comprehensive and complex as that of the United States exists in the absence of war. Ambitious minds in a democratic army, therefore, need not long for war. But they may long for an expanded military establishment—and for the extension of military functions far beyond those that can be properly defined as military.

Tocqueville reflected only indirectly on how the existence of a large military establishment could affect democracy. But he considered quite directly and extensively what war can do to a democracy and how a democracy is likely to respond to war. He pointed out that there are two dangers to democracy arising from war. First, he wrote: "Although war satisfies the Army, it annoys and often drives to desperation that countless crowd of citizens whose petty passions daily require peace for their satisfaction. There is therefore some danger that it may cause, in another form, the very disturbance which it should prevent." This apparently is a reference to internal disorder or even revolution. The record of American participation in wars, before the war in Vietnam, does not sustain Tocqueville's speculation. Most earlier wars were popularly supported. Rather than stirring domestic unrest, they served to ameliorate differences and at least to postpone domestic unrest. The condition of popular support or opposition must depend more on the nature of the war than on any basic theory as to the democratic response to war.

Second, he said: "Any long war always entails great hazards to liberty in a democracy. Not that one need apprehend that after every victory the conquering generals will seize sovereign power by force after the manner of Sulla and Caesar. The danger is of another kind. War does not always give democratic societies over to military government, but it must invariably and immeasurably increase the powers of civil government; it must almost automatically concentrate the direction of all men and the control of all things in the hands of the government. If that does not lead to despotism by sudden violence, it leads men gently in that direction by their habits." The clearest demonstration of this judgment followed World War II, especially with the establishment of the Central Intelligence Agency and the expansion of military intelligence—the one under civilian control, the other under military control. Each accumulated, illegally or extra-legally, information about American citizens. The kind of information-gathering which was tolerated during wartime was carried forward into peacetime, without so much as a nod to legality and without the sensitivity shown in the treatment of dogs that had been used in the Canine Corps. The dogs were carefully reconditioned before they were released into peacetime life. The military personnel and institutions were not so reconditioned or reordered.

There is grave reason to doubt that, outside of clear wartime conditions, a representative government and a democratic society can tolerate more than a very limited intelligence activity or operation. This is especially the case if the secrecy—and the almost unqualified choice of methods of deception, fraud, and violence—cannot be restricted to the limits of the international intelligence community, if they cannot be kept from spreading to the more formal and principled world of international relations and, more particularly, to domestic government and politics. Distinctions must be made if barbarism is to be contained. Assassination in wartime and within the intelligence contest of rival intelligence agencies is somewhat different from assassination during a cold war or in a time of political controversy. The evidence of the Watergate inquiry and subsequent investigations of the Central Intelligence Agency showed that the CIA was not restricted to intelligence areas, but was used in diplomatic areas previously accepted as being subject to more traditional rules of action. The same investigations showed that the methods and procedures of the Agency, developed and justified by some as proper in dealing with foreign countries, were—without much questioning of the act—transferred to domestic affairs and used in governmental and political activities.

Tocqueville offered two solutions to the problem of the restless Army. The first was that the Army should be democratic. This followed naturally, he thought, from democratic theory and experience. He believed that citizens would bring to the Army a taste for order and for discipline. "Once you have educated, orderly, upstanding, and free citizens, you will have disciplined and obedient soldiers." Since, as he believed, men of a democracy usually did not want to be soldiers, a democracy had to rely on conscription sooner or later to obtain enough soldiers. (The American experience has not quite borne this out. The measure of response has depended on the challenge of the war.) With compulsory military service, he wrote, "the burden is spread equally and without discrimination among all the citizens."

In a pure and fully supported democracy, one can assume that military service would be so respected and so sought after that, if not all men were needed, the soldiers might be chosen by lot. Those chosen might be looked upon, by themselves and by others, as especially favored. Under this condition of democratic dedication, volunteers would not be needed—and would not even be tolerated.

The experience of America in twentieth-century war has been with a mixed system of volunteers and conscripts. It has worked reasonably well, especially since in time of major wars the strength of the military has been drawn from the civilian population. The conscription system has overridden the volunteer system, but generally has done so in an open and nondiscriminatory way. Thus it has met the Tocqueville rule that "a democratic government can do pretty well what it likes, provided that its orders apply to all and at the same moment; it is the inequality of a burden, not its weight, which usually provokes resistance."

The inequality and discrimination of conscription laws and regulations during the Vietnam War did provoke resistance and protest, and in large measure moved the government into experimentation with the all-volunteer army. For practical purposes, this is a mercenary army. It does not reflect, as would a conscript army chosen at random, the civilization which is defended or represented by the army. The dangers that Tocqueville foresaw arising from a large and professionalized standing army must grow as that army becomes less democratic, less reflective of the general populace, and more isolated from society. Recent public suggestions about unionizing the armed forces are not surprising as the army becomes separated from society, from motives of patriotism, and from broad social identification.

Social control over military activities is likely to diminish with professionalization. That is not the case with conscripts. For, as Tocqueville observed, conscripts look forward to their return to civilian life. "In democracies it is the private soldiers who remain most like civilians; it is on them that national habits have the firmest hold and public opinion the strongest influence. It is especially through the soldiers that one may well hope to inspire a democratic army with the same love of liberty and respect for law as has been infused into the nation itself." There is a danger that a professional army will remove military activities at least one degree from the social and moral control of the civilian political society, and that initial decisions over military involvements will be left to the military. This tendency was manifest in arguments that only volunteers, rather than draftees, should serve in the unpopular Vietnam War.

In accepting the volunteer army, Americans have ignored at least three admonitions from Tocqueville. The first is that a volunteer army is likely to be drawn from the poorer and less-educated in the society, while what he called the "elite" avoid military service during peacetime. Second, a volunteer army is run by career officers. Third, the volunteer army "finally becomes a little nation apart, with a lower standard of intelligence and rougher habits than the nation at large. But this little uncivilized nation holds the weapons and it alone knows how to use them."

Tocqueville's second solution to the problem of a restless army was simply to reduce the army's size. "But that is not a remedy which every nation can apply," he observed.

A third point, not noted by Tocqueville, is that political direction bearing on war must always be precise and clear. The military must not be left in doubt; it must not be either tempted or pressured to develop its own political program and purposes. A powerful military institution inevitably expands into a policy vacuum—first in foreign affairs and then, if we look to the experience of recent years in Europe and in South America especially, also in domestic affairs.

The Vietnam experience is especially pertinent. In that war military men were called upon to act without clear political direction. In the early years of that war, the declared policy was to stabilize the government of South Vietnam. As military commitment increased in 1965, there was an escalation of policy to include prevention of invasion from the north. By 1966 American military strength in South Vietnam was of such magnitude that a more comprehensive purpose had to be given. The new purpose was to save all of Southeast Asia from communism and, beyond that, from domination by China. By 1967 the security of the

United States, its national honor, and the future of the free world were set as the real purposes of the war.

The principal failures in the Vietnam War were not military. Rather, they were failures by American civilian leaders to determine policy, to give direction and to set limits, to take the diplomatic actions necessary to bring the war to an end short of military showdown, and to act responsibly without regard to what such an end might be called—defeat, surrender, stalemate, or victory.

In a democracy, more than in any other system of government, war must be an extension of politics. Politics must not become an extension of war or of military power.

Tocqueville made at least two other significant observations about war and democracy. A democracy's goal is quick victory, reflecting, he said, the eagerness of democratic men for quick results. "No kind of greatness is more pleasing to the imagination of a democratic people than military greatness which is brilliant and sudden, won without hard work, by risking nothing but one's life." In World War II the desire for quick if not easy victory was manifest in such actions as the Patton drive and the conditions surrounding the use of atomic weapons against the Japanese. The same desire was manifest, but frustrated, during the Vietnam War.

Tocqueville also observed that democracies would find it very difficult to start a war, but also very difficult to end one, and that they would be under pressure to become involved in the wars of other democracies. Democracies, he said, were interdependent, so that "it is almost impossible for two of them to make war in isolation. The interests of all are so much entwined, their opinions and their needs so similar, that no one of them can stay quiet when the rest are in agitation. So wars become rarer, but when they do come about, they spread over a vaster field."

Certainly the United States was slow to enter World War I, and also slow to enter World War II. Yet our involvement in both seems to sustain Tocqueville's judgment that democracies cannot remain quiet when other democracies are involved in war. Making the world safe for democracy became a rallying cry of World War I. And we entered World War II at least partly in the name of democracy and the saving of it. In the

Cold War period, the Tocqueville observations seem to be less accurate. Although the wars have been smaller than world wars, our entrance has been quick and our withdrawal prolonged.

Since democratic wars are in large part ideological, admission of defeat is much more difficult; and a military attitude which will accept something short of total victory is difficult to maintain. Thus the United States, following what was labeled the "loss of China"—after a war in which we were only indirectly involved on the side of the losers—avoided admission of defeat by setting up a government in exile on Taiwan and maintaining it for more than twenty years, while at the same time refusing to acknowledge in diplomacy the existence of mainland China. In much the same way, after the failure of the Bay of Pigs invasion, the United States refused to acknowledge the diplomatic existence of Cuba.

Since World War II, there has been a marked change in the ideological stimulus to American military involvement. Response has been not so much one of democratic identification, but rather a negative response—an anticommunist response. Thus our intervention in the Dominican Republic in 1965 was not justified ideologically as an effort for democratic government, but as a move against communism. Our participation in the 1973 overthrow of the government of Chile, and our support of the takeover by a military junta, was not justified as a move to establish democracy in Chile, but rather as an effort to remove a Marxist government.

A third institutional force which creates problems for American democracy is the corporation, a creature of society which exists as a limited person by virtue of socially approved legal action. Because of the concentration of economic power and the magnitude of such power, because of the limited definition of "person" which constitutes the corporation, because of the diffusion of responsibility, and because of the escape from responsibility which is almost in the nature of the institution, the corporation has become a foreign force in American society. It is a source which is somewhat unmanageable and antidemocratic.

The historically projected process from noncompetitive feudalism to free, competitive capitalism to socialism is not evident. The process has been closer to a circular movement from feudalism to free, competitive capitalism and then back to a more sophisticated and more highly organized corporate feudalism. The new feudalism is not subject to laws designed for the theoretically free and competitive economy. Rather, it lends itself to negotiated settlements among the feudal powers, or between them and the central government. The central government is now democratically elected, in contrast with the kingly government that marked the controlling or arbitrating force in precapitalist feudalism.

The problem is complicated by the existence in a democratic society of the people's power to vote themselves a share of income or property. There has been a progressive removal of people from the traditional—one might say natural—condition of ownership, in which property can be physically defined as land, buildings, livestock, tools, and machinery. In its place there is a removed and documentary ownership, manifest in shares of stock or contracts or union agreements. This change seems to lead to a diminished sense of the rights of ownership and of the traditional claims to ownership (occupancy, prior inheritance, prior claim, and use). And it leads to another step in which the propertyless—the dispossessed or nonpossessors—move to vote themselves an increased share of what is produced by the whole community, without regard to private or state ownership.

Debate over the 1913 income-tax amendment raised the question of whether some persons could be required to pay a progressively higher tax on their income than others, and thus bear a relatively higher burden of support of society. The argument takes on another dimension when a progressive tax is used to raise revenue to provide income to persons who are not on public welfare, but who earn less than other tax-paying citizens. The negative-income-tax proposal, partially incorporated in the 1975 tax law, accepts this principle of redistributing wealth. A relative distinction, which is treated as an absolute, is that as long as redistribution is made from currently earned income (which usually includes income from wages, interest, dividends, and salaries), property is respected. According to this distinction, the danger of taking property without due process arises only when redistribution involves the capital holdings of those who are taxed. There is a warning about this trend in Tocqueville. "The chief and, in a sense, the only condition," Tocqueville wrote, "necessary in order to succeed in centralizing the supreme power in a democratic society is to love equality or to make believe that you do so. Thus the art of despotism, once so complicated, has been simplified; one may almost say that it has been reduced to a single principle."

The situation in England is instructive. A majority of the English people (whether made up of persons traditionally associated with labor or of persons associated with ownership) can vote themselves an increase in income from the income or the capital of the minority. The contest for political control centers in large measure on the issue of how wealth or income is to be shared and what claim that sharing will give to service and consumer satisfactions.

In the United States the contest has not reached that absolute level of showdown. It has been contained within a narrower range: for example, the contest between labor and management; the movement by those whose income depends directly on government payments (such as Civil Service employees, members of the military, and retired persons of both categories) to get increases in their income; and the efforts of those whose income depends in some measure on government policy (farmers, agricultural businesses, and regulated companies such as airlines and railroads) to change government policy so as to gain a larger share of the national income.

The last political test was in the campaign of 1972 when Senator George McGovern, the Democratic candidate, proposed a redistribution of wealth. Senator McGovern called for significant tax increases for the wealthy. At one point he suggested a 100 per cent tax on any inheritance over $500,000; later he retreated from that position and proposed a tax ceiling of 77 per cent on such inheritances. Senator McGovern also proposed abolition of the welfare system, to be followed by an automatic government grant of $1,000 to each American. Persons below the poverty level would keep the entire $1,000, while persons above that level would surrender an increasing share of the grant as their income (and thus their taxes) increased. There was much dispute over whether the very wealthy or the middle class would bear the principal burden of paying for the McGovern proposal.

In any event, the proposal was a factor in Senator McGovern's crushing defeat in the 1972 election.

We are approaching a point where a majority of the registered voters of the country could, if politically united, vote themselves an increase in income out of the earnings or capital of the whole society. The majority includes:

Social Security Recipients	33,000,000
Unemployment Compensation Recipients	8,560,000
Federal Civilian Employees	2,823,000
Federal Retirees	1,644,000
Federal Armed Forces	2,049,000

These groups total over 48,000,000 persons, whereas fewer than 82,000,000 Americans voted for President in 1976. Moreover, the number of people actually receiving significant government benefits is higher than indicated. For example, about 11,000,000 Americans receive benefits under the Aid to Families with Dependent Children Program. While children on welfare cannot vote, their older relatives can. Self-interest might dictate organization of all these groups into a voting bloc—especially if it were to be accepted, rightly or wrongly, that through failure of the economic system the retired were left without adequate support and the younger people were denied opportunity to work and earn a decent income.

Society's position against such majority action has been weakened by the power of eminent domain. This power has been more and more widely used to take private lands for public use or to direct such lands to private uses other than those to which they previously were put. When eminent domain was used chiefly to take land for military bases, government buildings, public roads, and the like, infringement on the sense of property was restricted. But when it was extended to provide right-of-way for corporate railroads, the sense of integrity of ownership was eroded. And when rezoning and increased taxation force land sales, changing concepts of ownership inevitably follow.

Evidence of public uneasiness and doubt about eminent domain was demonstrated during the Great Depression, when railroad right-of-ways, originally granted to the railroads through the exercise of government power, were taken over by the unemployed, by migrant workers, and by drifters seeking work. In the same way, such persons rode free on the railroads, contrary to law. And during the gasoline shortage of 1974, when filling stations closed early, car owners began to park their cars in the driveways of closed stations. This suggested, at least insofar as transportation and the automobile are concerned, a confused idea of where property ends and where use-right begins.

A fourth problem for democratic society, one observed by Tocqueville in its early stages, is the development of political parties. Beyond that, there has been a move away from representative government and an effort to institutionalize the political process in order to make it more workable as society has become more complex.

A significant retreat from representative government was signaled by the 1913 adoption of the Seventeenth Amendment, which provided for popular election of U.S. senators. Previously, senators were selected by men chosen from smaller population groupings within the respective states. (The system was comparable to the Electoral College process, by which electors chosen in the states meet to elect a President.) Party primaries were developed in the same period. In a variety of ways, they made easier a popular judgment on choice of candidates.

More recently, there have been demands for representation at conventions and in party offices on the basis of quotas numerically representing the racial, sexual, and age components of a party. Following the 1968 Democratic national convention, there was agitation for rule changes to insure more accurate representation of party membership at future conventions. A set of guidelines based on physical standards was adopted. By these standards, convention delegates are encouraged or required to reflect a proper ratio of persons based on age, sex, and race of party members. Yet such standards may leave unrepresented individuals or groups whose ideological position cuts across the lines of age, race, and sex. In principle, the perfect quota system would be one which selects delegates at random from among the total party membership. Those so chosen could then be allowed to make decisions for the party on issues and on candidates. A further extension of absolute, equalitarian democracy would be to have the candidates (assuming there was agreement among them on issues) chosen at random as the representatives of the party position.

The government of England, unable or unwilling to decide whether England should stay in the Common Market, presented the matter to the public in a referendum. The people strongly supported membership in the Common Market. The results suggested that the government was more afraid to act as a representative body than it should have been.

In the United States, dissatisfaction with the results of recent presidential elections, following unsatisfactory selection of candidates by the parties, has moved some political leaders to suggest that the solution is to have direct election of the President. Thus they reject the concept of representative government contained in the constitutional provision for the Electoral College.

There are several objections to proposals for direct popular election. The first is that the people might know more about the President than they do in the present system, but they might know even less of the important things that they should know about presidential candidates. Popular judgment of qualifications becomes more difficult as the issues of government become more complex.

A more rational and orderly response would be to perfect the representative process, so that persons better qualified or fully qualified to pass on presidential qualifications would pass that judgment. In the manner set forth in the Electoral College provisions of the Constitution, they would carry their recommendations to a limited constituency, taking responsibility for their recommendations as representatives of a political party or of a candidate, and (if supported in elections) voting their recommendations in the Electoral College.

To make such a process effective, changes in the Electoral College would be necessary. The current practice of having states vote as units in the Electoral College could be abolished. The original justification for the winner-take-all vote was partly political, for the smaller states believed they would have more strength if they voted as units. Moreover, there were cultural, economic, and social differences among the states which could be represented in unit votes. The early justifications no longer are valid. Differences between states have largely disappeared. In general, there are greater differences between blocs within individual states—between urban citizens and rural citizens, for example—than there are between states.

It would be better, in the interest of representative government, if the country were divided into some 2,000 to 2,500 presidential electoral districts. A presidential elector could be chosen by each district. Campaigns within the districts would be much the same as are political contests today. Parties would sponsor electoral candidates; and independent candidates would enter if they could meet reasonable standards for qualification. Runoffs might be necessary, as they are now necessary in some primaries. Each district would have about 100,000 persons, of whom approximately 70,000 might be eligible voters. The expense of campaigning in a unit with so few voters would be minimal. The results could well depend on the voters' confidence in the integrity and good judgment of the elector chosen. The elector probably would be well-known among the small constituency, someone who would be trusted by them and held responsible.

The important political meeting would not be a party convention, but rather the meeting of the Electoral College to choose the President of the United States. The President might be chosen by a straight party vote, if a majority of electors were from one party. On the other hand, he might be chosen by a coalition. But he would be the constitutional President of the country, with all of the constitutional powers to be exercised in a four-year term. The instability of parliamentary government under coalitions would not mark the presidency, since the presidential term is fixed. Partisanship in the Congress and in the presidency could be, if not eliminated, certainly reduced. The cost of campaigning, if the elector in the small district were made the key person, could be greatly reduced. Massive efforts to sell the presidential candidates nationwide would be less likely, and the expensive efforts to carry a whole state would no longer be necessary or profitable.

Overpersonalization of the office might also be less likely; and the consequent disposition on the part of persons, acting either with political motivation or with madness, to assassinate Presidents might decline, if not disappear. It has been a long time since 1812, the last time a British Prime Minister was assassinated, and a long time since there has been an attempt on the life of a Prime Minister. On the other hand, personalized leaders like Charles de Gaulle and recent Presidents of the United States have lived in constant danger of violent attack. Since a majority of Parliament is responsible for the continuation of a Prime Minister in office, the motivation for assassination is slight, because another would be elected in his place by the same members of Parliament. If presidential electors were known and accepted as responsible, the electorate might well blame them for the election of the President, rather than blaming the person chosen. It is unlikely that a madman would move upon a presidential elector.

The fifth serious challenge to the working of American democracy is presented by government agencies, popularly labeled the bureaucracies. The complexity of problems, rapidly changing conditions, leaders' desires to avoid political responsibility, and other factors have resulted in the establishment of special bureaus and agencies which combine legislative, judicial, and executive powers.

It is not wise to generalize about agencies or bureaus of government. Depending on the way in which they are organized, or because of their functions or methods, they vary significantly from one to another. In some the dynamism is internal and quite independent of outside control or direction. Others are a reflection of their directors, as was the case with the FBI under J. Edgar Hoover. Some are inevitably taken over by staff experts, and some become projections of their methodology, as in the case of the CIA. Some tend to become separate societies, relatively free of congressional or presidential or judicial control.

The clearest example of such independence is the Central Intelligence Agency. The Agency was designed principally as an intelligence agency for the executive branch of the government. It was anticipated that Congress would have only minimal knowledge of its operations and minimal control over those operations. It was assumed, however, that the Agency would operate within broad guidelines of national and international policy and would be subject to close executive surveillance. The executive branch soon found it convenient to transfer what should have been State Department operations to the Central Intelligence Agency; because if carried out by the CIA, the operations escaped ordinary congressional and public review and could be conducted by internally determined methods of operation. In the case of the CIA, methods which had been accepted and justified in wartime were transferred to cold war situations and even to standard diplomatic relations. Once the principle of secrecy is accepted, and once it is accepted that an agency can determine its own methodology, the agency tends to take on a life of its own—independent even of the executive branch, which theoretically and by statute is supposed to control it. In its freedom, the agency develops and executes policy quite independently. Recent disclosures of the CIA's role in possible political assassinations, and its possession of dangerous poisons long after it had expressly been ordered not to hold such materials, illustrate the danger of such independence. So do the disclosures that the CIA, specifically directed by statute to limit its operations to foreign intelligence matters, extended them to include domestic intelligence activities.

The Internal Revenue Service raises questions of a somewhat different nature. The search for answers leads to basic constitutional issues of privacy and freedom and due process under the law. The great complexity of American business and income-earning activities argues against a simple internal revenue code; so does the variety and mobility of Americans in locale, occupation, family, and other social relationships. To the extent that tax laws try to reflect this complexity, they must be complex and subtle. When it is impossible to draft laws of that refinement, the recourse is to grant discretionary authority to an agency—in this case, to the Internal Revenue Service.

It is customary, in moments of elation, to speak of the great virtue of the "voluntary" income-tax system of the United States and to compare the responsiveness of American citizens favorably to the response of taxpayers in countries like Italy. The record of response, insofar as records can be compared, does appear to be favorable. But the response should not be called "voluntary," for it is made under most severe threats of government action, both civil and criminal, against any citizen or corporation failing to pay taxes in keeping with IRS determinations. So aggressive is that agency that it has a record of losing only one quarter of the cases which are challenged in court. Yet its aggressiveness is justified as part of the threat which makes the "voluntary" system work. Federal taxation is the one major area of legal conflict in which the principal burden of proof is placed on the citizen who is challenged. It is also the one regular administrative operation (if one considers welfare administration to be irregular) in which privacy is least respected.

Of more limited scope are agencies such as wage/price control boards in which authority is usually shared in feudal or fascist manner among Big Government, Big Business, and Big Labor. Also significant to the economy is the Justice Department's Antitrust Division, which operates under a highly variable and agency-determined set of rules, and the Equal Employment Opportunity Commission, which is charged with enforcing the statute that forbids job discrimination based on race, sex, religion, or national origin.

The ultimate bureaucratizing of democracy was achieved by the 1974 Federal Election Campaign Act, which provided for government financing of presidential campaigns. The conditions for qualifying for such funds were set by law; and a Federal Election Commission, combining legislative, judicial, and executive roles, was set up to administer the law. The combination of roles made the Commission's work a magistrate's proceeding such as Jefferson and other Founding Fathers warned against. The Commission's procedures are like those against which the Declaration of Independence was written in protest.

Bureaucracy in a democracy is near perfection when the political process, through which government officials, policies, and control are to come, is controlled by a bureaucratic creation of the government itself. It is a manifestation of the tyranny of the majority in its purest form—that in which the majority tyrannizes itself.

Source Notes

NOTE: Two abbreviated titles are used extensively in the notes:

Journey: *Journey to America* (Tocqueville's notebooks)
Democracy: *Democracy in America* (Tocqueville's masterpiece)

Page 2   "We are meditating . . ." Gustave de Beaumont, quoted in George Wilson Pierson, *Tocqueville and Beaumont in America* (New York, 1938), pp. 47–48.

3   "It's a collection . . ." Alexis de Tocqueville, quoted ibid., p. 54.

3   ". . . we wandered about . . ." Beaumont, quoted ibid., pp. 54–55.

4   "an excellent man . . ." Tocqueville, quoted ibid., pp. 53–54.

4   "Our food would . . ." Beaumont, quoted ibid., p. 51.

5   "a tremendous steamship . . ." Tocqueville, quoted ibid., p. 55.

9   "One saw no oars . . ." Tocqueville, quoted ibid., p. 269.

10   "Nothing is more comfortable . . ." *Journey*, p. 210.

11   "Tocqueville and I . . ." Beaumont, quoted in Pierson, p. 547.

12   "All Jackson men . . ." Ronald E. Shaw, *Erie Water West* (Lexington, KY, 1966), p. 210.

17   "twenty very neat . . ." Tocqueville, quoted in Pierson, p. 246.

17   "these flowered wildernesses" Tocqueville, quoted ibid., p. 253.

17   "tranquil admiration . . ." Ibid.

18   "cut by hills . . ." Ibid.

18 "A majestic order . . ." Ibid., p. 262.

19 "In a few years . . ." Ibid., p. 278.

21 "the noble savage" John Dryden, *Almanzor and Almahide or, the Conquest of Granada by the Spaniards,* Part 1, Act 1, Scene 1.

21 "I was expecting . . ." *Journey,* pp. 203–4.

21 "small in stature . . ." Ibid.

22 "Having wandered . . ." Ibid., p. 205.

22 "When we got back . . ." Ibid., pp. 205–6.

23 "The record does not . . ." *F.P.C.* v. *Tuscarora Indian Nation,* 362 U.S. 99 (1960), 142.

25 "No, no . . ." Quoted in Pierson, p. 252.

25 "would rather live . . ." Quoted ibid., p. 255.

25 "the propriety of . . ." *Messages and Papers of the Presidents* (New York, 1897), Vol. 3, p. 1021.

27 "studded with cities . . ." Ibid., p. 1084.

27 "ranged by . . ." Ibid.

28 "they were inclined . . ." Edwin Arthur Miles, *Jacksonian Democracy in Mississippi* (Chapel Hill, NC, 1960), p. 69.

29 "a large troupe . . ." Tocqueville, quoted in Pierson, p. 595.

29 "The Chactas . . ." Ibid., p. 597.

29 "But we had . . ." Ibid., pp. 597–98.

30 "Brandy is the . . ." Sam Houston, quoted in *Journey,* p. 256.

30 "My view . . ." Ibid., p. 253.

30 "From whatever angle . . ." *Democracy,* pp. 338–39.

31 "Hear me . . ." Chief Joseph, quoted in Dee Brown, *Bury My Heart at Wounded Knee* (New York, 1970), p. 329.

33 "While tales of . . ." Murray L. Wax, *Indian Americans* (Englewood Cliffs, NJ, 1971), p. 67.

33 "It is the policy . . ." Quoted in U. S. Bureau of Indian Affairs, *Federal Indian Policies* (Washington, DC, 1975), p. 10.

34 "an important . . ." *Public Papers of the Presidents: Richard Nixon, 1973* (Washington, DC, 1975), p. 1023.

34 "Because termination is . . ." *Public Papers of the Presidents: Richard Nixon, 1970* (Washington, DC, 1971), p. 567.

37 "There is a law . . ." *Journey,* p. 255.

37 "The progress . . ." Quoted in Bureau of Indian Affairs, p. 10.

38 "New Directions" Ibid.
38 "New Trail" Ibid.
38 "equal citizenship . . ." Ibid.
38 "that the civilization . . ." Quoted ibid., p. 3.
38 "But to deny . . ." Ibid.
39 "The Pilgrims . . ." Sidney E. Mead, *The Lively Experiment* (New York, 1963), p. 4.
39 "There is no . . ." Stephen Vincent Benét, *Western Star*, quoted ibid.
39 "When I stood . . ." Francis Parkman, *The Oregon Trail*, quoted ibid.
39 "In all the . . ." Ibid., p. 5.
39 "Perhaps the Indians . . ." Bernard De Voto, *Across the Wide Missouri*, quoted ibid.
40 "New beginnings . . ." Quoted in "Indian Culture Hurt by Missions," Washington *Post*, May 2, 1975.
40 "demands appreciation . . ." (and subsequent quotations in same paragraph). Ibid.
43 "The law with us . . ." Quoted in *Journey*, p. 233.
43 "We try . . ." Quoted ibid., p. 91.
43 "I am very . . ." Ibid., p. 234.
43 "We do not . . ." Quoted ibid., p. 93.
43 "the Negro . . ." *Democracy*, p. 317.
44 "From birth . . ." Ibid., p. 319.
44 "have, if I may . . ." Ibid., p. 361.
44 "hardly recognized . . ." Ibid., p. 342.
44 "but customs . . ." Ibid., p. 343.
44 "In the South . . ." Ibid.
44 "will be no more . . ." Ibid., p. 351.
45 "the Negroes and . . ." Ibid., p. 355.
45 "leaving the Negroes . . ." Ibid., p. 358.
45 "the Negro race . . ." Ibid., p. 360.
46 "Either the slave . . ." Ibid., p. 363.
47 "Almost all . . ." *Journey*, p. 282.
47 "on the left bank . . ." *Democracy*, p. 346.
47 "No family . . ." Ibid., p. 375.
48 "In almost all . . ." Ibid., p. 343.
54 "I doubt . . ." Ibid., p. 96.
54 "In Europe . . ." Ibid.
55 "seemed to become . . ." Ibid., p. 250.
55 "that almost all . . ." (and subsequent quotations in same paragraph). Ibid., p. 225.

56 "In locking . . ." *On the Penitentiary System in the United States and Its Application to France*, p. 13.

57 "tracts containing . . ." Ibid., p. 51.

58 "experience alone . . ." Ibid., p. 52.

59 "At Auburn . . ." Ibid., p. 46.

60 "And before . . ." Ibid., p. 32.

61 "the smallest . . ." Ibid., p. 102.

61 "effective influence . . ." Quoted in *Journey*, p. 5.

61 "hardened" Quoted ibid.

61 "There were outcries . . ." Quoted ibid., p. 7.

61 "French prisons . . ." Ibid.

62 "often ineffective . . ." Ibid., p. 8.

62 "When Beaumont and Tocqueville . . ." Göran Printz-Påhlson, translated by Siv Cedering Fox, in *First Issue*, 1972.

63 "partisans did little . . ." David J. Rothman, *The Discovery of the Asylum* (Boston, 1971), p. 88.

63 "prison labor never . . ." Ibid., p. 104.

65 "cruel and unusual punishments" Eighth Amendment, U. S. Constitution.

66 "is overwhelmed . . ." Bernard Weiner, "The Clockwork Cure," *The Nation*, April 3, 1972, p. 434.

66 "reports out of . . ." Ibid.

67 "defective delinquents" "Md. Body Votes Patuxent Reform Bill," Washington *Post*, March 24, 1977.

68 "dormitory housing . . ." American Friends Service Committee, *Struggle for Justice* (New York, 1971), p. 33.

70 "I have studied . . ." U. S. Senate, Committee on the Judiciary, Subcommittee on National Penitentiaries, *Oversight Hearings on the Nature and Effectiveness of the Rehabilitation Programs of the U. S. Bureau of Prisons*, June 13–14, 1972, p. 53.

73 "it is not possible . . ." Thomas More, *The Utopia of Sir Thomas More*, edited by Mildred Campbell (New York, 1947), p. 61.

74 "is one of the things . . ." (and subsequent quotations in same paragraph). *Journey*, pp. 109–10.

74 "I do not believe . . ." Quoted ibid., p. 214.

75 "is indispensable . . ." Quoted ibid., p. 54.

75 "Religion regards . . ." *Democracy*, p. 47.

75 "Freedom sees . . ." Ibid.

75   "all Familists, Antinomians . . ." Nathaniel Ward, quoted in Mead, p. 13.

75   "The Jurisdiction . . ." John Cotton, quoted ibid.

76   "In the camp meeting . . ." Cushing Strout, *The New Heavens and New Earth* (New York, 1974), p. 106.

77   "'I am convinced . . .'" Joel Poinsett, quoted in *Journey*, p. 271.

78   "All sects are united . . ." Quoted ibid., p. 17.

78   "All the clergy . . ." *Democracy*, p. 449.

78   "They try to improve . . ." Ibid.

79   "The Indian . . ." *Journey*, p. 396.

79   "American civil religion" Russell E. Richey and Donald G. Jones, *American Civil Religion* (New York, 1974).

79   "The religious atmosphere . . ." *Democracy*, p. 295.

79–80   "Now it matters . . ." Jean Jacques Rousseau, *The Social Contract,* translated by G. D. H. Cole (Chicago, 1952), pp. 438–39.

80   "the American . . ." Will Herberg, "America's Civil Religion: What It Is and Whence It Comes," in Richey and Jones, p. 77.

80   "It is an organic . . ." Ibid., pp. 77–78.

81   "God sifted . . ." William Stoughton, quoted in Robert N. Bellah, *The Broken Covenant* (New York, 1975), pp. 41–42.

81   "Know this . . ." Edward Johnson, quoted in Eugene J. McCarthy, *Frontiers in American Democracy* (Cleveland, 1960), p. 47.

81   "Almighty Being . . ." George Washington, quoted in Robert N. Bellah, "Civil Religion in America," in Richey and Jones, p. 27.

81   "Invisible Hand" Ibid., p. 28.

81   "propitious smiles . . ." Ibid.

81   "I shall need . . ." Thomas Jefferson, quoted ibid., pp. 28–29.

82   "They came here . . ." *Public Papers of the Presidents: Lyndon B. Johnson, 1965* (Washington, DC, 1966), Book I, p. 72.

82   "Above the pyramid . . ." Ibid., p. 287.

82   "reads like a supplement . . ." William J. Wolf, "Abraham Lincoln and Calvinism," in George L. Hunt, ed., *Calvinism and the Political Order* (Philadelphia, 1965), pp. 155–56.

82   "loss of China" Dwight D. Eisenhower, quoted in William

Lee Miller, *Piety Along the Potomac* (Boston, 1964), p. 36.

82 "scandal-a-day" Ibid.

83 "only men . . ." Adlai E. Stevenson II, quoted in McCarthy, p. 51.

83 "Remember your own . . ." Dwight D. Eisenhower, quoted ibid.

83 "make a settlement . . ." Quoted ibid.

83 "future of all . . ." Joseph Martin, quoted ibid., pp. 51–52.

83 "One might say . . ." Miller, p. 34.

83 "Almighty God . . ." *Public Papers of the Presidents: Dwight D. Eisenhower, 1953* (Washington, DC, 1960), p. 1.

84 "is the mightiest . . ." Dwight D. Eisenhower, quoted in Martin E. Marty, "Two Kinds of Two Kinds of Civil Religion," in Richey and Jones, p. 147.

84 "Carpenters raced . . ." New York *Times*, January 19, 1953.

84 "The greatest demonstration . . ." Elmer Davis, quoted in Miller, p. 42.

85 "Whatever issue . . ." John F. Kennedy, text of speech printed in *U.S. News & World Report*, September 26, 1960, p. 75.

85 "before you and . . ." *Public Papers of the Presidents: John F. Kennedy, 1961* (Washington, DC, 1962), p. 1.

85 "that the rights . . ." Ibid.

85 "asking His blessing . . ." Ibid., p. 3.

86 "appropriates the vocabulary . . ." Charles B. Henderson, Jr., quoted in Marty, "Two Kinds of Two Kinds of Civil Religion," in Richey and Jones, p. 152.

87 "are a religious people . . ." Justice William O. Douglas, majority opinion in *Zorach v. Clauson*, 343 U.S. 306 (1952), 313.

88 "for the majority . . ." Quoted in *Journey*, p. 61.

88 "a profound indifference . . ." Quoted ibid., p. 70.

88 "bad taste" Miller, p. 47.

88 "vicious smear" Ibid.

88 "When God puts . . ." Ibid.

88 "such a cultural thing . . ." Mark O. Hatfield, quoted in Washington *Post*, May 3, 1974.

88 "They see . . ." Ibid.

89 "by the Christian community . . ." Ibid.

91 "I cannot help . . ." Leo Rosten, *Religions of America* (New York, 1975), pp. 20–21.

92 "prepares a people . . ." *Democracy*, p. 444.

92 "Every religion . . ." Ibid., pp. 444–45.

92 "will never succeed . . ." Ibid., p. 448.

96 "nation with the soul . . ." G. K. Chesterton, *What I Saw in America* (London, 1922), p. 12.

97 "The most extraordinary . . ." *Democracy*, p. 280.

98 "the land never . . ." *Journey*, p. 82.

98–99 "It is unusual . . ." *Democracy*, p. 554.

99 "the last trace . . ." Ibid., p. 54.

99–100 "In Philadelphia . . ." Edward Pessen, *Jacksonian America* (Homewood, IL, 1969), p. 116.

101 "It is acknowledged . . ." *Democracy*, p. 555.

101 "Hence, just while . . ." Ibid., pp. 556–57.

102 "no solidarity . . ." Ibid., p. 557.

102 "generally speaking . . ." Ibid., p. 558.

102 "When a workman . . ." Ibid., p. 555.

102 "What is one . . ." Ibid.

102 "is permanently . . ." Ibid., pp. 555–56.

102 "The territorial . . ." Ibid., pp. 557–58.

103 "What is one . . ." Ibid., p. 555.

103 "no subsidies" (and subsequent quotations in same paragraph). *Journey*, p. 287.

104 "The number of . . ." Ibid., p. 242.

104 "We are multiplying . . ." James Kent, quoted ibid., p. 243.

106 "beyond the time . . ." *Oddie v. Ross Gear and Tool Company*, 195 F. Supp. 826 (1961), 831.

106 "apply to . . ." Ibid.

106 "an obligation . . ." Ibid.

106 "In the process . . ." Richard J. Barnet and Ronald E. Müller, *Global Reach* (New York, 1974), p. 15.

109 "Pervading all nature . . ." Herbert Spencer, *Social Statics* (New York, 1866), pp. 352–55.

114 "to Maine" Philip Booth, "Maine," in his *The Islanders* (New York, 1961), p. 52.

114 "Man as a cog . . ." Erich Fromm, *The Revolution of Hope* (New York, 1968), p. 38.

117 "whether these . . ." Quoted in Anton-Hermann Chroust, *The Rise of the Legal Profession in America* (Norman, OK, 1965), Vol. 2, pp. 57–58.

117   "sprung from . . ." (and subsequent quotations in same paragraph). Quoted ibid., p. 60.

119   "who does justice . . ." Quoted ibid., p. 31.

119   "sentinels upon . . ." Quoted ibid., p. 82.

119   "no nobler end . . ." Ibid.

119   "the common . . ." *Enactments by the Rector and Visitors of the University of Virginia, 1825,* quoted ibid., p. 187.

119–20   "We must be . . ." Thomas Jefferson, letter of February 17, 1826, to James Madison, in *The Writings of Thomas Jefferson* (Washington, DC, 1903), Vol. 16, p. 156.

121   "Born among . . ." *Journey,* p. 320.

121   "are often defective . . ." *Democracy,* p. 231.

121   "In general . . ." Ibid., p. 232.

121   "that government . . ." Slogan quoted by Henry David Thoreau in the first sentence of his essay "Civil Disobedience."

121   "The law . . ." *Journey,* p. 233.

121   "In the new . . ." *Democracy,* p. 225.

121   "duels are still . . ." Ibid.

122   "not only . . ." Ibid., p. 241.

122   "In the United States . . ." Ibid., p. 240.

122   "There is hardly . . ." Ibid., p. 270.

122   "may be said . . ." Ibid., p. 150.

122   "The peace . . ." Ibid.

123   "if ever . . ." Ibid., p. 151.

123   "pack the court" James MacGregor Burns, *Roosevelt: The Lion and the Fox* (New York, 1956), p. 294.

123   "Private rights . . ." Ibid., p. 698.

125   "the American judge . . ." Ibid., p. 276.

126   "Our judges . . ." Albert Gallatin, quoted in *Journey,* p. 4.

130   "pay a price" *Public Papers of the Presidents: Richard Nixon, 1972* (Washington, DC, 1974), p. 987.

130   "The jurors . . ." Quoted in *Journey,* pp. 104–5.

130   "regarded as one . . ." *Democracy,* p. 273.

130–31   "I think . . ." Ibid., p. 275.

131   "I do not . . ." Ibid.

131   "hidden at . . ." Ibid., p. 264.

131   "instinctive preference . . ." Ibid.

136   "Subscribers who have . . ." Quoted in Louis W. Doll, *A History of the Newspapers of Ann Arbor, 1829–1920* (Detroit, 1959), p. 17.

138   "In America . . ." *Journey,* p. 286.

138   "and almost always . . ." Ibid., p. 281.

138   "these men . . ." Ibid., p. 283.

139   "PRISON DISCIPLINE . . ." Detroit *Courier*, June 23,
      1831.

139   "the editor . . ." Richard Hooker, *The Story of an Inde-
      pendent Newspaper* (New York, 1924), p. 16.

140–41 "To say the least . . ." Abraham Lincoln, letter of Febru-
      ary 25, 1847, to Andrew Johnston, in *The Collected Works
      of Abraham Lincoln* (New Brunswick, NJ, 1953), Vol. 1, p.
      392.

141   "Generally American journalists . . ." *Democracy*, p. 185.

141   "In America . . ." Ibid., pp. 183–84.

141   "It is pitiful . . ." *Journey*, p. 172.

141   "The hallmark . . ." *Democracy*, p. 185.

142   "destructive tastes" Ibid., p. 182.

142   "violence" Ibid.

143   "Take it to . . ." William L. Rivers, *The Opinion Makers*
      (Boston, 1967), p. 6.

143   "Give it to . . ." Ibid.

143   "reading more . . ." *Public Papers of the Presidents: John
      F. Kennedy, 1962* (Washington, DC, 1963), p. 376.

143   "Anybody may take . . ." *Democracy*, p. 185.

143   "it gratuitously . . ." Quoted in *Journey*, p. 13.

143   "Once the American . . ." *Democracy*, p. 186.

143–44 "It has been . . ." Ibid., p. 187.

144   "an oppressed citizen . . ." Ibid., p. 697.

144   "To cull . . ." Ibid., p. 183.

146   "For one thing . . ." John Kenneth Galbraith, "Grump's
      Fourth Law of Politics and Other Reasons Why We're So
      Confused," *New York*, May 22, 1972.

148   "Grey-jawed . . ." Jay Meek, "Massacre of the Villagers,"
      Poetry Northwest, Spring 1971, p. 40.

149   "Our reporters . . ." Richard S. Salant, quoted in Edward
      Jay Epstein, *News from Nowhere* (New York, 1973), p. ix.

149–50 "The newspaper . . ." Elmer Lower, quoted ibid., p. 44.

153   "the most natural . . ." *Democracy*, p. 193.

153   "Therefore the right . . ." Ibid.

153   "To make festivities . . ." Ibid., p. 189.

153   "to combat . . ." Ibid.

153   "If some obstacle . . ." Ibid.

157   "public interest" Ralph Nader et al., *Action for a Change*
      (New York, 1971), p. 86.

157   "private or special interests" Ibid., p. 6.

159–60   "Buttons, buttons . . ." Based on Andrei Voznesensky's "American Buttons," in his *Dogalypse: San Francisco Poetry Reading* (San Francisco, 1972), pp. 17–19; and "The Buttons of New York," in his *Little Woods* (Melbourne, n.d.), pp. 42–43.

162   "To take . . ." *Democracy*, p. 243.

162   "But if . . ." Ibid.

162   "Taxation without . . ." James Otis, as paraphrased by William Tudor, *The Life of James Otis* (1823; reprint ed. New York, 1970), p. 77.

163   "Tyranny begins . . ." Nathaniel Macon, quoted in Arthur M. Schlesinger, Jr., *The Age of Jackson* (Boston, 1945), p. 28.

163   "No sooner . . ." *Democracy*, p. 242.

164   "As the election . . ." Ibid., p. 135.

164   "The President . . ." Ibid.

164   "in the United States . . ." Ibid.

166   "corrupt bargain . . ." Marquis James, *The Life of Andrew Jackson* (Indianapolis, 1938), p. 442.

166   "So you see . . ." Andrew Jackson, letter of February 14, 1825, to William B. Lewis, in *Correspondence of Andrew Jackson* (Washington, 1928), Vol. 3, p. 276.

167   "America has had . . ." *Democracy*, p. 175.

168   "they managed things . . ." *Journey*, p. 64.

168   "Tariff oppressive . . ." Ibid., p. 180.

168   "Lacking great . . ." *Democracy*, p. 177.

168   "the ambitious . . ." Ibid.

168   "are an evil . . ." Ibid., p. 174.

168   "Small parties . . ." Ibid., p. 175.

169   "men of integrity . . ." *Journey*, p. 251.

169   "I cannot conceive . . ." Ibid.

169   "are held by . . ." Ibid., pp. 2–3.

169   "is a man . . ." *Democracy*, p. 278.

169   "common among . . ." Ibid., p. 197.

169   "seldom summoned . . ." Ibid.

169   "eloquent advocates . . ." Ibid., p. 201.

169   "how low . . ." *Journey*, pp. 267–68.

170   "in an often unequal . . ." *Democracy*, p. 179.

170   "show themselves . . ." Ibid., p. 497.

170   "drives to despair . . ." Ibid., p. 499.

171   "are frequently . . ." Ibid.

171   "they bear witness . . ." Ibid., p. 500.

171   "My opponent . . ." Quoted in *Journey*, pp. 74–75.

171   "in the West . . ." Quoted in *Journey*, p. 88.

171   "must descend . . ." Ibid., p. 268.

171   "dismissed 1,200 officials . . ." Quoted ibid., p. 90.

173   "To whip up . . ." Robert V. Remini, *The Election of Andrew Jackson* (Philadelphia, 1963), p. 111.

181   "How can one . . ." *Journey*, p. 158.

182   "Young Hickory" James, pp. 772, 775, 779.

182   "King Andrew I" Ibid., illustration facing p. 545.

182   "As in bygone times . . ." Ibid., p. 768.

183   "Its interior . . ." Gustave de Beaumont, quoted in Pierson, p. 664.

186   "Sir, of what use . . ." *Register of Debates*, 23rd Cong., 1st Sess., June 19, 1834.

187   "uncertainty and ineptitude . . ." John J. Rhodes, quoted in Washington *Post*, October 24, 1977.

187   "Nothing really has . . ." Ibid.

188   "Well: John Marshall . . ." Andrew Jackson, quoted in Horace Greeley, *The American Conflict* (Hartford, 1864), Vol. 1, p. 106.

189   "The naval force . . ." Levi Woodbury, "Annual Report of the Secretary of the Navy, Showing the Condition of the Navy in the Year 1831," in *American State Papers* (Washington, DC, 1861), Class VI: Naval Affairs, Vol. 4, p. 6.

189   "the Senate . . ." *Democracy*, p. 121.

189   "it cannot force . . ." Ibid.

191   "Of all the factors . . ." George E. Reedy, "Faceless Agents of Power," *The Nation*, January 1, 1973, p. 8.

192   "the Presidential position . . ." Ibid.

192   "That is why . . ." Ibid.

197   "Intrigue and corruption . . ." *Democracy*, p. 136.

197   "In the first . . ." Ibid.

198   "is much more . . ." Ibid., p. 108.

198   "high crimes" U. S. Constitution, Article II, Section 4.

198   "Great criminals . . ." *Democracy*, p. 110.

198   "ordinary men . . ." Ibid.

198   "No one has . . ." Ibid., p. 128.

201   "a negotiation . . ." Ibid., p. 131.

202   "American policy . . ." Ibid.

202   "consists much more . . ." Ibid., p. 228.

202   "difficult to co-ordinate . . ." Ibid., p. 229.

202 "has little capacity . . ." Ibid.

204 "that army consists . . ." Ibid., p. 126.

204 "How wonderful . . ." Ibid., p. 170.

204 "become the leading . . ." Ibid., p. 407.

204 "are born to rule . . ." Ibid.

205 "For armies are . . ." Ibid., p. 649.

205 "In the councils . . ." *Public Papers of the Presidents: Dwight D. Eisenhower, 1960–61* (Washington, DC, 1961), p. 1038.

206 "Missile gap" Theodore C. Sorenson, *Kennedy* (New York, 1965), pp. 610–14.

207 "ardently long . . ." *Democracy*, p. 647.

207 "because war makes . . ." Ibid.

207 "a little nation apart . . ." Ibid., p. 648.

208 "Pax Americana" U. S. Senate, Committee on Foreign Relations, *Hearings on Defense Department Sponsored Foreign Affairs Research,* Part 2, May 28, 1968, pp. 32–39.

209 "Although war satisfies . . ." *Democracy*, p. 649.

209 "Any long war . . ." Ibid., pp. 649–50.

210 "Once you have . . ." Ibid., p. 651.

210–11 "the burden . . ." Ibid., p. 651.

211 "a democratic government . . ." Ibid., pp. 651–52.

211–12 "In democracies . . ." Ibid., p. 652.

212 "finally becomes . . ." Ibid., pp. 648–49.

212 "But that is not . . ." Ibid., p. 651.

213 "No kind of . . ." Ibid., pp. 657–58.

213 "it is almost . . ." Ibid., p. 660.

215 "The chief . . ." Ibid., pp. 678–79.

Bibliography

"After a Rash of Take-Overs, New Worries About 'Press Lords.'" *U.S. News & World Report,* January 24, 1977.

Albion, Robert Greenhalgh. *Square-Riggers on Schedule: The New York Sailing Packets to England, France, and the Cotton Ports.* Archon Books, 1965 [first published in Princeton, NJ: Princeton University Press, 1938].

Alexander, Shana. "End of an Era?" *Newsweek,* May 12, 1975.

American Friends Service Committee. *Struggle for Justice.* New York: Hill & Wang, 1971.

Atkins, Burton M., and Harry R. Glick, ed. *Prisons, Protest, and Politics.* Englewood Cliffs, NJ: Prentice-Hall, Inc., 1972.

Bagdikian, Ben H., and Leon Dash. *The Shame of the Prisons.* New York: Pocket Books, 1972.

Bailey, Thomas A. *A Diplomatic History of the American People,* 8th ed. New York: Appleton-Century-Crofts, 1969.

Barnes, Peter, and Larry Casalino. *Who Owns the Land? A Primer on Land Reform in the USA.* Berkeley: The Center for Rural Studies, 1972.

Barnet, Richard J., and Ronald E. Müller. *Global Reach.* New York: Simon and Schuster, 1974.

Barnett, Stephen R. "Merger, Monopoly and a Free Press." *The Nation,* January 15, 1973.

Bateman, Carroll. *The Baltimore and Ohio: The Story of the Railroad That Grew Up with the United States.* Baltimore: Baltimore & Ohio Railroad Printing Plant, 1951.

Beaumont, Gustave de, and Alexis de Tocqueville. *On the Penitentiary System in the United States and Its Application to France.* Trans. by Francis Lieber. New York: Augustus M. Kelley, Publishers, 1970 [first published in Philadelphia: Carey, Lea & Blanchard, 1833].

Bellah, Robert N. *The Broken Covenant: American Civil Religion in Time of Trial*. New York: The Seabury Press, 1975.

Berger, Peter L., et al. "An Appeal for Theological Affirmation." *Worldview*, April 1975.

Berrigan, Philip. *Prison Journals of a Priest Revolutionary*. Comp. & ed. by Vincent McGee. New York: Holt, Rinehart & Winston, 1970.

Berry, Leonard J. *Prison*. Ed. by Jamie Shalleck. New York: Grossman, 1972.

"Big Money Hunts for Independent Newspapers." *Business Week*, February 21, 1977.

Binkley, Wilfred E. *American Political Parties: Their Natural History*, 4th ed. New York: Alfred A. Knopf, 1962.

Bishop, Robert L. "The Profits of Fusion," *The Nation*, May 8, 1972.

Bleyer, Willard Grosvenor. *Main Currents in the History of American Journalism*. Boston: Houghton Mifflin Co., 1927.

Bottini, Domenick A., et al., ed. *1977 Editor & Publisher International Year Book*. New York: Editor & Publisher Co., Inc., 1977.

Bowen, Frank C. *A Century of Atlantic Travel: 1830–1930*. Boston: Little, Brown & Co., 1930.

Brown, Dee. *Bury My Heart at Wounded Knee*. New York: Holt, Rinehart & Winston, 1970.

Burger, Warren E. "Incompetence in the Courtroom." *Intellectual Digest*, April 1974.

Cavan, Ruth Shonle. *Criminology*, 3rd ed. New York: Thomas Y. Crowell Co., 1962.

Chapman, William. "Native Americans' New Clout." *The Progressive*, August 1977.

Chesterton, G. K. *What I Saw in America*. London: Hodder & Stoughton, 1922.

Chroust, Anton-Hermann. *The Rise of the Legal Profession in America*, Vol. 2. Norman, OK: University of Oklahoma Press, 1965.

Chute, Marchette. *The First Liberty: A History of the Right to Vote in America, 1619–1850*. New York: E. P. Dutton & Co., 1969.

Clark, William H. *Railroads and Rivers: The Story of Inland Transportation*. Boston: L. C. Page & Co., 1939.

Cohen, Felix S. *The Legal Conscience*. Ed. by Lucy K. Cohen. New Haven: Yale University Press, 1960.

Cole, Donald B. *Jacksonian Democracy in New Hampshire, 1800–1851*. Cambridge: Harvard University Press, 1970.

Commons, John R., et al. *History of Labour in the United States*, Vol. 1. New York: The Macmillan Co., 1918.

Conrad, Alfred H., et al. "Slavery as an Obstacle to Economic Growth in the United States: A Panel Discussion." *Journal of Economic History*, December 1967.

Cronin, Thomas E. "Putting the President Back into Politics." *Washington Monthly*, September 1973.

———. "The Swelling of the Presidency." *Saturday Review of the Society*, February 1973.

Damon, Allan L. "Presidential Expenses." *American Heritage*, June 1974.

David, Paul T., et al. "Origins of the National Convention System." *The Politics of National Party Conventions*. Washington: The Brookings Institution, 1960.

Debo, Angie. *A History of the Indians of the United States*. Norman, OK: University of Oklahoma Press, 1970.

Deloria, Vine, Jr. *Custer Died for Your Sins: An Indian Manifesto*. New York: The Macmillan Co., 1969.

Denniston, Lyle. "Disputes Worry Justices." Washington *Star*, May 26, 1975.

Disco, Sally, and Susan Meyers. "Legal Supermarkets." *Harper's*, July 1973.

Doll, Louis W. *A History of the Newspapers of Ann Arbor, 1829–1920*. Detroit: Wayne State University Press, 1959.

Driver, Harold E. *Indians of North America*. Chicago: University of Chicago Press, 1961.

Dunbar, Seymour. *A History of Travel in America*, Vols. 2 & 3. Indianapolis: The Bobbs-Merrill Co., 1915.

Dupuy, E. Ernest. *The Compact History of the United States Army*. New York: Hawthorn Books, Inc., 1961.

Duscha, Julius. "A Free and Accessible Press." *The Progressive*, January 1974.

Eaton, Clement. *Henry Clay and the Art of American Politics*. Boston: Little, Brown & Co., 1957.

Emery, Edwin. *The Press and America: An Interpretative History of the Mass Media*, 3rd ed. Englewood Cliffs, NJ: Prentice-Hall, Inc., 1972.

Epstein, Edward Jay. *News from Nowhere: Television and the News*. New York: Random House, 1973.

Etzioni, Amitai. "A Nation of (Too Many) Laws." Washington *Post*, January 12, 1975.

Evans, Eldon Cobb. *A History of the Australian Ballot System in the United States.* Chicago: University of Chicago Press, 1917.

Filler, Louis. *The Crusade Against Slavery, 1830–1860.* New York: Harper & Brothers, 1960.

Fisk, Margaret, ed. *Encyclopedia of Associations,* Vol. 1. Detroit: Gale Research Co., 1977.

Footlick, Jerrold K. "Do-It-Yourself Lawyers." *Newsweek,* June 16, 1975.

Foreman, Grant. *Indian Removal: The Emigration of the Five Civilized Tribes of Indians.* Norman, OK: University of Oklahoma Press, 1932.

Franklin, John Hope. *From Slavery to Freedom: A History of Negro Americans,* 4th ed. New York: Alfred A. Knopf, 1977.

Frazier, E. Franklin. *Black Bourgeoisie: The Rise of a New Middle Class in the United States.* New York: Collier Books, 1962.

Freund, Paul A. "Public Aid to Parochial Schools." *Harvard Law Review,* June 1969.

Friedman, Lawrence M. *A History of American Law.* New York: Simon and Schuster, 1973.

Fritsch, Albert J. *The Contrasumers: A Citizen's Guide to Resource Conservation.* New York & Washington: Praeger Publishers, 1974.

Fromm, Erich. *The Revolution of Hope: Toward a Humanized Technology.* New York: Harper & Row, 1968.

Galbraith, John Kenneth. "Grump's Fourth Law of Politics and Other Reasons Why We're So Confused." *New York,* May 22, 1972.

Gammon, Samuel R., Jr. *The Presidential Campaign of 1832.* New York: Da Capo Press, 1969 [first published in Baltimore: The Johns Hopkins Press, 1922].

"Getting There Is Half the Fun." *U.S. News & World Report,* May 16, 1977.

Geyer, Alan F. *Piety and Politics: American Protestantism in the World Arena.* Richmond: John Knox Press, 1963.

Gilmore, Grant. "The Storrs Lectures: The Age of Anxiety." *Yale Law Journal,* Vol. 84, 1975.

Goldfarb, Ronald L., and Linda R. Singer. *After Conviction.* New York: Simon and Schuster, 1973.

Goodwin, Richard N. "Clipping White House Wings." *Washington Post,* March 17, 1974.

Granito, Anthony R. *A Fire Officer's Guide: Company Leadership and Operations.* Boston: National Fire Protection Association, 1975.

Green, Mark J. "The Ethics of Powerlaw." *Newsweek,* June 16, 1975.

Hamilton, John Maxwell. "Ombudsmen for the Press." *The Nation,* March 16, 1974.

Hanlon, William T. "Whose Ox Was Gored at Wounded Knee?" *America,* March 16, 1974.

Hanson, Robert P., ed. *Moody's Industrial Manual.* New York: Moody's Investors Service, Inc., 1977.

Herman, Edward S. "The Income Counter-Revolution." *Commonweal,* January 3, 1975.

Hertzberg, Hazel W. *The Search for an American Indian Identity: Modern Pan-Indian Movements.* Syracuse: Syracuse University Press, 1971.

Heyl, Erik. *Early American Steamers,* Vol. 2. Buffalo: Erik Heyl, 1956.

Hofstadter, Richard. *The Idea of a Party System: The Rise of Legitimate Opposition in the United States, 1780–1840.* Berkeley and Los Angeles: The University of California Press, 1969.

Hooker, Richard. *The Story of an Independent Newspaper: One Hundred Years of the Springfield Republican, 1824–1924.* New York: The Macmillan Co., 1924.

Hugins, Walter. *Jacksonian Democracy and the Working Class: A Study of the New York Workingmen's Movement, 1829–1837.* Stanford, CA: Stanford University Press, 1960.

Hunt, George L., ed. *Calvinism and the Political Order.* Philadelphia: The Westminster Press, 1965.

Hunter, Louis C. *Steamboats on the Western Rivers: An Economic and Technological History.* New York: Octagon Books, 1969 [first published in Cambridge, MA: Harvard University Press, 1949].

Hyer, Marjorie. "From Pulpit, Sen. Hatfield Calls on Nation to Repent." Washington *Post,* May 3, 1974.

Irwin, John. *The Felon.* Englewood Cliffs, NJ: Prentice-Hall, Inc., 1970.

Jackson, George. *Soledad Brother: The Prison Letters of George Jackson,* 2nd ed. New York: Bantam Books, 1972.

Jacob, Herbert. *Justice in America: Courts, Lawyers, and the Judicial Process.* Boston: Little, Brown & Co., 1972.

James, Marquis. *The Life of Andrew Jackson.* Indianapolis and New York: The Bobbs-Merrill Co., 1938.

Johnson, Haynes. "The Press: A Lack of Vigor." Washington *Post,* June 24, 1973.

Jones, Archer, and Paul H. Hoepner. "The South's Economic Investment in Slavery." *The American Journal of Economics and Sociology,* July 1967.

Jones, William H., and Laird Anderson. "Press Concentration" and

"Owners of 2 or More Daily Papers." Washington *Post*, July 24, 1977.

Kennedy, John F. Speech in Houston, TX, September 12, 1960, reprinted in *U.S. News & World Report*, September 26, 1960.

Kobre, Sidney. *Foundations of American Journalism*. Westport, CT: Greenwood Press, 1970 [first published in Tallahassee, FL: Florida State University, 1958].

Kuh, Richard H. "Mediocrity on Olympus: The Politics of Criminal Justice." *The New Leader*, January 8, 1973.

Lapham, Lewis H. "The Temptation of a Sacred Cow." *Harper's*, August 1973.

Leacock, Eleanor Burke, and Nancy Oestreich Lurie, eds. *North American Indians in Historical Perspective*. New York: Random House, 1971.

Lee, Alfred McClung. *The Daily Newspaper in America*. New York: The Macmillan Co., 1937.

Levine, Stuart, and Nancy Oestreich Lurie, eds. *The American Indian Today*. Deland, FL: Everett/Edwards, Inc., 1968.

Little, Hugh. *Volunteer Fire Training Manual*, 2nd ed. New York: Arco Publishing Co., 1967.

Litwack, Leon F. *North of Slavery: The Negro in the Free States, 1790–1860*. Chicago: University of Chicago Press, 1961.

Livermore, Shaw, Jr. *The Twilight of Federalism: The Disintegration of the Federalist Party, 1815–1830*. New York: Gordian Press, 1972 [first published in Princeton, NJ: Princeton University Press, 1962].

Lloyd's Register of Shipping, for 1832. London: C. F. Seyfang; reprinted by the Gregg Press Limited.

Lubenow, Gerald C. "The Action Lawyers." *Saturday Review*, August 26, 1972.

Lytle, William M. *Merchant Steam Vessels of the United States, 1807–1868: "The Lytle List."* Ed. by Forrest R. Holdcamper. Mystic, CT: The Steamship Historical Society of America, 1952.

McCarthy, Eugene J. *Frontiers in American Democracy*. Cleveland: World Publishing Co., 1960.

McCormick, Richard P. *The Second American Party System: Party Formation in the Jacksonian Era*. Chapel Hill: University of North Carolina Press, 1966.

McLaughlin, Robert. "Giving It Back to the Indians." *The Atlantic*, February 1977.

Mayer, Martin. *The Lawyers*. New York and Evanston: Harper & Row, 1967.

Mead, Sidney E. "In Quest of America's Religion," in Alan Geyer and Dean Peerman, ed. *Theological Crossings*. Grand Rapids: William B. Eerdmans Publishing Co., 1974.

——. *The Lively Experiment: The Shaping of Christianity in America*. New York: Harper & Row, 1963.

Mears, Walter R. "The Debates: A View From the Inside." *Columbia Journalism Review*, January/February 1977.

Miller, William Lee. *Piety Along the Potomac: Notes on Politics and Morals in the Fifties*. Boston: Houghton Mifflin Co., 1964.

Mitford, Jessica. *Kind and Usual Punishment: The Prison Business*. New York: Alfred A. Knopf, 1973.

Moltmann, Jürgen, et al. *Religion and Political Society*. New York: Harper & Row, 1974.

Morison, Samuel Eliot. *The Oxford History of the American People*. New York: Oxford University Press, 1965.

Morris, Richard B. "Andrew Jackson, Strikebreaker." *The American Historical Review*, October 1949.

Nadworny, Milton J. "New Jersey Workingmen and the Jacksonians." *Proceedings of the New Jersey Historical Society*, July 1949.

Nichols, Roy F. *The Invention of the American Political Parties*. New York: The Macmillan Co., 1967.

"One Hundred and Sixty-seven Groups Own One Thousand and Forty-seven Dailies: Seventy-one Percent of Total Circulation." *Editor & Publisher*, July 9, 1977.

Osborne, John. "White House Watch: The Other Carters." *The New Republic*, February 26, 1977.

Oswalt, Wendell H. *This Land Was Theirs: A Study of the North American Indian*. New York: John Wiley & Sons, 1973.

Paneth, Donald. "Newspapers in Chains." *The Nation*, May 8, 1972.

Pearce, Roy H. *The Savages of America: A Study of the Indian and the Idea of Civilization*, rev. ed. Baltimore: Johns Hopkins University Press, 1965.

Pechman, Joseph A., and Benjamin A. Okner. *Individual Income Tax Erosion by Income Classes*. Washington: The Brookings Institution, 1972.

Pessen, Edward. *Jacksonian America: Society, Personality, and Politics*. Homewood, IL: The Dorsey Press, 1969.

——. "The Working Men's Party Revisited." *Labor History*, Fall, 1963.

Phillips, Kevin. "Busting the Media Trusts." *Harper's*, July 1977.

Pierson, George Wilson. *Tocqueville and Beaumont in America*. New York: Oxford University Press, 1938.

Pollard, James E. *The Presidents and the Press*. New York: The Macmillan Co., 1947.

Porter, Pat. "Why Indians Stay Poor." *WIN*, January 24, 1974.

"President's Fleet of Planes Cut." Washington *Star*, March 4, 1977.

Reedy, George E. "Faceless Agents of Power." *The Nation*, January 1, 1973.

———. *The Twilight of the Presidency*. New York and Cleveland: New American Library and World Publishing Co., 1970.

Remini, Robert V. *The Election of Andrew Jackson*. Philadelphia and New York: J. B. Lippincott Co., 1963.

———. "Election of 1832," in Arthur M. Schlesinger, Jr., ed. *History of American Presidential Elections, 1789–1968*, Vol. 1. New York: Chelsea House Publishers and McGraw-Hill Book Co., 1971.

———. *Martin Van Buren and the Making of the Democratic Party*. New York: W. W. Norton & Co., 1970.

Richey, Russell E., and Donald G. Jones, ed. *American Civil Religion*. New York: Harper & Row, 1974.

Rosten, Leo, ed. *Religions of America: Ferment and Faith in an Age of Crisis*. New York: Simon and Schuster, 1975.

Rothman, Daniel J. *The Discovery of the Asylum*. Boston: Little, Brown & Co., 1971.

Schlesinger, Arthur M., Jr. *The Age of Jackson*. Boston: Little, Brown & Co., 1945.

Shackford, James A. *David Crockett: The Man and the Legend*. Ed. by John B. Shackford. Chapel Hill: University of North Carolina Press, 1956.

Shaw, Ronald E. *Erie Water West: A History of the Erie Canal, 1792–1854*. Lexington: University of Kentucky Press, 1966.

Sisson, Daniel. *The American Revolution of 1800*. New York: Alfred A. Knopf, 1974.

Smith, Chesterfield. "The Lawyers" (Interview). *Intellectual Digest*, March 1974.

Smith, Elwyn A., ed. *The Religion of the Republic*. Philadelphia: Fortress Press, 1971.

Smith, James D., and Stephen D. Franklin. "The Concentration of Personal Wealth, 1922–1969," a paper presented to the American Economic Association, New York, December 1973.

Spencer, Herbert. *Social Statics*. New York: D. Appleton & Co., 1866.

Stampp, Kenneth M. *The Peculiar Institution: Slavery in the Ante-Bellum South*. New York: Vintage Books, 1956.

Stanford, Phil. "A Model, Clockwork-Orange Prison." *New York Times Magazine,* September 17, 1972.

State of California, Health and Welfare Agency, Department of Corrections. "Characteristics of Felon Population in California State Prisons by Institution, June 30, 1976." N.P.: August 19, 1976.

Stinnett, Ronald F. *Democrats, Dinners and Dollars.* Ames, IA: Iowa State University Press, 1967.

Strout, Cushing. *The New Heavens and New Earth: Political Religion in America.* New York: Harper and Row, 1974.

Sullivan, William A. "Did Labor Support Andrew Jackson?" *Political Science Quarterly,* December 1947.

Taft, Donald R., and Ralph W. England, Jr. *Criminology,* 4th ed. New York: The Macmillan Co., 1964.

Taylor, George Rogers. *The Transportation Revolution, 1815–1860.* New York: Rinehart & Co., Inc., 1951.

Teeters, Negley K., and John D. Shearer, *The Prison at Philadelphia: Cherry Hill.* New York: Columbia University Press, 1957.

Temin, Peter. *The Jacksonian Economy.* New York: W. W. Norton & Co., 1969.

Terkel, Studs. *Working.* New York: Pantheon Books, 1974.

Tocqueville, Alexis de. *Democracy in America.* Trans. by George Lawrence, ed. by J. P. Mayer. Garden City, NY: Doubleday/Anchor, 1969 [first published in New York: Harper & Row, 1966].

——. *Journey to America.* Trans. by George Lawrence, ed. by J. P. Mayer. Garden City, NY: Doubleday/Anchor, 1971.

Treisman, Eric. "The Last Treaty." *Harper's,* January 1975.

Tugwell, Rexford G. *The Enlargement of the Presidency.* New York: Doubleday & Co., 1960.

U. S. Bureau of the Census. *Current Population Reports,* Series P-60, No. 107, "Money Income and Poverty Status of Families and Persons in the United States: 1976" (Advance Report). Washington: U. S. Government Printing Office, September 1977.

——. *Current Population Reports,* Series P-20, No. 307, "Population Profile of the United States: 1976." Washington: U. S. Government Printing Office, April 1977.

——. *Current Population Reports,* Series P-20, No. 304, "Voter Participation in November 1976." Washington: U. S. Government Printing Office, December 1976.

——. *Historical Statistics of the United States: Colonial Times to 1970.* Washington: U. S. Government Printing Office, 1975, Parts 1 and 2.

———. *Statistical Abstract of the United States.* Washington: U. S. Government Printing Office, 1977.

U. S. Bureau of Indian Affairs. "Facts on American Indians and Alaskan Natives." Washington: Bureau of Indian Affairs, November 1977.

———. *Famous Indians: A Collection of Short Biographies.* Washington: U. S. Government Printing Office, 1974.

———. *Federal Indian Policies . . . from the Colonial Period Through the Early 1970's.* Washington: U. S. Government Printing Office, 1975.

———. "Restoration of Land to Indians." Washington: Bureau of Indian Affairs, November 1975.

U. S. Commission on Civil Rights. "Staff Memorandum: Constitutional Status of American Indians." Washington: Commission on Civil Rights, March 1973.

———. *The State of Civil Rights: 1976.* Washington: U. S. Government Printing Office, February 15, 1977.

———. *The Unfinished Business: Twenty Years Later . . .* Washington: U. S. Government Printing Office, September 1977.

U. S. Department of Agriculture, Economic Research Service. *Food Consumption, Prices, and Expenditures, Supplement for 1975.* Washington: U. S. Department of Agriculture, January 1977.

———. *National Food Situation.* Washington: U. S. Government Printing Office, September 1977.

U. S. Department of Labor, Bureau of Labor Statistics. *The Employment Situation: October 1977.* Washington: U. S. Department of Labor, n.d.

U. S. Government Accounting Office. Elmer B. Staats, Comptroller General of the United States, Letter of June 6, 1974, to Hon. William Proxmire, dealing with military personnel assigned to the President and Vice President.

U. S. Law Enforcement Assistance Administration. *Prisoners in State and Federal Institutions on December 31, 1975 (National Prisoner Statistics Bulletin).* Washington: U. S. Government Printing Office, February 1977.

———. *Sourcebook of Criminal Justice Statistics—1976.* Washington: U. S. Government Printing Office, February 1977.

U. S. National Archives. Record Group 41, New York Register No. 46, February 18, 1829, and New York Register No. 155, June 9, 1830 (certificates of registry for the ship *Havre*).

U. S. Office of Management and Budget. *The Budget of the United*

States Government: Fiscal Year 1979. Washington: U. S. Government Printing Office, 1978.

———. *Special Analyses: Budget of the United States Government, Fiscal Year 1979.* Washington: U. S. Government Printing Office, 1978.

U. S. Presidents. *Public Papers of the Presidents of the United States.* Washington: U. S. Government Printing Office, various eds.

U. S. President's Commission on Law Enforcement and Administration of Justice. *The Challenge of Crime in a Free Society.* New York: E. P. Dutton & Co., 1968.

U. S. Senate, Committee on the Judiciary, Subcommittee on National Penitentiaries. *Oversight Hearings on the Nature and Effectiveness of the Rehabilitation Programs of the U. S. Bureau of Prisons,* June 13–14, 1972.

———. *Priorities for Correctional Reform Hearings,* May 13–20, 1971.

Waddell, Jack O., and O. Michael Watson, ed. *The American Indian in Urban Society.* Boston: Little, Brown & Co., 1971.

Wagner, Dale E. *A Concise History of American Campaign Graphics, 1789–1972.* Washington: Public Policy Research Associates, 1972.

Wax, Murray L. *Indian Americans: Unity and Diversity.* Englewood Cliffs, NJ: Prentice-Hall, Inc., 1971.

Weiner, Bernard. "The Clockwork Cure." *The Nation,* April 3, 1972.

Weisberger, Bernard A. *The American Newspaperman.* Chicago: University of Chicago Press, 1961.

Weston, Florence. *The Presidential Election of 1828.* Washington, DC: The Ruddick Press, 1938 (Ph.D. thesis at the Catholic University of America).

"When Their Power Failed." *Time,* October 4, 1976.

White, Leonard D. *The Jacksonians: A Study in Administrative History, 1829–1861.* New York: The Macmillan Co., 1954.

"Why It Will Be Hard to Stay 'Just Plain Folks.'" *U.S. News & World Report,* January 24, 1977.

NEWSPAPERS OF THE 1830S

Courrier des États-Unis (New York)
Detroit Courier (Michigan Territory)
Journal du Havre (Havre, France)
Louisville Public Advertiser (Kentucky)
National Intelligencer (District of Columbia)
New York American (New York)

New York Daily Advertiser (New York)
Newport Mercury (Rhode Island)
Ohio State Journal and Columbus Gazette (Ohio)
Rochester Daily Advertiser (New York)
Washington Globe (District of Columbia)

Index

Tͻ